The story of oneself is embedded in the history of the world, an overall narrative within which all other narratives find their place. That history is a movement toward the truth becoming manifest, a movement toward intelligibility. But in the course of discovering the intelligibility of the order of things, we also discover why at different stages greater or lesser degrees of intelligibility remain.

Alasdair MacIntyre,
Three Rival Versions of Moral Enquiry

Hannah's Child

A Theologian's Memoir

Stanley Hauerwas

WILLIAM B. EERDMANS PUBLISHING COMPANY

GRAND RAPIDS, MICHIGAN / CAMBRIDGE, U.K.

Published 2010 by
Wm. B. Eerdmans Publishing Co.
2140 Oak Industrial Drive N.E., Grand Rapids, Michigan 49505 /
P.O. Box 163, Cambridge CB3 9PU U.K.

Printed in the United States of America

15 14 13 12 11 10   7 6 5 4 3 2 1

Library of Congress Cataloging-in-Publication Data

Hauerwas, Stanley, 1940-
    Hannah's child: a theologian's memoir / Stanley Hauerwas.
        p.   cm.
    ISBN 978-0-8028-6487-1 (cloth: alk. paper)
    1. Hauerwas, Stanley, 1940- 2. Theologians — United States —
    Biography.   I. Title.

    BX4827.H34A3   2010
    230'.044092 — dc22
    [B]

                                                  2009044729

www.eerdmans.com

To Adam and Paula

Contents

On Being Stanley Hauerwas

I did not intend to be "Stanley Hauerwas." I am aware, however, that there is someone out there who bears that name. Stanley Hauerwas is allegedly famous. How can a theologian, particularly in our secular age, be famous? If theologians become famous in times like ours, surely they must have betrayed their calling. After all, theology is a discipline whose subject should always put in doubt the very idea that those who practice it know what they are doing. How can anyone who works in such a discipline become famous?

Nonetheless, in 2001 *Time* magazine named me the "best theologian in America." It is true that when David Reid, at the time the publicist for Duke Divinity School, came to tell me that I was to be so named my first response was, " 'Best' is not a theological category." My response was not an attempt to be humble. I do not think you can try to be humble. I was simply responding to the absurdity of it all.

Those who know me did not miss the irony of the occasion. After all, I have made a career criticizing the accommodated character of the church to the American project. I am then rewarded for being the great critic of America by one of the standards of American life? We live in a strange world, but I have tried to make the most of it, that is, I have tried to use *Time*'s designation as a form of secular power that might be used for God's good purposes.

Still, the Stanley Hauerwas of *Time* magazine is not the Hauerwas "out there" about which I worry. No, the Hauerwas with which I have more trouble identifying is the Christian Hauerwas. I do not want to be misunderstood. I certainly count myself a Christian. Or, more accurately, I have friends who count me as a Christian. I have, moreover, tried to live a life I hope is unintelligible if the God we Christians worship does not exist.

I believe what I write, or rather, by writing I learn to believe. But then I do not put much stock in "believing in God." The grammar of "belief" invites a far too rationalistic account of what it means to be a Christian. "Belief" implies propositions about which you get to make up your mind before you know the work they are meant to do. Does that mean I do not believe in God? Of course not, but I am far more interested in what a declaration of belief entails for how I live my life.

It may be that I am not that interested in "belief" because God is just not "there" for me. God is "there" for some. God is there for Paula, my wife; for Timothy Kimbrough, the rector of Holy Family Episcopal Church; for Sam Wells, my friend. But God is not there for me in the same way. Prayer never comes easy for me. I am not complaining. I assume this to be God's gift to help me think hard about what it means to worship God in a world where God is no longer simply "there."

Charles Taylor has characterized "our age" as one of "exclusive humanism." God is a "hypothesis" most people no longer need — and "most people" includes those who say they believe in God. Indeed, when most people think it "important" that they believe in God, you have an indication that the God they believe in cannot be the God who raised Jesus from the dead or Israel from Egypt.

I am a card-carrying citizen of "our age." I live most of my life as if God does not exist. You may think: "Surely that is a piece of self-deprecating garbage. It must be the case that 'the best theologian in America' is a robust Christian. Who, after all, has stressed the difference God makes for making Christians more than Stanley Hauerwas? If he is not sure what it means for one to be a Christian, where does he get off saying things like, 'The first task of the church is not to make the world more just but to make the world the world'?"

I do think that the first task of the church is to make the world the world. That means, of course, that I need all the help I can get to recognize that I am "world." But I sometimes worry that my stress on the "Christian difference" may be my attempt to overcompensate for my lack of "faith." That still does not seem to get the matter right. It is not that I lack faith, but that I always have the sense that I am such a beginner when it comes to knowing how to be a Christian.

"How" is the heart of the matter for me. When I first read Kierkegaard, I was quite taken with his suggestion that the "what" of Christianity is not the problem. It is the "how." I have spent many years trying to say that we cannot understand the "what" of Christianity without knowing "how" to be Christian. Yet then I worry about the how of my own life.

I have written this memoir in an attempt to understand myself, something that would be impossible without my friends. I have had a wonderful life because I have had wonderful friends. So this attempt to understand myself is not just about "me" but about the friends who have made me who I am. It is also about God — the God who has forced me to be who I am. Indeed, trying to figure out how I ended up being Stanley Hauerwas requires that I say how God figures into the story, and this is a frightening prospect.

IN HIS LOVELY BOOK *THE ART OF TIME IN MEMOIR*, SVEN BIRKERTS OBSERVES that "there is no faster way to smother the core meaning of a life, its elusive threads and connections, than with the heavy blanket of narrated event." Accordingly, he suggests that memoir begins not with event but with an intuition of meaning, that is, with "the mysterious fact that life can sometimes step free from the chaos of contingency and become story." In contrast to an autobiography, Birkerts suggests, memoir is not a sequenced account of a life but the telling of the stories that have given a life its internal shape. Thus the memoirist must try to discover the nonsequential connections that make the contingencies of a life intelligible. Birkerts suggests that intelligibility requires the attempt to master one's life by "a filling out of a meaningful design by circumstance, and that this happens once events and situations are understood not just in themselves but as stages *en route* to decisive self-recognition."

Birkerts's insightful account of the art of memoir sounds themes that have been at the heart of my work — contingency, time, memory, character. I worry, therefore, that what I have written here might be just more of "my work" disguised as memoir. Or, more accurately, I worry that if readers take this memoir to be an explanation of "my work," then it may have the same effect on them as Anthony Trollope's autobiography had on his audience. Toward the end of his life, Trollope wrote his autobiography and instructed his son to publish it after his death. I think Trollope, the master of character, wrote the book in part because he could not resist developing one last great character study in which he was the subject. The book, however, did his reputation no good. His "public" would not forgive him for his frank avowal that he wrote for money. Trollope was a better novelist than I am a theologian, so I have less at stake, and, in any case, I cannot resist trying to understand how I became Stanley Hauerwas. Moreover, I am not writing only for myself, but for those who have been kind enough to take me seriously over the years. I am not sure I am the most reliable reporter of how I have come to think the way I think, but I hope my way of "showing the connections" will invite friends, old and new, to take pleasure in the life God has given me.

CHAPTER 1

Being Saved

Where to begin? Not with the beginning, but with the decisive "decision," that is, what I did because I could not get myself "saved." I became a theologian because I could not be saved. I was baptized at Pleasant Mound Methodist Church in — you will not be surprised — Pleasant Mound, Texas. Pleasant Mound was just that — a small mound just outside Dallas on which sat a small, white, framed Methodist church. I lived in Pleasant Grove, which was not far from Pleasant Mound. The Texans who insisted that these places were "pleasant" exemplify the proclivity of Texans to reassure themselves through exaggeration that it was a good thing to be a Texan. Of course, in the Texas heat even a small group of trees, a pleasant grove, could be quite pleasant.

Pleasant Mound Methodist was Methodist, but like most folks in that area we were really Baptist, which meant that even though you had been baptized and become a member of the church, you still had to be "saved." Baptism and membership were Sunday morning events. Saving was for Sunday nights. Sunday night was an hour hymn sing, a time for "personal prayer" at the altar rail, a forty-five minute to an hour sermon, and then a call to the altar for those convicted of their sin. If you came to the altar, it was assumed that you had struck up a new relationship with God that was somehow equivalent to being saved. I wanted to be saved, but I did not think you should fake it.

I am not sure how old I was when I began to worry about being saved, but it was sometime in my early teens. I had begun to date a young woman who also went to Pleasant Mound, which meant I was beginning to sin. I was pretty sure I needed saving, but I just did not think I should try to force God's hand. All this was complicated for me because the church was at the center of my family's life.

Pleasant Mound and Pleasant Grove were growing. A new church building was needed. The old church stood on a prime bit of property; at least, it was a prime piece of property for a gas station. After much deliberation, the old church was sold to make way for the gas station. The money from the sale made it possible to buy property and build a new brick church. My father, a bricklayer, became the general superintendent of the building project. Trained by my father to labor for bricklayers, I helped build the church in which I could not be saved.

I thought the church to be a grand building. We even had something called a sanctuary. Actually, it was not a sanctuary but a fellowship hall that was to serve as a sanctuary until we got enough money to build a sanctuary, which, as it came to pass, never happened. My father's funeral would be in the fellowship hall that served as a sanctuary. Still, as a kid I thought it was a special place. How else was I to explain my father's willingness to work for less so that the church could be built, when he never made that much to begin with?

Our minister was Brother Zimmerman. Brother Zimmerman had actually gone to college and maybe seminary, but he preferred to be called "Brother" to show, I suspect, that even though he was educated he was not all that different from the rest of us. He was thin as a rail because he gave everything he had to being a minister. I remember him as a lovely, kind man, but he believed we did need to be saved. Indeed, for a few summers after the new church was completed, Brother Zimmerman would erect a tent beside the church so that we could have the yearly revival. I remember that it was thought to be quite an honor for a clergyman from another nearby Methodist church to be asked to preach our revival. Despite the honor, the clergyman needed to be from a church nearby because we could not pay travel. It was never clear to me why we needed to be revived, but you could always count on some members of the church, and they were often the same people year after year, being saved. I sometimes think they wanted to be saved in order to save the preacher, because it was assumed that the Word had not been rightly preached if no one was saved.

So there I sat Sunday night after Sunday night, thinking I should be saved, but it did not happen. Meanwhile, some of the youth were "dedicating themselves to the Lord," which usually meant they were going to become a minister or a missionary. I am not sure how this development among the youth of Pleasant Mound began, but it was not long before several kids, a bit older than I was, had so dedicated their lives. So finally one Sunday night, after singing "I Surrender All" for God knows how many times, I went to the altar rail and told Brother Zimmerman that I wanted to dedicate my life to the Lord. I thought that if God was not going to save me, I could at least put God in a bind by being one of his servants in the ministry. When I took that trip to the altar, I assumed I was acting "freely," but in fact I was fated to make that journey by a story my mother had told me.

MY MOTHER AND FATHER HAD MARRIED "LATE." MY MOTHER DESPERATELY wanted children. She had a child that was stillborn — something I learned when I was looking through her "effects" after she had died. It was then that I discovered my original birth certificate, which indicated the previous birth. But my indomitable mother was not deterred by the loss of a child. She had heard the story of Hannah praying to God to give her a son, whom she would dedicate to God. Hannah's prayer was answered, and she named her son Samuel. My mother prayed a similar prayer. I am the result. But I was named Stanley because the week before I was born my mother and father saw a movie — *Stanley and Livingstone.*

It was perfectly appropriate for my mother to pray Hannah's prayer — but did she have to tell me that she had done so? I could not have been more than six, but I vividly remember my mother telling me that I was destined to be one of God's dedicated. We were sitting on the porch of our small house trying to cool off at the end of a hot summer day. I am not sure what possessed Mother to unload her story on me at that time, but she did. My fate was set — I would not be if she had not prayed that prayer. At the time, God knows what I made of knowing that I was the result of my mother's prayer. However, I am quite sure, strange servant of God though I may be, that whatever it means to be Stanley Hauerwas is the result of that prayer. Moreover, given the way I have learned to think, that is the way it should be.

Was I not robbed of my autonomy by my mother's prayer? Probably. But if so, I can only thank God. Autonomy, given my energy, probably would have meant going into business and making money. There is nothing wrong with making money, but it was just not in my family's habits to know how to do that. All we knew how to do was work, and we usually liked the work we did. As it turns out, I certainly like the work Mother's prayer gave me.

Mother told me only that Hannah had Samuel because she had promised to dedicate her son to God. I do not know if Mother knew that Samuel was to be a Nazirite or that he would be the agent of God's judgment against the house of Eli. On the Sunday evening when I dedicated myself to the Lord, I certainly did not think that I was assuming a prophetic role, and I am by no means a Nazirite: I have drunk my share of intoxicants, and I am bald. Some might think, however, given the way things have worked out, that I have played a Samuel-like role and challenged the religious establishment of the day. It is true that I have tried, with no more success than Samuel, to warn Christians that having a king is not the best idea in the world, at least if you think a king can make you safe.

But I have never tried to be Samuel. I did not even know the story of Samuel before I went to seminary. I certainly have not tried to be "prophetic," as I am sometimes described by others. Toward the end of his life, Samuel asked the people he had led to testify against him if he had defrauded or oppressed anyone, or taken a bribe. They responded that Samuel had not defrauded or oppressed anyone, nor taken anything "from the hand of anyone." If I have any similarity to Samuel, I hope people might cast it in terms like these.

After leaving Samuel with Eli, Hannah rejoiced that God had made her victorious over her enemies, who had derided her for being childless. It is a wonderful victory song, not unlike the great songs of God's triumph over the rich and powerful sung by Miriam, Deborah, and Mary. I should like to think that I have tried to do no more than remind God's people that, as Hannah sang:

> There is no Holy One like the Lord,
> no one beside you;
> there is no Rock like our God.
> Talk no more so very proudly,

let not arrogance come from your mouth;
for the Lord is a God of knowledge,
and by him actions are weighed.

It would take years for me to understand the significance of songs such as Hannah's. But I would have never known such songs could be sung without Mother's prayer. Of course, it did not work out the way my mother or I thought it might. When I finally dedicated my life to God I assumed, and I expect my mother assumed, that I would be a minister. But that was not to be. I tried. But the trying only made me feel silly.

For example, it was assumed by those at Pleasant Mound Methodist that if you had been "called" you were ready to preach. So it was not long after my walk to the altar rail that I found myself preaching on Sunday night. I was scared out of my wits. I did not have a clue. Out of desperation, I went to the church library and found a book entitled *A Faith for Tough Times*, by someone named Harry Emerson Fosdick. I do not remember which of his sermons I used, but I think it involved an attack on hypocrisy. It gives me great pleasure to remember that my first sermon was stolen from a Protestant liberal.

The expansion of the congregation at Pleasant Mound meant that we needed an associate pastor. A man named Raymond Butts was appointed to the church. He was better educated than anyone I had ever known. From him I learned that if you were going into the ministry you probably ought to read books. So I started to read, but I had no idea what I was reading. Most of the books in the church library were about the Bible. I remember one that tried to use archeological evidence to prove that all the events recorded in the Bible, particularly the flood, really happened. Not only had the flood really happened, but the ark was visible in ice on the top of a mountain in Turkey.

That the church had such a book in the library did not mean that we were fundamentalists. You have to be smart to be fundamentalists, and we were not that smart. We did not even read the Bible that much, though I remember that Mother bought a Bible, a red-letter Bible, from a door-to-door salesman. It was a large Bible. Mother gave it the place of honor in the house; that is, it sat on top of the TV.

I assume I soaked up the stories of the Bible in Sunday school and through hearing sermons. I vividly remember the flannel board that the teacher used to illustrate Sunday school lessons in which we were told stories such as Abraham's sacrifice of Isaac. The teacher reassured us that Isaac would be OK by putting a ram in the bush at the top of the flannel board. It came as quite a shock to me years later to be reminded by Kierkegaard that God had not told Abraham there was to be a ram in the bush.

The stories of the Bible and the stories of the family were intertwined. The family loved to tell the story of how Billy Dick, my six-year-old cousin, reacted to the story of the crucifixion at Sunday school by shouting out, "If Gene Autry had been there the dirty sons of bitches wouldn't have gotten away with it." Of course, we knew you should not say "sons of bitches," particularly in Sunday school, but Billy Dick, the son of Dick, my father's youngest bricklaying brother, was simply using the language of "the job."

I came to read the Bible only because of a program sponsored by the Dallas Public Schools. The Linz family, a Jewish family who had a chain of jewelry stores in Dallas, funded a program for the study of the Bible. The program was administered by the public schools — this was not yet a culture of "exclusive humanism." There was a study guide for each of the testaments. We met every Saturday morning at Pleasant Mound to review the material. The whole point was to take an exam at the end of the study of each testament, hoping you would do well enough to win a "Linz Pin." I won a Linz Pin for the New Testament, but I do not think I made the required score of 90 to win one for the Old Testament.

My range of reading, however, was expanding. I had discovered Cokesbury bookstore in downtown Dallas. I do not know how that happened, but I was enthralled by that store. On the upper floor they sold cheesy liturgical ware and outfits, but the first floor was lined with books. They even had a bargain table of books. I spotted a book by B. David Napier called *From Faith to Faith.* I had no idea who Napier was, but even if I had known he was a scholar of the Old Testament it would have done me no good, because I had no idea what it meant to be a scholar of the Old Testament. I read the book and understood just enough to figure out that the Bible was not exactly straightforward history. I began to think that I needed to think.

Being Saved

I stumbled on a book by Nels F. S. Ferre that gave me some idea of what thinking might look like. In *The Sun and the Umbrella: A Parable for Today*, Ferre made the astounding observation that Christ, the Bible, and the church could just as easily be used to hide the sun as to reveal God. I had no idea that I was being introduced to Plato's cave, disguised as a religious parable. I was impressed. Indeed I was more than impressed, because I was beginning to think that maybe all this Christianity stuff was not all it was cracked up to be. I began to think that I might not want to be a Christian at all. But I kept that thought to myself.

Of course, all this was complicated by the trials of simply growing up. I thought I was in love. I was trying to negotiate high school, which was no mean trick given the fact that I did not play football. Football in Texas, then as now, is everything and more that has been captured by the film *Friday Night Lights*. Where you played on the team determined your "making out" rights after the game. I could not be on the team because I worked for my father in the summers. To play football you had to begin practice in August, and I could not take off work to do that. The best I could do was to be a cheerleader. In short, I was not part of the in-crowd at Pleasant Grove High, nor at W. W. Samuel High, which is what we became after we were taken into the city of Dallas.

For most of my high school class, graduation from W. W. Samuel was the end of their education. But because I had dedicated my life to the ministry, I had been told by Reverend Butts that I should go to college. No one in my family had ever gone to college. The only college graduates I knew were my teachers and ministers. All going to college meant to me was that I should study in high school because you needed good grades to get into college. So I studied. I even discovered that I loved to read history, in particular the history of England. There was a world beyond Pleasant Grove.

I applied to two colleges — Hendrix in Conway, Arkansas, and Southwestern University in Georgetown, Texas. In truth, I was not sure I wanted to go to college at all. I did not want to leave my girlfriend, fearing that in my absence she would find someone new. Moreover, given my doubts about Christianity, I was not sure why I was going in the first place. But the ball had started rolling down the hill, and it would have been hard to explain to my parents why I did not want to go to college. Admitted to both schools, I chose to go to Southwestern primarily because it was closer, making it possible for me to get home more often to see my girlfriend. That reason quickly evaporated, because she did soon find someone else. I was heartbroken for a week or two.

College, even one as small and undistinguished as Southwestern, was a new world for me. Only by going to college did I discover that I came from the working classes. My roommate, for example, had come to Southwestern to pledge a fraternity. I had never heard of a fraternity. When asked if I was going to go through rush, I had to ask what that was. When told that it meant you go to parties, I thought it was probably a good thing. It did not occur to me that I was supposed to try to get a "bid" — whatever that was.

I did, however, meet Joe Wilson, who later became a bishop in the Texas Methodist church, at the Phi Delta Theta party. We talked about the search for the historical Jesus. I thought it a really good thing that guys got together to explore such matters, so I became a pledge of Phi Delta Theta. The great benefit of being a member of a fraternity was that I had to learn the Greek alphabet. I never moved into the fraternity house.

I think it may have been at Southwestern when I first began to realize that I never quite "fit in." I always seem to be in the "in between." I am working class, but I have spent a life in the university teaching students who do not come from the working classes. I am a Protestant who is probably more Catholic than many Catholics — though that may be a deep self-deception. I am deeply conservative, but I am drawn to extreme positions. Southwestern was my first training ground for learning how to negotiate a world that I loved, but also one in which I would never quite belong.

Although I am now a chaired professor at a major research university, I still do not feel at home in the academy. I am sure that feeling has everything to do with class, but I also suspect that the sense I have had of never "fitting in" has been a way to resist being taken in by my "success." I would like to think that I have never been able to develop an arrogance my accomplishments might justify; even so, this is more likely the result of a fear of power, and not a matter of virtue.

Being Saved

Such matters, of course, were far in the future. I had no idea that going to college might put me in a position to be part of a different class of people, of the power elites, and to have money. I thought I was going to college to learn to think. I was fortunate, therefore, that there was someone at Southwestern who was a teacher. His name was John Score. He made my life possible.

During my senior year in high school, my mother and I had gone to Southwestern to look it over. Sent to Reuter Hall to see what the dormitory was like, we were welcomed by a man named John Score. I had no idea that he would become a decisive influence in my life. He was the son of the past president of Southwestern. He was the rector of Reuter Hall because he was single, had not yet completed his dissertation, and no doubt needed the money. I think he thought I might be different because while he was showing us the dorm I mentioned that I was reading H. Richard Niebuhr's *Christ and Culture*. I have no idea what John thought about a kid who said he was reading Niebuhr, but I suspect it at least suggested to him that I was not completely normal.

John never told me what to do. He was far too wise to do that, but he guided me through Southwestern and life. I became one of the assistants to the rector in Reuter Hall, which consisted primarily of letting people into their rooms because they had lost their keys or were drunk. They had usually lost their keys because they were drunk. Southwestern students, of course, officially did not drink, but this was central Texas. Beer, particularly at Joe's in Walberg, Texas, was simply part of life. One of the few times I remember John getting mad at me was when my roommate and friend, Dan Adamson, and I got drunk and stole the Walburg, Texas, sign and put it up in our room. He made us return it.

I had gone to Southwestern to major in history, but I soon discovered that history, at least at Southwestern, was not all that interesting. Southwestern was a mass of requirements in introductory courses. I fell in love with novels, but John's Introduction to Philosophy made me *the* philosophy major at Southwestern. John's basic training was in theology, but he was part of a four-person Religion and Philosophy Department, and he was designated to teach philosophy.

At the time, however, I did not appreciate his intellectual background. He had gone to Southwestern and then to Garrett Theological Seminary in Chicago. At Garrett he had studied under Philip Watson, who was one of the early theologians influenced by theological developments in Sweden associated with Anders Nygren and Gustaf Aulen. That put John Score on the conservative side of Protestant liberalism. He then went to Harvard to do his Ph.D., but for reasons that were never clear to me he left Harvard for Duke.

At Duke he worked under Robert Cushman, who was the dean of the divinity school as well as a major Wesley scholar and theologian. Cushman had gone to Yale, where he seems to have been influenced by the remarkable Robert Calhoun, a historical theologian who more or less thought that Plato was one of the church fathers. Mr. Cushman's book on Plato, *Therapeia,* confirmed Calhoun's judgment. The heart of Cushman's argument in *Therapeia* was that to understand Plato properly you had to recognize the interdependent character of knowledge and virtue, because any apprehension of the ultimate structure of Being, as he contended, is "conditioned upon *ethos* or the right state of balance of affection within the soul."

That is how John taught me to read Plato. John was writing his dissertation, however, on Wesley. I think he had trouble finishing the dissertation because he was not that interested in Wesley. His argument was that the accounts of Wesley's life that centered on Wesley's Aldersgate "experience" (when he felt his heart to be strangely warmed) failed to do justice to the significance of Wesley's field preaching for shaping his fundamental theological views. In an odd way, John's argument was an elaboration of Cushman's account of Plato: knowledge, in this case of God, requires a lifelong transformation of the self. Although I still thought of myself as "not a Christian," I was beginning to think that through the study of philosophy there might be something to this Christian stuff.

John offered six semester-long seminars in which we read Frederick Copleston's *History of Philosophy,* along with the primary texts. There were never more than two or three students in the seminars. I am sure our discussions were often ill formed, but I had no idea what a marvelous education I was getting until I went to Yale Divinity School and discovered how well John had prepared me. John also taught a range of other courses. I remember falling in love with Paul Tillich in Modern Religious Thought, but that love affair ended when I wrote a long research paper on Blaise Pascal for another course. Even more important for me was a course on the philosophy of history in which I read everything I could get my hands on by R. G. Collingwood.

The courses I was taking with John were important, but just as important was John's willingness to include me in his life. He was an unconventional man who lived conventionally. He never married, though he would have liked to; but after his father's early death, he cared for his mother. This was a great boon for me, because his mother lived in Dallas. Every summer John moved to Dallas to live with his mother while allegedly working on his dissertation. In fact, life was too interesting for John to let the completion of a dissertation get in the way of his taking advantage of going to movies, concerts, and art exhibits, or reading novels and eating meals. And he often invited me to join him.

I would lay brick all day, come home, clean up, and then drive to University Park, where John and his mother lived. John loved the movies. Bergman was a mainstay. My parents loved John, and he often came out to have a meal with us. The distance between Pleasant Grove and University Park was not more than ten miles, but the names represent different worlds. I often laid brick in Highland Park and University Park on houses that when finished I would never be allowed to enter, because I lived in Pleasant Grove. Yet because of John's wonderful generosity, and because he himself was not an insider to the world of University Park, I never noticed that I was an outsider in this world.

John was even a Methodist, but that did not prevent him from being a Christian. He was, after all, the son of his father, who, before he became president of Southwestern, had been the pastor of First Methodist, Fort Worth. Mrs. Score was one of those classic Methodist spouses who knew every charge in the conference, as well as who wanted to move where. John was ordained, though I do not think I ever saw him celebrate. He went to church at First Methodist, Georgetown, but complained about the preaching. As a result, he drove frequently to Austin on Sunday mornings to hear Billy Morgan at University Methodist or Carlyle Marney at University Baptist. He often took me with him.

John never tried directly to make me rethink my presumption that I was not a Christian. He was too wise for that. Rather, I slowly learned by his example that to be a Christian meant that you could never protect yourself from the truth. John loved Nietzsche because he admired Nietzsche's ability to get to the heart of the matter. John was a Texan;

he had little use for bullshit. Some, I suspect, would have confused his ability to call it like he saw it with cynicism, but he was not a cynic. He was not a cynic because, like Nietzsche, he had a passion for the truth.

Intellectually, my greatest strength is that there is nothing in which I am not interested. Intellectually, my greatest weakness is that there is nothing in which I am not interested. That strength and weakness I learned from John, who, I am happy to say, did finally finish his dissertation. My reading habits I also learned from him. I am a gregarious reader. I suspect this reflects the insecurity that comes from my feeling that I do not belong in the university. I simply was not brought up in that trade, so I have always worked from the presumption that there is something else I need to learn. Yet I hope it is the case that my insecurity is bounded by the sheer joy I find in the complex simplicity of the world discovered through reading.

Philosophy and religion were not all I studied at Southwestern. In fact, I learned to love science too. I did not do well in chemistry because I could not find my unknown; but I loved geology. Southwestern was perfectly located for fossil collection, and I loved collecting, which prepared me well for coming to understand later why the development of geology as a science was such an extraordinary achievement. Theologically, to discover that rocks have a history is of major importance. Darwin helped us recover the significance that humans are animals, but I remain fascinated by geology — and I do not think that is simply because I am a Texan. In Texas, geology means oil.

There was a physicist, Bob Brown, at Southwestern who complained that he could never understand what philosophers said because philosophers knew nothing about physics. So some of us associated with religion and philosophy asked him to give us a physics course, which he did. It was a two-semester course in which we learned physics through the history of physics. I spent a month looking through a telescope to measure the movements of the moons around a planet in order to determine the mass of the planet. I suspect that if I had been at a research university, I would never have received the education Southwestern made possible.

I was, of course, also taking the regular regime of courses in "religion": Old Testament, New Testament, church history, and modern theology. That meant I was well formed by the discourses of liberal theology — whether that perspective was acknowledged or not. I was impressed by what I was learning. I did not quite understand that I was being taught how Protestants, particularly Protestants in Germany in the eighteenth and nineteenth century, had put the world together; but I was sure that if I did turn out to be a Christian, I would certainly be a liberal.

I BEGAN TO GO TO CHURCH AGAIN. NOT ONLY DID I GO WITH JOHN, BUT DURing the summers I began to go to Casa View Methodist in Dallas. I had somehow discovered that this was a liberal church. Even professors from Perkins School of Theology at SMU went to Casa View. Everyone knew that Perkins was the hotbed of Protestant radicals because Schubert Ogden taught there, and Ogden had mixed up that strange cocktail of Rudolf Bultmann with a twist of Charles Hartshorne. The pastor at Casa View was a wonderful man named Will Bailey. He basically gave us a diet of existentialism disguised as Christianity, but I was intrigued.

I even joined the church on a retreat at the notorious Faith and Life Community in Austin. The Methodist maverick, Joe Matthews, and the Presbyterian, Joe Slicker, had joined forces to create a radical Christian community to challenge the status quo. The status quo certainly needed challenging, but the combination of psychotherapeutic insight and liberal theology was not sufficient to sustain a challenge to the status quo for the long haul. The Faith and Life Community, however, participated in protests against segregation and in the process attracted people like Tom Hayden.

I remember feeling quite manipulated during the weekend retreat at the Faith and Life Community. I was, after all, a philosophy major. Matthews and Slicker, who thought they were theological radicals, were actually, like so many Protestant liberals, pietists in existential drag. They were determined for you to confess that the intense group sessions you experienced had changed your life, just as revivalists were never content unless you converted. But if I could not be saved at Pleasant Mound, I sure as hell was not going to be saved at the Faith and Life Community in Austin, Texas.

I was, however, increasingly drawn to the study of theology. I was not sure I was a Christian, but I certainly liked thinking about what Christians allegedly thought about. So I started to think about going to seminary. I did not know enough to know that you might skip seminary and go directly to graduate school. Everyone I knew who thought about the difference God might make for how you thought had gone to seminary, so I assumed that was what I should do.

I was attracted to Yale because H. R. Niebuhr taught there. Reading philosophy had helped me recognize that I probably did not know enough to be an atheist, but I still did not understand how an intelligent person could believe in God or be part of a religious tradition. Two books were decisive for making me reconsider that judgment — Martin Buber's *I and Thou* and H. Richard Niebuhr's *The Meaning of Revelation*. Buber gave me a way to think "God" that had never occurred to me. Niebuhr gave me a way to think "Jesus" that seemed to meet some of the challenges mounted in the name of history. Because Niebuhr was at Yale I thought I should go there. It never occurred to me that seminaries were places you went to study for the ministry. I just thought that is where you went to explore further whether this stuff was true or not.

I told Wilfred Bailey about my desire to go to Yale. He said that before I made up my mind, he wanted me to speak to a friend of his at Perkins. That friend turned out to be Schubert Ogden, who was kind enough to see me. I had read his *Christ without Myth* and, of course, thought that if I was going to be a Christian I would be one without myth. But I was somewhat taken back by Ogden's suggestion that it would be a bad thing to go to Yale. Instead he suggested I go to Chicago, because Chicago provided the broad spectrum of theological perspectives that someone like me needed. He said if I went to Yale I would just turn out to be another Barthian. He was certainly right about that. I have never regretted it.

Of course, there were other forces in play by the time I went to Yale. My life at Southwestern was not reducible to courses and books. Do not forget that I was a member of Phi Delta Theta. The fraternity's main business was having parties. You were supposed to have a date to go to the party. I did date, but I was not very good at it. Early in my senior year, I asked Anne Harley to go to one of the parties. I am not sure why, but it seems she had decided that I was the one she wanted. Being the horny young Texan I was, I assumed that was a good idea.

Being Saved

Anne was bright and, at least it seemed to me, quite pretty. She was not a committed student. Rather than study, she would spend hours playing bridge in the Union at Southwestern. She had dated a number of my friends, but those relationships had not gone anywhere. I have no idea why she was attracted to me, but we were both seniors, and I suspect she might have thought that if she was to find a husband at school she needed to make some decisions.

I have never known how to negotiate women. That I use those terms suggests how frightened I am of women. Do women need to be "negotiated"? I hope not, but I am never sure I know what women want. I think I need to know what women want because I was raised to think that my job as a male is to give women what they want. I am sure I learned that lesson from my mother. I have always assumed that my task is to make the world all right for any woman who is kind enough to love me. Paternalistic scripts die hard in the souls of Southern males.

Sex, of course, often plays a role, making these matters even more complex. I am a romantic all the way down. As a student at Southwestern, I assumed that you could have sex with someone only if you loved them. I did not want to have sex and then face the necessity of thinking I was in love. Anne and I were not "going all the way," but I suspect that I was sure I loved her because I loved playing around.

As graduation approached, we began talking to our parents about getting married. When I left for New Haven, Anne had moved to Dallas and was living with my parents. We planned to be married at the end of my first year in seminary, but we were too impatient for that. We married at the end of my first semester at Yale. My mother had tried to tell me that she thought something was not quite right about Anne. She worried that Anne had trouble getting up in the morning to go to work. She worried about Anne's "grouchiness." But I attributed the concerns to the fact that she was my mother. Mothers are not supposed to like their daughters-in-law. It turned out Mother was right to worry.

CHAPTER 2

Work and Family

Good God, I thought, this is a long way from Pleasant Grove. Of course, being a Texan meant that the thought could not go unsaid, so I blurted out, "This is a long way from Pleasant Grove!" I feel certain the Flemish Catholics at the Catholic University of Leuven had never heard of Pleasant Grove, Texas, my hometown. But there I was, standing in a lecture room absolutely packed to the ceiling with faculty and students who had come to hear me give a lecture entitled "The Non-violent Terrorist: In Defense of Christian Fanaticism." The lecture was not only a defense of Christian nonviolence, but also a critique of developments in Catholic moral theology, developments that had begun at Leuven. I was a long way from Pleasant Grove.

The thought that I am a long way from Pleasant Grove is one I often have in academia. I have been teaching at Duke for over twenty-five years, but I still find myself thinking, "This is a long way from Pleasant Grove." I cannot repress that thought because of the distance between Pleasant Grove and places like Leuven and Duke. The kind of Christian I am, the kind of academic I am, the kind of person I am, has everything to do with that distance. That distance, moreover, creates the space that makes the story I have to tell possible.

The distance between Pleasant Grove and Leuven may or may not have something to do with what it means for me to be a Christian, but I am certain it has shaped what it means for me to be an academic. I was raised to "just get on with it." If you smashed a finger loading a scaffold with brick, which I did many times, there was no time to dwell on the pain. You stuck the finger in a can of turpentine, not a good idea as it turned out, and just got on with it. I was able to live twenty-four years with a mentally ill spouse because I learned early on that you just have to get on with it.

The word used for lives that just get on with it is "work." I cannot remember any time in my life that I did not have work to do. I never felt oppressed, even as a child, by the fact that I was expected to work, because I assumed, given the example set by my parents, that work was what everyone did. Insofar as I can remember, I had a happy childhood. Of course the question of whether I should be happy simply did not come up. We did not have time to be unhappy, because we had to work. We did not have much money, but I am not sure we thought we had to work to make money. I think we worked because that is what we did. If "working class" describes anyone, it certainly describes my parents.

Some of my earliest memories are memories of helping my mother in the garden. I was no more than four or five, but I learned early that there is a right and wrong way to hoe. Mother was left-handed, so teaching me how to hoe right-handed was not easy. But I learned. It never occurred to me to wonder why we needed a garden. We needed to have a garden because we had to eat. Our half acre of North Texas black gumbo soil grew not only Johnsongrass in great supply but also beans, okra, corn, collards, and anything else Mother planted. But you had to hoe the rows, and that was good work for a young boy.

I am not sure how Daddy had come to own that half acre in Pleasant Grove, but in 1943 or 1944 we set up shop on that piece of land. I lived there until I went to college in 1958. Before moving to Pleasant Grove, we had lived in an area aptly named Urbandale. We lived in a duplex. A family of twelve lived on the other side. The kids took great delight in beating me up for no apparent reason, other than sheer meanness. The straw that broke the camel's back was the day the kids put tacks in the driveway to flatten the tires on my father's car. Mother, who always made the decisions in our family, decided it was time to move.

Daddy bought a house that had been condemned by the city and had it moved to the lot in Pleasant Grove. He paid a hundred dollars for the house, which included having it moved. Mother insisted that the house be put on the back of the lot because she thought someday they would build a larger house "up front." That never materialized, but as I grew up, Daddy added a bathroom, a "living" room, and finally a room for me. We used an outdoor privy for at least five years. Neighborhood kids knocked it over every year at Halloween, and every few years we had to move it because the hole filled up. Verdant circles of green grass would then appear where the hole had been. I loved to roll in these patches of grass with my dogs, and since I was expected to "keep the yard," I had to cut the same grass with a push mower, which was not easily done.

I also had to keep the Johnsongrass in the front under control. It could grow six feet high, and the stalks were tough. It was my job, using nothing but a sling, to keep it cut, in part because one of Mother's plans was for me to grow a garden of black-eyed peas and okra, which I could then sell to the neighbors. We had a hand push plow that I used to make the rows of peas and okra. I then put grocery bags of black-eyed peas (shelled) and okra in my wagon and delivered them to the neighbors. I was six.

I sold a bag of peas and okra for thirty cents. After a full summer of peddling my produce, I had made thirty-six dollars. That is a hell of a lot of peas and okra. Mother made me start a bank account because she said I needed to learn to save money. I did save what I made, but I wanted a watch. She let me buy one for thirty dollars. It was the first thing I ever owned.

At six, I started to go to school. The schools in Pleasant Grove were "common schools," which meant they were not good enough to be certified by the state. The school rooms were converted barracks used during the war. I was able to walk to school — barefoot. During the winter we did wear shoes, which was a big deal for me because it turned out I was unbelievably flat-footed. Shoes hurt. Trying to correct my feet meant, moreover, that I had to wear "high top" shoes that earned me no end of derision from my classmates.

I could not read when I went to school, and I had trouble learning to read once I got there. I also seem to have had a "behavioral problem." I was an only child. I craved attention. And like my mother, I seldom shut up. Punishment for talking out of turn and other forms of misbehavior was to be sent to the cloak room, where you sat in the dark. Teachers also used the paddle often. Indeed it was assumed that males had to receive at least one spanking a week or they lacked "spirit."

I finished first grade unable to read, or at least I could not read well. But sometime in the second grade I discovered baseball. Actually, I discovered I loved to read books about baseball. There were a number of novels about baseball players in the little library the school possessed. I systematically started to read every book in the library about baseball. I particularly liked novels about players who were not very talented or good but through hard work became the stars of their team. I had every intention of following their example.

For some reason I wanted to be a first baseman. I went out for the Little League team, but I was not an immediate success. I spent hours throwing a scruffy hardball against the garage my father had built out of block left over from a job he had done somewhere. That was the way I learned to catch. I became pretty damn good, but I never learned to hit. I played church softball into my sixties, when my knees gave out, and I could still catch pretty well.

My baseball and gardening summers came to an end when I turned seven or eight. It was time for me to join my father on the job. All my family knew was brick. The only time Daddy did not lay brick was during the war. Daddy had a talent for exactness that landed him a war-related job grinding bombsights. It was a job declared to be essential to the war effort, which meant he was never drafted. But as soon as the war was over he returned to what the family did: laying brick. My grandfather was a bricklayer. My father had five brothers. They were all bricklayers.

I HAVE NEVER BEEN CLEAR ABOUT THE FAMILY HISTORY. ALL I KNOW IS THAT my grandfather came to Alabama from Minnesota because there was family in northern Alabama that owned and ran a brick factory. Granddaddy worked at the factory, but he had the audacity to run off with and marry a Coffee. The Coffee family had been the slave-owning aristocrats of the area. There was even a Coffee plantation. It seems the Coffee family was none too pleased by their new son-in-law. They tried to make the best of a bad situation. The family published an article in the Florence, Alabama, newspaper welcoming the newly married couple back home after they had eloped. The article reports that my grandfather and grandmother had taken a train to Knoxville, Tennessee, where they were married. The name of the traveling salesman who had witnessed the marriage was given in the article, ensuring that the marriage had actually taken place.

The Coffee family may have been trying to come to terms with the marriage, but Granddaddy was not about to come under the power of the Coffee family. So it was not long before he escaped Alabama by moving to Texas. He moved from one small Texas town to another for a number of years. He may have done so because he was trying to make a living by laying brick, as well as doing a little ranching on the side. No doubt there was a limited amount of work for a bricklayer in the small towns in which they lived. But it may also be the case that Granddaddy had a streak of independence that kept him on the move until he finally came to Dallas.

Grandmother and Granddaddy had six sons: Clarence, Bill, George, Rufus, Coffee, and Dick. They all became bricklayers. Grandmother reasserted the pride of her family by naming my father Coffee. She also seems to have chosen him to be the one set aside to grow old with her, assuming that he would not marry. She was not prepared, however, to face the white-trash energy of my mother. Indeed, I am not sure if any of us were ever prepared to face the reality of my mother. I surely was not.

The best way I know to introduce my mother is to share the letter I wrote to my grandsons when she died. My wife, Paula, and I were in Bern, Switzerland, when I learned my mother was soon to die. I knew she might die while I was gone. Adam, my son, and I had been to see her the week before I left to go to Europe, and we had said good-bye to her. She was ninety-two and suffering from memory loss, but she knew in general who we were. There was a lovely sweet moment we had together. We were sitting in the sun. Mother was in her wheelchair going to sleep off and on. Adam asked if there was anything we could do for her. She responded, "No, I just like to listen to ya'll talking to one another." My mother, who seldom quit talking long enough to listen, ended up wanting to listen.

My adopted brother had called to tell us it did not look as if Mother would live long. All Paula and I could do in Bern, Switzerland, was to wait. Like my mother, I am not good at waiting. I had to do something. So I wrote the following letter to my grandsons on learning of my mother's death.

Dear Joel and Kendall:

Your great-grandmother died May 2, 2006. You never got to know her well, so I thought it might be good to tell you something of her life. Such telling is one of the ways we learn to acknowledge gifts that have made us possible. It is also important to be connected to the past. Your great-grandmother certainly had much to do with making me who I am — for good and ill. Someday to understand who you are you will discover a bit of Great-grandmother was passed on to you.

Your great-grandmother was born in the central part of the state of Mississippi. The closest town was Kosciusko, which had been named after a Polish general in the American Revolutionary War. Mississippi was a state of the Confederacy and the exemplification of what is described as the "deep South." The South was determined by slavery and poverty. African Americans were treated horribly in Mississippi, but those who often mistreated African Americans were also poor. Indeed, in the South there was even a name to describe poor whites; they were called "white trash." Your great-grandmother came from white trash. She was not trash, but she was certainly poor. Her father eked out a living on hardscrabble land by growing cotton. Joanna, your great-grandmother, grew up picking cotton. It was hard work. They also raised chickens and grew crops for food. Joanna did chores to help her family survive.

When she was ten her mother died and her father soon married one of his cousins. Joanna's life would never be the same because her stepmother took little interest in the children from the previous marriage. Moreover, Joanna's father could be quite cruel. As a result, Joanna and her sister ran away when they were in their early teens to live with their mother's brother. He was called Uncle John Andrew, and his wife was named Ophilia. Joanna always regarded them as her real parents.

Somehow Joanna managed to graduate from high school. But she had to make a living. So she sold magazines across the South as well as worked for people as a housekeeper. It has never been clear to me how she got to Texas, but she told me that her sister, Wildean, had gone to Texas and suggested that Joanna join her. She worked for a year in Wichita Falls, Texas, and then got a job in Dal-

Work and Family

las in a home for what were then called "unwed mothers." A friend at the home introduced her to my father, Coffee Hauerwas, and a courtship began. Of course he was not my father when they began dating, but Joanna clearly knew she had met the man she wanted to marry.

There was just one problem: Coffee's mother did not want him to marry. He was one of six brothers, all of whom were bricklayers. His mother thought one of her sons should take care of her in her old age, and Coffee, whose name was her maiden name, was the one she chose for the task. However, your great-grandmother was a determined woman, and she was determined to marry Coffee. I do not know how she accomplished that task, but she did.

Determination, energy, hard work, and an unrelenting desire to do for others are the traits that characterized Joanna's life. Hard work was also at the heart of Coffee's life. They were never well-off, but they never wanted for anything, because they worked hard. Your great-grandmother often thought, however, that Coffee was not sufficiently self-assertive, so she constantly pushed him to be more aggressive, particularly when it came to business. But Coffee usually went his own way, which meant your grandmother was right — many for whom he worked took advantage of him. He was a craftsman of the first order, able to lay up beautiful brick jobs, but he never made any money — or at least he made only enough to get by. But get by we did. We always kept a garden, and you could always eat the wild kale and mustard that grew in the ditch behind the garage.

Mother and Daddy were late to marry, but they wanted children. Joanna had trouble getting pregnant. She prayed to God that she would dedicate her child to God if he would give her a child. She got the idea from the story of Samuel in the Bible. She did have me, and some years later told me that story to explain how I came to be. I often think that it was fine that she prayed to God for a son, but did she have to tell me? That she did so no doubt has something to do with my having become a theologian.

Joanna was always present in my life — too present. It was as though she was determined to see that I got every advantage she did not get. So she was always on the PTA and the "homeroom mother." Everywhere I turned she was there. As I grew up, I found it quite tiresome and embarrassing. She just could not refrain from trying to make life better for those with whom she came in contact and, in particular, better for me. But I was saved from Mother by my father, by being put on "the job" when I was seven or eight. Once I went on the job I was no longer under Mother's constant desire "to help."

I need to be clear. Many of the things Mother did were good. It was good she started the Cub Scouts so that I could be a Scout. It was good she worked in Sunday school and church to ensure my involvement. But her constant doing, her unrelenting energy, could get old. Looking back on it, I am not sure how manipulative she was, but she certainly used every strategy to get you to do what she was sure was good for you, whether you knew it or not. It was as if she feared you might not love her if she was not doing for you. She had no rest in her.

But, God love her, there was also no malice in her. Rather, she had the wounds from a past of poverty and class. She feared those who seemed to be "above" her, and the only way she knew to "beat them" was to do more. She did much good, but I wish she had gotten more pleasure and fun out of life. Still, I can say that because of her and my father's lack of regard for their own interest, they gave me a life they could not imagine was possible. They did so, moreover, because they were Christians.

Church was a constant reality for your great-grandmother. She had been raised Baptist, but it was never clear to me how much she had learned about Christianity. Daddy was a Methodist, so they became Methodist and, in particular, members of Pleasant Mound Methodist Church. This was in Texas, and the church was a white-framed building on a small hill with a graveyard in the back. Later a new church would be built, and your great-grandfather would become the general superintendent for the construction of the building. Joanna worked equally hard to see that the church became all it could be. Our lives centered around the church.

That your great-grandparents spent so much time at church had everything to do with their extraordinary generosity. They did not have much, but they gave what they had, and, more important, they gave themselves. Poor people often do not have money, but they do have time. Mother and Daddy gave time to church and to me. They also gave me a brother, Johnny Medlock, whom they befriended and raised during my last years in high school and when I went to college. That was one of their most precious gifts.

I left home when I was twenty-one. I went to college and graduated to go on to Yale Divinity School. You will have some sense of what a precious gift it was for my parents to want me to go to college and then to Yale. It meant I increasingly became part of a world they could not understand, but they "let me go on." Letting go is not easy, but they did it. They tried to understand and participate in my life as best they could, but it was not easy. Their participation was made even more difficult by my wife, Anne, who did not like people like my parents. Anne did not like many people, because she did not like herself.

I think it fair to say that after I left home your great-grandmother was a little lost. She was not quite sure what she would do. What she did was try to run Daddy's life. They were growing older, and the aches and pains began. She went to school to become a practical nurse. It was important for her, and she poured her whole being into becoming a nurse. The only problem was that she diagnosed every small problem Coffee had as being more serious than it was. Poor Daddy was condemned to having his own nurse.

One other annoying habit of your great-grandmother was her constant talking. She could go on forever. She just would not shut up, repeating the same thing over and over again. Poor Daddy became the primary recipient of what she had to say. Fortunately, as he became older he became increasingly deaf. Who says God does not have a sense of humor? Yet they made a life, a quite wonderful life, together.

After my father retired they moved to Arkansas to live outside Mena. As usual, with much hard work, they created a home and a garden. They lived in a trailer. Your father visited them in Arkansas several times. His visits, I suspect, were some of their fondest memories. They got to be with their grandson, whom they dearly loved. And in a manner, they got to share their life with him. They taught him how to fish and grow potatoes, tomatoes, and green beans.

However, the place in Arkansas was too hard to maintain after they grew older, so they moved to Carthage, Texas, to be close to Donresia and Acie. Donresia was Aunt Dean's daughter, whom Mother and Daddy helped raise for some years. She was like a sister to me. Carthage was a good place for them to be, but your great-grandmother worried about Coffee's health and thought they needed to be closer to good health care. So she moved them back to Dallas. It was a good idea to the extent that there they were closer to Johnny, but a bad idea because your great-grandfather was no longer close to any woods or a place to fish.

In December 1992, they were to move to a retirement home, but your great-grandfather died the night of the move. After the funeral, your great-grandmother moved to C. C. Young, where she lived for the next fourteen years. As usual, she could not do enough for those around her. She put in flowers and cared for her fellow residents. For five years she did very well, but then her memory began to fail. Yet she continued to try to do for others.

Even in death she tried to be of use. She wanted her body to go to medicine in the hope that those training to care for others might learn from her. I confess that I never particularly approved of that decision, but she felt strongly about it. This meant we could not have a funeral after her death. I suspect that is one of the reasons I feel it necessary to write you this letter. She was always afraid she might not be remembered, but I cannot, nor do I desire, to forget her life.

Of course, we will all be forgotten someday. We are dust and to dust we shall return. But we believe that God desires each one of us to be his friend. Your great-grandmother has now entered into a friendship with God about which we can rejoice. She lived life full-throttled, forging for us a life-enhancing life. God has now given her the rest that was so often missing in her life. She has joined Coffee, whom she deeply loved, in the love that moves the sun and the stars.

Coming to the end of this letter I cannot help but feel the inadequacy of what I have written. If only I could through words give you a sense of the vitality and energy of your great-grandmother. If only I could give you a better sense of what it meant to emerge from racism and poverty to see African Americans as friends. If only I could elicit the love your great-grandparents had for one another, me, Johnny, and your father. But I cannot. Yet I hope this letter gives you some hint of the genuine goodness, the sheer unmerited gifts, your great-grandfather, Coffee, and your great-grandmother, Jo-anna, were.

Love,

Granddad Hauerwas

The tone of this letter is no doubt the result of my sense of guilt at not being present when my mother died. Johnny was there, and I am eternally grateful to him for being with her as she died. Yet I think most of what I say in the letter is true. Mother was a pain in the ass, but she meant well. To this day I have a great deal of trouble "being cared for" by anyone. Mother's desperate attempt to force you to love her by caring for you continues to shape my emotional habits of resistance.

She had a raging chaotic intelligence that had never been disciplined by a decent education. Moreover, she could not learn because she never shut up long enough to listen. She was manipulative, but she lacked the subtlety that a good manipulator needs. For example, she would say — "You need to be good to Mr. X because you may need his help in the future." That she was so explicit about her strategies of manipulation almost makes them charming — but not really. Rather, her attempt to make so many of her relationships matters of exchange witnesses to her deep insecurity, an insecurity born of profound poverty. More precisely, Mother's insecurity derived from the often inarticulate sense that she had no power to ensure her survival in a hostile world. Her only hope was to make people like or love her by what she did for them.

I AM NOT SURE I KNEW IT AT THE TIME, BUT EARLY IN MY LIFE I AM SURE I wanted to find a way to escape from my mother. Home meant Mother. "The job" meant my father. So I was quite happy when Daddy began taking me to the job. I must have been seven or eight years old when I began to spend my summers on the job. I was, of course, still expected to do my chores at home, but being taken to "the job" meant I was becoming a man.

The work was hard, and hard men did the work. The hardness was manifest in the language they used, a language that I learned quickly and that was constitutive of the work we had to do. Few sentences began or ended without "fuck this" or "fuck that." I suspect that Daddy tried to use less profanity when I was around, but he sure had an expressive way of saying "shit." Of course, such language was the language of "the job." You were never supposed to talk that way in church.

For many years, however, I did use the language of the job in contexts of school and church. I did so in part, I think, because I did not want to lose my bearings — my sense of where I had come from. That said, I suspect my use of profanity was more complex than simply an attempt to stay connected with my working-class roots. I also used the language of the job in school and church because I discovered that speaking this way upset the pious, and I took delight in that result. I hated the hypocrisy that niceness cloaks. As I grew older, however, I found my reputation for having a foul mouth to be more of a burden than a blessing, so I did my best to let such language return to being that of "the job."

When Daddy first took me to the job, I was not strong enough to be a laborer. I was also overweight. I suspect the latter was due partly to the unending fried food we ate. So I began by sitting on the scaffold catching brick thrown by the other laborers. Pitching brick was one of the essential skills for a bricklayer's helper because there was no other way to get brick onto the scaffolds. My father could not afford to buy a hoist. So someone on the ground would swing four to six bricks between his legs and fling them to a height of twenty-five feet. If thrown well, the bricks would stay together in a gentle arc and come to rest in the catcher's hands. The catcher would then stack the brick on the scaffold. As a catcher, I had to learn how the bricks were best positioned so that the bricklayer could grasp the brick, cut a head joint, and lay the brick with an economy of motion. That there is a right and wrong way to stack brick means that every task associated with laboring for bricklayers is a skill you must learn.

By the time I was ten, I had learned the full range of skills necessary to be a bricklayer's "helper." I learned quickly how to build scaffold, how to joint, how to shake up the mud on the boards, and even how to chop mud. The latter was the most important and best paid skill among those who were laborers. Mud had to be consistent from one batch to the next, or the mortar between the brick would not be the same color. You do not know what hot is until you are slacking lime to mix with sand on a hot Texas summer day. I did it many times.

The mud maker, moreover, had to know how to chop the mud appropriate to the brick being laid. If, for example, the brick was a porous common brick, the mud needed to be "wet" because the brick quickly soaked up the moisture. If the bricks were "clinkers," that is, bricks that were extra hard because they had come from the bottom of the kiln, the mud needed to be stiff; otherwise the bricks would float on the mud. I was never as good as Mr. Henry, the Hauerwas family's ancient mud maker, but I sure as hell tried to be good at hoeing the mud.

I loved working for my father. I loved the bond hard work established between workers. You need to understand. I was usually the only white guy doing the work of a laborer. Blacks labored. Whites laid brick. But Daddy was from the old school. You could lay brick only after you had learned all the skills necessary to be a good bricklayer's helper. So I was a white guy who did the work of blacks.

I bonded with the other laborers because we had a common enemy — bricklayers. For example, if the bricklayers did not work fast enough, the mud on the boards would dry out, making it necessary for the laborers to shake up the mud. In the hot Texas sun, the mud dried out readily enough without the bricklayers' help. So if a bricklayer took a minute to shoot the shit with someone, it meant that our work as laborers increased. Yet the bricklayer was king. Those of us who had to work "on the ground" had to put up with whatever bricklayers wanted to dish out. As a result, I got to know the men with whom I worked in a quite unusual manner, given the normal segregationist patterns that shaped life in the South.

I also believed that because I was my father's son I had to work harder than anyone else. I did not want anyone to think that I had my job because I was my father's son. And work I did. It was not long before I could push more brick in a brick bar than anyone on the job. I could also load a scaffold using brick tongs (a pincher device that allows you to lift ten to twelve bricks at a time) quicker than anyone else. My Uncle George said I was a lazy worker because I would rather load a brick bar with twice the normal load than make two trips. There was some truth to that, but it always turned out that you had to make two trips anyway.

I became quite strong, and I think Daddy was quite proud of my ability to work. I would sometimes overhear him telling other men on the job that I was his son and that I could outwork ten blacks. Racism was a peculiar thing on the job. Segregation was assumed, but the hard work we had to do meant that it was impossible to avoid getting to know one another. My father worked within the world as he found it, but his regard for Mr. Henry, Isaac, Fred, and George Harper meant that he never used the racist habits that shaped our lives to justify the cruelty embedded in the assumed "normal."

That I was such a good laborer was a roadblock to my learning to lay brick. Daddy hated to lose me as a laborer. He also did not want me to start making a bricklayer's wages, fearing I might be tempted not to go to college. But by the time I was sixteen, I wanted to learn to lay brick. Daddy started to teach me how to lay brick by spreading mud and laying brick on a board in the back yard. God knows how many four-foot-high walls I built, tore down, only to build again. That is the way you learned how to lay brick.

The secret of bricklaying rests in how you spread the mud. You have to cut the mud off the board with your trowel just right, so that when you spread the mud, you do not get it on the face of the brick you have just laid. The mud then must be "frogged" in a manner that essentially lets the brick lay itself. Frogging involves making a trench in the mud so that when the brick is laid the mud pulls the brick level, down to the line. Good bricklayers seldom touch the brick with their trowel. They lay the brick by the feel of their hand. I knew I would never know how to lay brick like my father and his brothers. They were craftsmen. I was always in too much of a hurry to be a really good bricklayer. I could lay a thousand brick a day, which at the time most bricklayers thought to be the norm. I loved jobs where, in the language of a bricklayer, all you could see of the bricklayer was "ass and elbows," which meant you could lay brick without ever having to stop to build a lead or to work around doors or windows.

God knows what possessed us to work so hard. We were quite literally covered in sweat from the beginning to the end of the day. And we smelled like shit, because the sweat often soured, giving everyone on the job a tangy odor. I rather liked the smell, particularly when it offended the people who would come to the job to supervise what we were about. Because we sweat so much we had to drink water constantly. We kept the water in a wooden keg that we tried to keep cool by putting ice in it early in the morning. The ice would seldom last longer than a couple of hours, but hot water was better than no water at all. I soon learned from George Harper never to go to the keg without using the trip to carry back material that the bricklayers would soon need. In short, never waste a motion. If you did, you would not make it to the end of the day.

The etiquette of the keg was not ambiguous. There were two cups (which often looked just alike), one for blacks and one for whites. But if I was at the keg and a bricklayer was using the white cup, I did not have time to wait. So I often drank from the black cup, not to challenge racism but because I was thirsty, in a hurry, and did not give a damn. My mother was concerned about this because she was afraid I might get a "disease." I had no idea what she meant. What she meant, I found out later, was that most blacks had syphilis. If I had known what she meant, I could have corrected the error in her thinking.

To be sure, sex was a constant topic on the job, but you talked about it more than you could do it. It was not without reason that bricklayers called the block we laid, particularly the 8x8x16s, "birth control block." Lay those suckers all day and see if you have energy left after work for any extracurricular activity. At best, you can clean up, eat, and go to bed. Often after laying block all day I could not stop my left hand from cramping all night. And I was young. Think what it meant for men in their fifties to lay block all day. Of course, that did not stop anyone on the job from bragging about their sexual conquests.

The hardness of the work meant that you were expected to keep up your end. If a bricklayer slacked off, then the bricklayer working the other end of the line had to do more work. Daddy always worked the line because he set the pace for us all. He was slight, but God could he lay brick. He could spread mud down the course in a manner I could only envy. A flick of the wrist and he had spread mud over eight brick. The men that worked for him admired his skill and respected his honesty. They seldom tried to cheat him.

I loved the men that worked for my daddy. Bricklayers are extremely independent. They know they have a skill others need but do not have. They are not about to put up with bullshit. Piss them off, and they will gather their tools, walk off the job, get drunk, and then find another job. Screw you. At the same time, however, they know they are trapped. They make a good wage, but no one can lay brick forever. So how do you survive for the long haul? The work after a while will destroy the body. Then what do you do? What you do is drink and look for some angle.

Consider Jesse Womack. Jesse was a man of extraordinary intelligence, a slick bricklayer, and a hard worker, but he was also an alcoholic who never found a way out. He constantly came up with schemes that would make him rich. Once when we were laying brick at a meatpacking plant, a horrible job, Jesse got the idea that he could turn the cow horns into lamps. Using glass shards, he slicked one horn after another so that they could be a base for a table lamp. The lamps were, of course, kitsch, but the horn illumined by light from the inside could be quite beautiful. Jesse was good at making the lamps, but he was no salesman. He ended up with a lot of lamps in his house — and it was a small house.

I will never forget Bearhunter, who got his name because he claimed to have killed a bear with his bare hands. He also claimed to have walked across China after his plane was shot down in World War II. We did not believe any of his stories, but we enjoyed them. Then there was Benny Simons. He was a laborer with whom I worked for two or three years. Benny was part American Indian, part black, and part white. I loved to work with Benny because he worked as hard as I did.

One time Benny and I were building scaffold on a warehouse in the Trinity River bottom in Dallas. The bricklayers had topped out a wall that must have been thirty or forty feet high. Benny and I had to move the scaffold from the section that was completed to the next section. Rather than throwing the boards down to the ground to carry them to the next section, we were trying to do the job quicker by walking along the completed wall. These boards were sixteen foot long and only God knows how heavy they were. Just as Benny began to walk along the wall with one of the boards, a wind blew Benny off the wall. He fell the full thirty or forty feet, and the board landed smack on top of him. I thought for sure that was the end of Benny, but he just got up cursing a blue streak and came back up on the wall. Benny, like my Uncle Rufus, could curse in sentences. I always liked it when he called me "a sorry little son of a bitch pissant." God knows what ever happened to Benny. He had a penchant for getting involved with women who were often married to someone else.

THEN THERE WERE MY UNCLES. THEY WERE NOT EXACTLY NORMAL. UNCLE Rufus was probably the best bricklayer of the lot, but he was always trying his hand at something else that usually did not work out. Once he got mad at a lady who had hired him to build some kitchen cabinets; he was a wonderful woodworker, but he installed them so high she could not reach them. Uncle Rufus also had the gift of creative cursing. We once had an exchange in which I gave as good as I got, making him complain to Aunt Christine, his wife, that I had cursed him out that day. Aunt Christine called Mother, who told me I had upset Uncle Rufus. Women, for quite understandable reasons, had a hard time imagining what the job must be like.

Then there was my uncle George. Uncle George was a piece of work. He was always "into something." For a while it would be Boy Scouts. Then there was the Masonic Lodge. I dare not forget coon hunting and the raising of bluetick hounds. He also made rifles for a while by hand. He built several houses out of block. He lived in one and rented the others. In the one in which he lived, he built a beehive into the chimney so he could watch the bees make honey. Of course, they finally got loose in the house, but it did not deter my uncle George from thinking it a good idea. My aunt Sally was from Commerce, Texas, so I guess she knew what she got when she married my uncle George. Still, she put up with a hell of a lot.

Uncle George was a beautiful bricklayer, but he did not like to work all that hard. At various times, he and my father tried to be partners in a common business, but Daddy was never able to put up with Uncle George's tendency to come to work only when he felt like it. It was not as if Uncle George was lazy. He was just interested in all these other things. And he would often prevail on my father to be interested in what he was interested in.

That is how I learned to coon hunt. Daddy and Uncle George took me out to hear the dogs run. We sat around the campfire and listened for the dogs to hit the trail. Then we talked about which dog was leading the pack. The coon would finally go up a tree, which meant the dogs would howl rather than bark. Then we left the campfire to go where the coon was treed so we could cut down the tree. The poor coon would then be at the mercy of the dogs. It was a cruel sport. I never took to it.

Uncle George once captured a baby coon and decided to try to tame and raise it. Racky finally ran away, but not before throwing all of Aunt Sally's dishes on the floor. Uncle George still missed him. He also got my father into the Masonic Lodge. By this time I was in divinity school, and I had no use for the Masonic Lodge. With my usual bluntness I told my father he could join the Masonic Lodge but he sure as hell would not be buried as a Mason. He soon was an inactive Mason. I do not know if his decision to leave the Masons was due to my remark or not.

Under the influence of Uncle George, daddy spent one winter restoring a World War II issue Springfield 30-06 for use as a deer rifle. As part of the restoration, he made a beautiful walnut stock. I came home the summer of my second year from Yale, and the first thing Daddy did was show me the gun. I had, of course, grown up with guns. I was sure, moreover, that Daddy had restored this gun for me. I acknowledged the beauty of the weapon, but then said, "Daddy, you realize that someday we are going to have to take these goddamn things away from you people." Talk about becoming an Eastern shit. Daddy, of course, said little in response.

Years later I wrote about the incident in a chapter in one of my books. I always gave my books to my folks, and about a year later Mother found the story of Daddy and the gun and called me. On the phone Daddy said, "I still do not know what I am going to do with that goddamn thing." I said, "Don't worry; I will take care of it." And I did. I gave the gun to David Toole, a former student and friend who is from Montana and knows how to use a gun. Just as important, he knows the story that goes with the gun. Paula and I are godparents of his son, Gabe, who hopefully will also know the story of the gun.

My mother was often unhappy with Uncle George. When I was thirteen or fourteen, he took several of us on a scouting trip to Mena, Arkansas. I remember he drove a great big Mercury. We left early, so it was still dark. On the way, he cursed out another driver because he had failed to dim his lights. Uncle George used words that were unusual even for me. It never crossed his mind that he had not dimmed his own lights. We boys noticed, but we knew better than to say anything.

Uncle George was taking us to a homestead one of my great-uncles had developed when, during the Depression, the government was giving land away in Arkansas. Uncle Nick had been an artist in Chicago who, we were told, had a fondness for the bottle. His wife, in an effort to get him away from bad influences, had encouraged him to go to Arkansas. Uncle George and Daddy had visited Uncle Nick when they were boys. Later, on a camping trip to Arkansas, they found Uncle Nick's place. It was grown up something terrible; the log cabin was in bad repair; and the people living there were none too nice. We are talking Hatfields and McCoys. But Uncle George was not deterred. He convinced them to sell the place to him and my dad for five hundred dollars.

The homestead was at the base of Blue Mountain, one of the highest mountains in Arkansas. We got to the property about three in the afternoon. We boys were full of energy, so we suggested to Uncle George that we climb to the top of Blue Mountain. It never occurred to us that he would agree, but he thought it was a great idea, so off we went. We did not get to the top until midnight. Uncle George thought we might stay up there until morning, but the wind was howling and we were cold. So we started down. It was pitch dark. We got separated and hopelessly lost. I avoided falling off several cliffs, but that did not save me from the ever present briar patches. As a result, by the time I made it back to Uncle Nick's place I was scratched up from head to toe. I was just grateful to have made it back. I made it back finally by following a fence row. Uncle George thought it a wonderful adventure. My mother, assessing my body, wanted to kill him.

My mother's animus soon faded. How could you stay angry at this man-child? Moreover, Mother always loved Aunt Sally, Uncle George's wife. My mother also loved Aunt Christine, who was married to Uncle Rufus. Aunt Christine was pure country. She and Uncle Rufus had five children, which seemed a lot. Bobby, their oldest son, was a bit younger than I was, but when he got older he and I labored together. Bobby never learned to lay brick. Besides me, only Uncle George's son Don learned to lay brick. But Don was married six times, twice to the same lady, so he had to find other ways to make a living. The sad truth is that no one in the family continued the family tradition.

THAT NONE OF US BECAME BRICKLAYERS OR EVEN BRICK CONTRACTORS HAD everything to do with the changes in the world around the family Hauerwas. Bricks and those who lay them are expensive. Increasingly, buildings were designed to avoid the need for such craftsmen. My father retired early, partly because his back had done all the bending it could do, but also because he could not compete with newly arriving immigrants. They not only worked as hard as we did but did so for less money. That is when Mother and Daddy moved to Arkansas and lived in a mobile home just outside Mena. Daddy, who had spent a lifetime building brick homes for others, ended up living in a prefabricated trailer. He never complained about living in a trailer, but that he lived in a trailer has always seemed to me an indication that something had gone fundamentally wrong.

In his memoir *Stone Mad*, stonecutter Seamus Murphy reflects on his training in the trade. He begins with the observation that life is change, which leads us to use our past as a yardstick to examine the future. People in trades such a stonecutting take pride in the past, in the fact that they are part of a tradition of those who have gone before, whose handiwork can be seen in town and village. Those shaped by the craft tradition work to conserve modes of life that they have learned are constitutive of achieving the good ends to which their craft is dedicated. Murphy fears that the future holds little in store for people like him. Concrete has replaced stone, which means that a craft like stonecutting, which requires that apprentices be trained over years in the diverse skills necessary to deal with the unanticipated challenges of the craft, cannot be sustained.

My father understood that the world was changing; and therefore he never wanted me to follow him into bricklaying. Yet the training I received left an indelible mark on everything I do. I assume change is inevitable, but I am deeply conservative. My understanding of what it means to be conservative is shaped by the craft tradition. My criticism of liberal political presumptions is based in my presumption that politics, like laying brick, is a wisdom-determined activity. Liberalism too often is the attempt to have concrete replace stone in an effort to avoid the necessary existence of a people with wisdom.

Commenting on the craft of stonecutting and on the training required to work with stone, Seamus Murphy observes: "With hammer, mallet and chisel we have shaped and fashioned rough boulders. We often curse our material, and often we speak to it kindly — we have come to terms with it in order to master it, and it has a way of dictating to us sometimes — and then the struggle begins. We try to impose ourselves on it, but we know our material and respect it. We will often take a suggestion from it, and our work will be the better for it." In like manner, I think of theology as a craft requiring years of training. Like stonecutters and bricklayers, theologians must come to terms with the material upon which they work. In particular, they must learn to respect the simple complexity of the language of the faith, so that they might reflect the radical character of orthodoxy. I think one of the reasons I was never drawn to liberal Protestant theology was that it felt too much like an attempt to avoid the training required of apprentices. In contrast, Karl Barth's work represented for me an uncompromising demand to submit to a master bricklayer, with the hope that in the process one might learn some of the "tricks of the trade."

My MOTHER AND FATHER RETIRED, BUT THEY CONTINUED TO WORK. THEY planted a garden that would feed half of Mena. Mother was sure they needed a "bunkhouse" in preparation for visitors. Daddy built the bunkhouse out of rock picked up on their property. It is a stunning rock job that I suspect few people even know is there. He also built a bridge out of the same material, in order to secure the entrance to their property. Again, I wonder if many people notice the craftsmanship that went into that artful curve over an undistinguished creek. Formed by years of "doing it right," my father could not do anything halfway.

Mother and Daddy lived in Mena four or five years before moving to Carthage to be with Acie and Donresia. Adam and I helped them move. It was a good move, because Daddy could help feed the animals Donresia and Acie owned. He had also been befriended by a cat that had walked out of the Arkansas woods and claimed him as "hers." She had a bob tail, so Daddy named her "Bobby." They brought her to

Texas, and the three of them had a few good years together there before my mother moved them to Dallas.

Daddy died on December 31, 1992. His birthday was December 24. He had just turned 84. We had all come to Texas to celebrate his birthday and Christmas. I was to give a paper in Israel in early January, so Paula and I left Texas after Christmas to journey to Israel, as well as take a trip up the Nile. Arriving in Aswan, I was given a message to call Adam. It proved impossible to make a call from Aswan, so I did not learn of Daddy's death until we returned to Cairo. It took us three days to get back. I had always known that when my father died I should preach his funeral. I am not sure why I knew that, but the trip home gave me time to write this sermon.

Christ's Gentle Man

A Sermon on the Occasion of My Father's Funeral

Revelation 7:9-17
Matthew 5:1-12

My father was a good, kind, simple, gentle man. He did not try to be gentle, for there was no meanness in him. He was not tempted to hatred, envy, or resentment. He was kind and gentle, possessing each virtue with a simplicity that comes only to those who are good through and through. It was simply his gift to be gentle, which he gave unreservedly to those of us fortunate to be his family and friends.

That his gentleness came so effortlessly helps us understand better Jesus' beatitudes. Too often those characteristics — the poor in spirit, those that mourn, the meek, those who hunger and thirst for righteousness, the pure in heart, the peacemakers, and the persecuted — are turned into ideals we must strive to attain. As ideals, they can become formulas for power rather than descriptions of the kind of people characteristic of the new age brought by Christ; for the beatitudes are not general recommendations for anyone but describe those who have been washed by the blood of the Lamb. It is they who will hunger and thirst no more, having had their lives transformed by Christ's cross and resurrection.

Thus Jesus does not tell us that we should try to be poor in spirit, or meek, or peacemakers. He simply says that many who are called into his kingdom will find themselves so constituted. We cannot try to be meek or gentle in order to become a disciple of this gentle Jesus, but in learning to be his disciple some of us will discover that we have been gentled. Jesus' gentleness is nowhere more apparent than in his submission to the cross and, even there, in his wish that no harm would come to his persecutors. But it is no less apparent in his willingness to be touched by the sick and troubled, to be with the social outcasts and the powerless, and, in his time of agony, to share a meal with his disciples that has now become the feast of the new age.

Part of the difficulty with the beatitudes is that some of the descriptions seem problematic to us — in particular, we do not honor the meek. To be meek, or gentle, is, we think, to lack ambition and drive. Gentleness, at most, is reserved for those aspects of our lives we associate with the personal, but it cannot survive the rough and tumble of "the world." Yet Jesus is clear that his kingdom is constituted by those who are meek and gentle — that is, by those who have learned to live without protection. Gentleness is given to those who have learned that God will not have his kingdom triumph through the violence of the world, for such a triumph came through the meekness of a cross.

It is surely fitting and right that upon the death of my father we celebrate all that his gentle presence meant in our lives. It is fitting and right that we mourn the loss of his presence. Yet he would be the first to remind us that his life should be celebrated and mourned just to the extent that we remember his gentleness as a gift made possible by Christ. The great good news of this day is that my father's life made sense, that his life was possible, only because our gentle savior could not be defeated by the powers of hate and violence. My father's life is intelligible only as we see in his gentleness the gentleness of our Lord.

For example, in one of the climactic moments of my father's life, when he was honored for supervising the building of Pleasant Mound Methodist Church, the first words he said were: "I would like to say that I am only human, the one we should be thanking is

Almighty God. He is the one that gave it to us. Words will not let me express myself." He thanked Don Ragsdale, the construction committee, and Don Wallace, who "did the best electrical job he had ever overseen." He thanked all the Christian business firms with whom he had been doing business over the years and who gave material at cost. He closed saying he had already received the thanks necessary. "I just thank God and praise God for it."

Simple but eloquent words. They but embody the simplicity and eloquence of his gentle life. His life was like the beauty he taught me to see in a solid brick wall whose bed joints were uniform and head joints true. The simple gentleness of my father rested in the sense of the superior good that comes to those whose lives are honed by a craft. My father was incapable of laying brick rough, just as he was incapable of being cruel. It literally hurt him to look at badly done brick work, just as it hurt him to see cruelty.

Like his gentleness, his sense of craft was also out of step with the spirit of the times. The world wanted work done quickly and cheaply. The world wanted shortcuts. The world wanted him to build houses of brick so soft that they would melt from watering the yard. He was incapable of such work, so he was not rewarded as the world knows reward. Yet he lived well, secure in the knowledge that he never built a house with a "hog in the wall" — that is, with one course more on one side of the house than the other.

There is a rock building back in the woods outside Mena, Arkansas, that my father and mother built. Few people will ever see that building, though it is one of the most stunning rock jobs I have ever seen. My father and mother could not have built it otherwise, for to do so would have offended my father's sensibility. To lay rock well you must see each rock individually, yet in relation to what may be the next rock to be laid. To see each rock in this way requires a humility founded on the love of the particular. This is the humility that characterized my father's life. And it was perhaps nowhere more apparent than when you walked with my father through the woods.

My father never saw "nature" in the abstract. He saw this tree or plant, this stream or river, this sky against these particular clouds. As one who spent his whole life in the construction of buildings, he seemed to prefer those aspects of our existence that we could not make. Thus he would talk endlessly, and he seldom talked endlessly, about what a wonderful ash tree this was, or about the wonder that a post oak leaf is so different from a red oak. It was my father who found the holly tree hidden in the woods at our home in Chapel Hill, a tree I had walked by many times but never seen.

I think the wonder he possessed was what made him so fond of children. He did not see children as potential adults. Rather, he enjoyed their wonder. When they found an extraordinary rock, he too thought the rock, common though it was, extraordinary. If they liked the rock enough to share their discovery with him, then indeed it was extraordinary. I think children loved my father because they sensed in him the gentle wonder that, unfortunately, many of us lose in the name of being "grown up." He loved to teach us to fish or hammer a nail, and he could do it with all the patience such teaching required. Though I have to say that I think teaching me to lay brick tested that patience to its limits.

Jesus' gentle life was challenged by the fractious and contentious character of his own people, the power of Rome, and the incomprehension of his followers. My father's gentleness in many ways had a more serious challenge — namely, Texas. Texans have not been a people known for their meekness or gentleness. We are a flinty people, formed as we are by a dry wind that blows across a hard land. We are not known for our humility, but for our bluster.

My father was a Texan, and he had some bluster to him. Like all Texans, he liked to brag — particularly around carpenters. Yet try as he would to be a Texan, his gentleness prevailed. You could feel it in the stories he told of riding his horse to school each day as a young boy. He loved school, but even more he loved that horse. It was that same love, I suspect, that made Bobby, the bobtail cat that walked out of the Arkansas woods, choose my father to be her companion in life. My father accepted that choice as inevitable, and he and Bobby seemed to understand one another in a manner that made the rest of us "outsiders."

I suspect such tenderness also had much to do with one of my father's major failings as a Texan — a failing, I might add, that none of us ever explicitly acknowledged. Truth be known, trained as he was from an early age to hunt, he was a terrible shot. My hunch is that his deficiency in this respect did not derive from lack of skill, but had more to do with his love of animals. One of my earliest memories is of him deferring to a neighbor the shooting of a dog that was suspected of being mad. His gentleness simply would not let him assume the role of a hero. Even mother was sometimes frustrated by this deficiency, as she could not understand how he could miss the ducks that landed on their tank in Arkansas. I suspect he just could not bring himself to kill birds, numerous as they were, whose beauty he so admired. Of course, armadillos rooting up his azaleas was quite a different matter.

Perhaps a more determinative challenge to my father's gentleness derived from the fact that Texas, at least the Texas in which he was raised, was also "the South." He inherited habits that separated blacks from whites. Yet those habits could never flourish in his soul. That his gentleness prevailed even here I think had much to do with the unavoidability of the comradeship forged from the crucible of unbelievably hard work. The years he worked with Mr. Henry and George Harper meant that he could never believe that their goodness should be ignored on the basis of their color. He, like all of us, lacked the practices to know how the community formed through hard work could be carried forward in other aspects of our lives, but he also knew the sadness with which we must live in the absence of such practices.

The work that he loved, the work that wreaked havoc on his body, was also a challenge to his gentleness. One side of his hands was worn smooth by the millions of times he held the rough material he laid. Work had made the other side as hard and course as the mortar that results when lime and cement are mixed. The hardness of the material, the hardness of the work, can make bricklayers "hard men." "The job" is no place for the faint of heart or for those of refined speech or taste.

Yet even there my father remained my gentle father, working as hard as the men he paid, dealing fairly with their weaknesses and strengths, enjoying the "characters" — the Clarence Boduskys, the Jesse Womacks, the Tiptons, Bearhunter, Bobby, and, of course, my uncles: George, Rufus, Dick, Tommy, and Bill. He loved and was loved in a world embarrassed to acknowledge that love was even present. Hard men will cry unashamedly when they hear that "Mr. Coffee" is dead, because they know they will not see his like again on "the job."

No one knows the gentleness that characterized this man's life more than my mother. She knows that in spite of the tiredness that often gripped his life he never failed to have time for any of us. He never thought that in doing so he was sacrificing his own interest, as his love for us was his interest. The tender love my mother and father embodied in their marriage reached out and gave me a brother. That they did so is not surprising, since their love was one in which there was no fear of the stranger.

That such gentleness constituted my father's life must surely be the reason God chose to give him such a gentle death. He lived peacefully, and he died peacefully. Of course his dying does not feel gentle for us who loved him. We rightly feel a loss, knowing that such gentle souls are all too rare. How are we to live without him?

But the great good news is that he has joined the other saints of God's kingdom gathered around the throne. He is among those who now worship God, continually sheltered as they are by the one who alone is worthy of worship. He has joined the great communion of saints, the same communion that we enjoy through God's great gift of this meal of gentleness. For in this meal we are made part of God's life and thus share our lives with one another. So we come filled with sadness, yet rejoicing that God, through lives like my father's, continues to make present Christ's gentle kingdom.

I was fifty-two when my father died. I feel quite sure that I needed all fifty-two years to be able to preach that sermon. I wanted the sermon to be eloquent, because I think his life exemplified the simplicity that is the heart of eloquence. Yet that sermon, my ability to write that sermon, was not without cost: it meant I was a long way from Pleasant Grove and the world of my parents.

My FATHER'S GREAT GIFT TO ME, MY MOTHER'S GREAT GIFT TO ME, A GIFT I did not recognize until later, was their willingness to let me go on. I did not feel my separation from them as I went through college. I was, after all, returning home every summer to lay brick. I was vaguely aware that I was being initiated into a world of books and institutions with which they were unfamiliar. It was only when I went to Yale that I began to sense that my new world was one my parents had no resources to understand, or enter.

They tried. In particular, my mother tried. Her trying, however, often led to some trying moments for me. I was once giving a lecture to clergy in Dallas, and I thought she might like to be present. I had made some reference to abortion, which Mother failed to understand. Hers was the first hand raised in the question period. Drawing on her experience as a nurse, she said I was clearly wrong about abortion. I responded stupidly by saying that she clearly did not know what she was talking about. Needless to say, I lost any persuasive power I might have had over the attending clergy.

My father would have never said anything. He was proud of me. He was glad I was a professor. But once Adam was born, he became the focus of my mother's and father's attention. They longed to be with him. They had times together, but I was in a difficult marriage to a difficult person who did not like my parents. I was caught. I was too much my father's son to know how to negotiate the conflict. As a result, my parents never got to enjoy their grandson in the way they so rightly desired.

Yet there was a connection between my world and theirs — we were Christians. They let me go on; they let me enter a world foreign to them, because they thought I was serving God. Yet I did not feel any psychological pressure from them to be more Christian than I was prepared to be as I worked my way through Yale Divinity School and Yale Graduate School. I assumed that my parents would never want me to be anything other than straightforward. Bullshit was not allowed. Plain speech and plain thinking was the hallmark of their life, and I took it to be the hallmark of my life. I should like to think that this is still true of how I think and write.

I do not know whence it came, but I have a passion for truth. I do not want to lie to others or myself. I want to know the truth about the way things are. I hope I am a Christian because what we believe as Christians forces an unrelenting engagement with reality. That my parents let me go is a testimony to the truthfulness of their lives. Without lives like theirs, the life I have led, a life shaped by books, is threatened by unreality. I try to remember where I came from.

Indeed, I not only try to remember, but I hope my life exemplifies what I learned on the job. I am often asked how I get done all I get done. The answer is simple — I work. I get up at five every morning and I work till six every evening. I do not waste time. If I have fifteen minutes, I can read this or that. It is the same principle as never going to the keg without carrying back some block. To be so determined can be oppressive for others, as well as for me, at times. Thanks to Paula I have learned to rest — a little. But I work because I love the work I have been given to do.

Yet it remains true that the work I have been given to do is work that is a long way from Pleasant Grove and the job. I often think of a scene from the movie *Breaking Away*. The movie is set in Bloomington, Indiana, and is focused on a young student at the university who is in training for a bike race. The movie explores what it means for the young bike rider to grow up, as he attempts to break away, not from other bike riders in a race, but from his family and his upbringing. His attempts to break away create tensions with his father, who is a "cutter" — the derogatory name given to the "townies" who make their living cutting the stone in quarries that surround Bloomington.

The scene I find so powerful has the son and father walking across the university campus. They pass a large building, and the son, in an effort to make conversation, observes that he has a class in this building. His father replies that he cut the stone for that building and then adds, "I've always wondered what it looks like on the inside." His son is absolutely bewildered. He cannot believe his father has never seen the inside. He asks why. "Because," his father says, "it wouldn't be right." "Cutters" do not go into the buildings they build.

I have spent my life in buildings built by people like my father, buildings in which the builders have felt they do not belong. Class matters. I am a long way from Pleasant Grove and the job, but I have no desire to leave Pleasant Grove or the job behind. I think that has meant that I have been interested only in what matters. I have never sought to have a career. I am an academic because to be an academic has given me time to think about matters that should matter. What I hope and pray is that the way I have tried to think and write may in some small way help sustain lives as good as my parents. My father was a better bricklayer than I am a theologian. I am still in too much of a hurry. But if the work I have done in theology is of any use, it is because of what I learned on the job, that is, you can lay only one brick at a time.

CHAPTER 3

Studies

It was 1962. I was twenty-two. I had never been farther north than Mena, Arkansas. But I was going to divinity school at Yale University in New Haven, Connecticut. I remember finding myself on the Garden State Parkway, fearing that I would make a wrong turn and never make it to New Haven. Newark, New Jersey, was not where I wanted to spend the rest of my life. I had never seen row upon row of apartment buildings. I thought, "If this is what it's going to be like, I will never make it 'up here.' " But I did somehow find my way to the Merritt Parkway and New Haven. If going to Southwestern was an entry into a new world, Yale was doubly so. I had no idea what I was getting myself into.

The divinity school at Yale is "up the hill" from the university. The architecture is Georgian, and it looks like a miniature copy of the University of Virginia. The divinity school was built during the Depression, with money left over from the building of Sterling Library, or so the story goes. John William Sterling, who had given the money for new buildings at Yale, allegedly was an agnostic who would not have been all that pleased, as we say in the South, that his money was used to build the divinity school. But he died in 1918 and could not protest. I do not know if that story is true, but those of us who made up the student body at the Sterling Divinity Quadrangle rather liked the idea that the school had been named after an agnostic.

That the divinity school was up on the hill and looked different from the rest of the university suggests, at least symbolically, the intellectual distance between the university and the divinity school. Innocent as I was, it never occurred to me that the divinity school might be regarded by many in the university as "not the university." I simply assumed that the divinity school was where you went to investigate whether the stuff Christians say they believe is true. I did not understand that Yale University itself had no use for Christianity, which is to say that theology was not a legitimate subject in the university. I thought I had come to Yale University to study theology. I had a lot to learn.

It may seem quite inconceivable, but I had not figured out what it meant to go to a divinity school. It had not come home to me that divinity schools were where people go to study for the ministry. Indeed, I was quite surprised to learn that many of my fellow students were there to become ministers. I even discovered that I was expected to work in a church.

I did not want to work in a church, which meant that I had a hell of a time getting a job. John Oliver Nelson (or JON, as he liked to be called), the dapperly dressed person in charge of fieldwork at the divinity school, told me, "You're a rough cut diamond, but you don't need to be quite so 'rough cut.' For example, you don't need to tell them that you're not sure if you like children. Don't forget, Hauerwas, we need to get you a job." Class issues were also involved. JON told me that a minister from Greenwich who had interviewed me suggested that I simply "would not do."

But thanks to JON, I did get a job. He matched me with a minister who he thought might overlook my obvious class problems. His name was Dick Smeltzer. He was the pastor of Hamden Plains Methodist Church in Hamden Plains, Connecticut. Dick was a remarkable man who thought theology mattered. In the interview, he asked me two questions: did I have a car? and what side was I on in the Barth-Brunner debate? I let him know that I did have a car, and that I was on Barth's side. I got the job. It turned out that Dick loved to argue theology, and he was on Brunner's side. It was also the case that the last person who had worked at the church did not have a car, and so Dick had to take them back and forth. My job was to teach Sunday school to a class of sixth-graders and to run the Methodist Youth Fellowship. I was not particularly good at either, but at the end of my two years at Hamden Plains the kids I taught gave me a volume of *Church Dogmatics* III.4.

THAT I WAS DRAWN INTO THE LIFE OF THE CHURCH, OR AT LEAST A CHURCH, by entering the divinity school at Yale may suggest to people who know of my emphasis on the centrality of the church for Christian theology that it all began at Yale. And indeed, I am sure that the seeds of the way I do theology were sown during the education I received in the divinity school. It would be a mistake, however, to assume that the way I think represents something called the "Yale School of Theology," as some people have come to call it. Yale did make all the difference for how I think, but I had no idea at the time that Yale represented a "position."

I came to Yale during a time of transition. H. Richard Niebuhr had retired and died the year before. Roland Bainton had also retired, though he was ever present and often seen peddling his bicycle around the campus. Robert Calhoun was in his last years. I had one of the last courses in the history of theology that he would teach. I never took a course from George Lindbeck, who was in Rome at Vatican II. I had only one course, Christology, from Hans Frei. Thus it would not be quite right to say that these remarkable men were my teachers. Nonetheless, I had a wonderful education at Yale, and I have spent a lifetime trying to think it through. I am not sure if I became a Christian at Yale, but I certainly began to be a theologian because of what I learned there.

For example, I think I had one of the best introductions to Old Testament possible. Brevard Childs taught the first semester, which concentrated on the Pentateuch. I will never forget his lectures on Genesis. We read Gerhard von Rad and Martin Noth, as well as John Bright and G. Ernest Wright. Accordingly, for interpretation of Old Testament texts we were expected to take seriously questions concerning how the history of Israel was to be reconstructed. I remember one of our seminars turned on the question of whether Abraham, who may or may not have existed, was a camel or ass nomad. Mr. Childs thought it quite amusing when I suggested that, being unable to keep up on that debate, I might just as well read the text without the presumption that the meaning of the text depended on historical reconstruction.

Mr. Childs was amused because he was beginning to develop the hermeneutics of canonical criticism that would become his mark on the field. At the time I was not quite sure what to make of his proposal. Later I came to worry that his approach might be a way to reinstitute an emphasis on *sola scriptura*, the Protestant doctrine that the Bible is the ultimate authority for faith. However, I had read enough R. G. Collingwood to worry equally about the way "history" was used to tell us what really happened. In addition to his emphasis on the shape of the canon instead of the historical reconstruction of the text as a guide to interpretation, Mr. Childs also suggested that the early church, precritical readings of Scripture might have something important to tell us. A wonderful man named Richard Kenny, who unfortunately died young, was the graduate assistant in the course. He wrote his dissertation on the manna traditions as read through the church fathers. Because of Dick I was introduced early on to the revolutionary idea that we might again learn to read Scripture theologically by attending to how the fathers read the Bible.

Walther Zimmerli taught the second semester of Old Testament. He was a visiting scholar from Zurich, and at the time was acknowledged as one of the great scholars of the prophetic literature. By the time I finished studying the prophets with Mr. Zimmerli, I could not distinguish between the prophetic word and Karl Barth. What was so remarkable about these remarkable men was not only their extraordinary erudition, but that they actually thought the text was about God. At the time, I do not think I appreciated the significance of this fact, but their example has stayed with me.

Paul Meyer taught New Testament. It was a relatively conventional course in which we spent more time on the relationship between the Gospels of Matthew, Mark, and Luke — the so-called Synoptic Problem — than I care to remember. We actually read Kirsopp Lake. Mr. Meyer, however, was at his best when he lectured on Romans. It was just at the time when scholars were beginning to question the Lutheran reading of Paul. I cannot remember if Krister Stendahl's article "The Apostle Paul and the Introspective Conscience of the West" had been published, but the challenge to the Lutheran emphasis on justification was certainly part of the course.

The graduate assistant for New Testament was Wayne Meeks, who was writing his dissertation on the use of the Old Testament in John's Gospel. I am not sure, but I believe it was through Wayne that I began to pick up hints that "Judaism" was not just some precursor to Christianity that Christians could leave behind. I seem to remember that we even read Frank Cross, to challenge the presumption that Judaism was a priest-ridden, legalistic religion. It began to occur to some of us that what Christians believe is unintelligible without the continuing presence of the Jews. Certainly much was made of Romans 9–11 as central for how Paul was to be understood.

I do not know why or how the Jews became so important for me. Growing up, I had known only one Jew, Max Goldblatt, who owned a store that seemed to sell everything. In particular, he sold model airplanes that I loved to assemble and fly. He was a lovely man who was extremely kind to me. My parents had told me he was a Jew, but I had no idea what that meant. Jews and Catholics, as far as I was concerned, came from another planet.

Before Yale, in college, I had become convinced that one of the decisive challenges concerning the truthfulness of Christianity was the failure of Christians to stand against the Shoah. I do not remember how I came to that conclusion, but I think reading Nietzsche had convinced me that how Christians lived surely must be crucial for understanding how, if at all, what Christians say they believe might be considered true. That Christians not only had prepared the ground for the Shoah through centuries of persecution, but also had conspired in the murder of the Jews, I took as a decisive indicator that Christianity did not meet the demands for truthfulness.

It therefore came as quite a shock to me to discover in Julian Hartt's systematic theology course at Yale that Barth had seen more clearly than most the perversion of National Socialism. I was not prepared for the idea that Christianity itself might harbor such a critical lens about affairs in the world. Barth later confessed that Dietrich Bonhoeffer understood better than he had that the persecution and murder of the Jews was the most decisive indicator of the demonic character of the Nazis. Barth, however, because of his recovery of the Christological center of the Christian faith, did rightly recognize the Nazis for who they were. I was impressed.

Mr. Hartt was from a long line of Methodist pastors. He had been raised in South Dakota because his father, a Methodist minister from Maine, had thought it important to bring Jesus to South Dakota. His lectures in systematic theology, which were allegedly expositions of the Apostles' Creed, were exercises in dialectical brilliance, cultural insight, and wicked humor. He was as philosophically astute as he was theologically brilliant. We read Austin Farrer and Karl Barth. I was mesmerized by Hartt. Indeed, I suspect that if anyone cares enough to try to understand the way I do theology they will discover that I am a pale imitation of Hartt.

I think one of the lasting lessons I learned from Hartt was a respect for the language of the faith. For example, Hartt would spend a number of lectures trying to analyze why the first article of the creed would have us say, "I believe in God, the Father." Father? Why Father? How could we possibly know that God is the Father before we know that God is the Creator? Hartt would run through countless variations on what "Father" could possibly mean in such a context. He would then finally make the move I came to associate with Barth: what we should learn from the creed's placement of "Father" prior to "Creator" is that the first article cannot be separated from the second. Accordingly, the doctrine of creation is necessarily an eschatological doctrine; that is, we know there was a beginning because we have seen the end in Christ. Creation is not "back there." Rather, it names the character of all divine action. God does not need to "intervene" in creation because creation is charged with the grandeur of Christ. I was beginning to understand that learning to speak Christian is an invitation to see the magical wonder of existence.

Mr. Hartt, moreover, never let us forget, and here Farrer was all important, that massive metaphysical claims are entailed in the connection between the first and second articles. Early on I was beginning to understand why Aquinas was right that only God is pure act. Only in God are existence and essence one. Accordingly, our language about God is necessarily analogical, which means that theology has the task of helping the church not say more about God than needs to be said.

I was again extraordinarily fortunate to have a talented graduate assistant in systematic theology. Robert King was writing his dissertation on Christology and identity descriptions. Suddenly I began to see the importance of issues in philosophical psychology for the work of theology. I read Gilbert Ryle's *The Concept of Mind* and began to wonder about the implications of that great book for presumptions about Jesus' "messianic consciousness," a prominent debate in New Testament scholarship at the time. In short, I was beginning to make connections that I have been working out for my whole life. In particular, it became clear to me that questions surrounding how to understand the person and work of Christ are integrally related to our understanding of what it means for us to be human.

Old Testament, New Testament, and systematic theology were two-semester courses. My fourth course in the first semester was taught by Paul Holmer, a new faculty member from the University of Minnesota. He was a philosopher. I took his course on Kierkegaard. Mr. Holmer was not only tall but large in every sense of the term. He filled any room, even a lecture hall, he entered. He was thoroughly a Midwesterner and used this fact, when it pleased him, to disguise his cultural sophistication. He was, for example, the first person I came to know who loved opera. But Mr. Holmer's first loves were Kierkegaard and Wittgenstein. I never developed a love for opera, but I certainly came to love Kierkegaard and Wittgenstein.

I read as much Kierkegaard as I could get my hands on. I was sure Kierkegaard was right to put the stress on the "how" of the faith as necessary for understanding the "what." Put differently, I was learning from Holmer's account of Kierkegaard (as well as from Hartt) that theology is best understood as a form of practical reason. Moreover, I learned from Kierkegaard that the truth of practical reason is Christ, and thus practical reason cannot be constrained by the accommodated form of the church identified with Christendom.

Barth, in a late reflection on Kierkegaard (whom he identifies as this "gallant witness to the truth"), observes that Kierkegaard is a teacher whose school every theologian must enter — once. From Kierkegaard we learn that the God who is the "infinite qualitative difference" from us has said "yes" to us in Christ. Barth, however, thinks it best that we enter Kierkegaard's school only "once," because the very character of Kierkegaard's attack on the human-centered pietism of his day had the ironic effect of fortifying a quite similar pietism in ours.

Some may wonder if Kierkegaard really exerted such an influence on me, because I seldom reference him. It is a good question, but I think he always haunts me. In truth, I decided early on that Kierkegaard is one of those figures that require you to live with them on a daily basis if you are to "use" their work well. I decided I would live with others, partly because I simply did not want to negotiate the unending scholarly debates surrounding Kierkegaard. I have never pretended to be a scholar.

Yale Divinity School had different tracks students could choose. Most chose the ministerial track. I chose to be on a track that would put you on a trajectory toward a Ph.D. and college or university teaching. That track required a sequence of courses on religion and the intellectual life. The final course I took my first year was on the history of the university taught by Edward Dirks. It was not an intellectually exciting course, but it gave me an opportunity to read, for example, Hastings Rashdall's history of the university.

What a year! I was exhilarated. More importantly, I was fully engaged. At no time did I think, "Why am I doing this? I'm not even sure if I'm a Christian." Indeed, I lost interest in whether I was or was not a Christian. I simply found what I was reading to be about matters that mattered. This is what I wanted to do with my life. This is what I hope my life has been. I have never looked back nor regretted what I have been given.

Oh, on December 29, 1962, I got married. That is about as much thought as I put into that decision. Only God knows what I thought I was doing. Of course, I thought I was in love. I know I was at least in lust. We were supposed to be married the summer after my first year in seminary, but I was lonely, and Anne was not happy in Dallas. So sometime during the first semester we decided to be married at the Christmas break. Anne did all the wedding plans. We were married in San Antonio at her home church. We drove straight to New Haven, and into hell.

It was not hell at first. It just worked out that way. In truth, I simply had no idea what I was doing by getting married. It just seemed like something you did along the way. I had started to date Anne our senior year in college. I had little sense of the complexity of human relationships. Anne seemed to want me, and that was enough for me. Her father managed "Five and Dime" stores, so she seemed more middle class than I was. That did not bother me, though it came to bother her.

Her mother was a disturbed person. She spent her days in a bathrobe, seldom leaving their modest suburban house. She was not without talent and spent much of her time painting flowers. It would turn out that Anne had inherited both her mother's talent and her inability to negotiate life. Early on Anne enlisted me to protect her from her mother. It was a role I played gladly. After all, I am a southern male. We think that one of our primary roles in life is to make the world safe for "our women." It is a role that is destructive not only for those who play it, but also for the women we allegedly protect.

Anne's mother was "religious." I am not sure what that meant except that she had a fascination with the pastor of their church. She brought up Anne to serve the church. Accordingly, she insisted that Anne major in Christian education in college in order to prepare her for a lifetime service in the church. This was well before the time when women could think of being ordained. Anne resisted both her mother and the church. I could not blame her, and in fact I was quite sympathetic, but I was not prepared for how her hatred of mother and church would finally become a hatred of me.

I guess we were "happy" at first. We had little money. I had found a place for us to live not far from the divinity school. We occupied an attic apartment that we got for free in exchange for babysitting the couple's three children, keeping the snow shoveled, and doing the yard work. That arrangement proved to be a disaster. The couple was not only inconsiderate but more than willing to exploit us at every turn.

Part of the difficulty with the arrangement was that Anne had started to work as a customer representative for Connecticut Blue Cross. It was too much to ask of her — caring for three obnoxious children and starting a new job. Anne was smart, but that did not mean she had good judgment, particularly about other people. But being self-absorbed, I failed to pick up on her inability to negotiate peer relationships. I thought everything was fine. I had everything I wanted — the bedroom and books. I am not sure if Anne knew what she wanted.

After three months in the apartment, we were able to move into divinity school housing. Life seemed good. We were surrounded by people like us, that is, young and newly married. We did what young couples did together — eat and go to the movies. Anne was an excellent cook. We made friends, and our life together seemed to be set. At that time I did not have a clue that I was married to a seriously ill person. All I knew was that one of my roles in life was to try to make her happy.

I WAS EXPECTED TO WORK IN A CHURCH NOT ONLY DURING THE SCHOOL YEAR but during the summer, which was the last thing I wanted to do. Church work did not seem like work to me, and I thought I needed to make more money than churches paid. During the school year I had read about the worker-priest movement in France after World War II. So I convinced JON that I should spend my summer as a worker-priest. I could not get a job laying brick because of the power of the unions, but JON found me a job at G & O Manufacturing.

G & O made various forms of radiators and coils for heating units. I was trained to run a huge punch press. The press stamped copper into fins that were then threaded onto copper pipes. I then ran an expander through the pipes to hold the fins in place. Thus it is that I learned to make the heating units that run along the wall next to the floor boards. I had never worked inside. I had never worked around machinery. I had never worked in a place so loud that you could not hear yourself think. But it was a job, and I needed a job.

It was piecework, and the management had never seen anyone work the way I worked. I could turn out more tubing than they thought possible. I could do so even though the press "scrapped" constantly. When that happened I had to turn the machine off, reach into the jaws of the press, and draw out the material that had prevented the copper from going through the press. It was dangerous work. You lived in fear that you might forget to turn the press off and lose your fingers or hand. I was damn lucky. I managed to work at G & O for three summers, at night during the school year, and every holiday. Through it all I never lost even a finger. I came close once, when a helper moved a lathe table before he was supposed to. I was reaching for a lead "bullet" to put in the end of the tube. It had fallen into the bottom of the lathe, and my finger got caught. But I was lucky — all I lost was the skin from the first knuckle up. I still have the scar.

Because of the pace I kept, it was not long before the "timers" were sent to retime me. It seems they thought I was making too much money. The shop was about half black and half white. An African American named Al Reasoner was my foreman. He had been raised in South Carolina and was the son of a Presbyterian minister. He thought it fascinating that I was in divinity school. We were destined to become good friends. I complained to Al about the retiming, and he had it stopped.

Studies

I was beginning to understand why labor unions were needed. The social gospel took on new significance.

Indeed, the next year I went to the AFL-CIO convention in New York. A man named Charlie Weber had come to the divinity school to meet students who were interested in exploring the relationship between religion and labor. He worked for the religion and labor council of the AFL-CIO. I was the only person who turned up. He drove me to New York, where I heard an extraordinary speech by Walter Reuther. I had never heard anyone speak with such passion.

This was 1962. The time was conservative. That I was the only student from Yale to attend the convention confirms that Yale was a conservative school. Times would soon change. In the meantime, we were in the early years of urban renewal. Richard Lee had been elected mayor of New Haven. I was drawn into New Haven democratic politics because two of the faculty, Bill Muehl and Bill Miller, were running for town council. Robert Dahl's book *Who Governs* was required reading. That book was not only a study of New Haven but a defense of pluralist politics as the form of democratic polity.

One of my close friends in the divinity school was Butch Henderson. Butch was from Muleshoe, Texas. We took an instant liking for one another, often trying to destroy one another on the tennis court. We were drawn to the efforts of Mr. Muehl, who taught preaching, and Mr. Miller, who taught social ethics, to remake New Haven politics. So we became the "machine" that helped them get elected. Our duty was to patrol Whaley Avenue on election day to "pick up people," a euphemism for helping African Americans get to the polls, which were located in a school in a largely white section of town.

Butch and I thought we were liberals pursuing the most progressive politics available. The Sixties had not yet arrived. We caught hints that urban renewal might be a form of "Negro removal," but we assumed that we were working to make New Haven a model city. We thought we were activists. We thought we were the embodiment of the kind of politics Reinhold Niebuhr's work envisaged. We had a lot to learn; and what we had to learn politically, I discovered, had significant theological implications. I suspect that learning the limits of pluralist politics may have prepared me to read John Howard Yoder.

UNDER THE INFLUENCE OF MR. HARTT'S THEOLOGY COURSE AND MR. HOLmer's course on Kierkegaard, I had decided that theology was best done as a form of practical reason. Of course metaphysical issues were constitutive of theological claims, but such issues were best approached indirectly. So I looked forward to concentrating in "ethics" for the rest of my time at Yale. James Gustafson's introductory course in Christian ethics was required in the second year, but I would have taken the course required or not. For me it was a gateway to the world I wanted to make my life.

Early in the course I challenged Mr. Gustafson's use of H. Richard Niebuhr's distinction in *The Meaning of Revelation* between internal and external history. I was at Yale studying theology because of that book, but under the influence of Collingwood I had become increasingly suspicious of Niebuhr's attempt to distinguish an outer history of things from an inner history of selves. I worried that this distinction might be problematic for the actual practice of history, and I was also beginning to think that it might have unhappy Christological implications. In many ways, everything I have done subsequently has been a continuation of that set of issues.

I fear that some people may interpret the much later antagonistic exchanges between me and Gustafson as indications that I do not think of myself as his student. Nothing could be further from the truth. I am his student, and I owe him much. I am sure it was from Jim that I first began to think that character and the virtues were crucial for understanding the moral life. I am also sure that my insistence that ethics be theological is a theme I learned from him. Our theologies differ, of course, but that our theologies differ, and that we each care about the difference, reflects our common commitment to the difference theology should make.

I did and did not anticipate our later differences. I was at Yale when Jim wrote *Christ and the Moral Life*. Indeed, Jim Childress and I are thanked in the preface for help in checking references and proofreading. I learned a great deal from the book and assumed that Jim's focus on Christ more or less aligned him with Karl Barth, and not Reinhold Niebuhr. I remember, however, being disappointed in the conclusion of the book, where Jesus seems to do no more than confirm what we might know on other grounds. I began to wonder if Jim thought that

Jesus was but the exemplification of what it means to trust that we can trust in trust. I sensed that he, like H. Richard Niebuhr, might have developed a Christology that was, at the very least, "thin."

I do not want to give the wrong impression. At the time, I certainly did not have a well-worked-out Christology. Indeed, I still do not. I am not even sure I believe in anyone having a well-worked-out Christology. So it was not as if I was in a position to test Gustafson's "orthodoxy." I think the difference had more to do with how I was coming to understand the task of theology.

The presumption of many scholars at the time was that the task of theology was to make the language of the faith amenable to standards set by the world. This could be done by subtraction: "Of course you do not have to believe X or Y"; or, by translation, "When we say X or Y we really mean . . ." I was simply not interested in that project. From my perspective, if the language was not true, then you ought to give it up. I thought the crucial question was not whether Christianity could be made amenable to the world, but could the world be made amenable to what Christians believe? I had not come to the study of theology to play around.

I am not sure why I thought like this, but I suspect it had something to do with being a bricklayer. I simply did not believe in "cutting corners." I was attracted to Barth because he never cut any of the corners. He never tried to "explain." Rather, he tried to show how the language works by showing how the language works. There is a "no bullshit" quality to Barth's thought that appealed to a bricklayer from Texas and that seemed to me the kind of straightforwardness Christian claims require.

Listening to Hartt, I had come to appreciate the complexity of the simple beliefs we have as Christians. Reading Barth with Hartt had forced me to realize that a claim such as "Jesus is Lord" requires constant variations to be said rightly. Every volume of the *Church Dogmatics* is an exercise to show the connections necessary to say one thing well. From Barth's perspective, therefore, the task of theology can never come to an end. Paul Tillich had to finish his *Systematic Theology*. Barth could not finish *Church Dogmatics*, because if he had finished he would have had to start over.

During this second year at Yale, in addition to Mr. Gustafson's course on Christian ethics, I was also taking Mr. Holmer's philosophical theology seminar. The first semester consisted in our reading slowly Wittgenstein's *Tractatus Logico-Philosophicus* and *The Blue and Brown Books*. The second semester we read the *Philosophical Investigations*. I also took another course with Mr. Dirks on theology and the intellectual life in which I concentrated on Wittgenstein. God knows if I knew what I was doing, but I thought I saw connections between Barth and Wittgenstein just to the extent that they refused to "explain."

Mr. Holmer was a Swedish pietist disguised as a philosopher. Of course, the disguise was also who he really was. He loved Wittgenstein as much as Kierkegaard. To read Wittgenstein with him was a spiritual exercise. I often tried to resist, but I was learning much in the process. For example, reading Wittgenstein with Mr. Holmer meant that I was never tempted to think Wittgenstein had a theory of meaning about how words are used. Years later I would spend a year reading the *Investigations* with the philosophers at Notre Dame only to discover how much I had learned from Mr. Holmer.

One of the most valuable things I gained from Mr. Holmer was an understanding of intellectual work as investigation. It is so tempting to think you need to have a "position" if you are to be a "thinker." Positions are also useful if you are to make it as an academic. Theology in modernity, moreover, has been position driven. Thus you are a Tillichian, a Bultmannian, a liberal, a conservative, a Barthian (if you can ever understand what that might entail), a process theologian, and so on. That many theologians think they need to have a position is, I suspect, the result of the loss of ecclesial identities. But reading Wittgenstein with Mr. Holmer helped me see that positions far too easily get in the way of thought.

I realize that it may seem quite odd for me to speak of not having a "position," given the fact that many of my theological and ethical colleagues would characterize me as someone with a strong position. This characterization is not entirely unfair; nonetheless, it is wrong. It is true that I am a pacifist, but that does not mean my pacifism is a "position." Positions too easily tempt us to think that we Christians need a theory. I am not a pacifist because of a theory. I am a pacifist because John Howard Yoder convinced me that nonviolence and Christianity are inseparable.

Studies

ONE OF THE CLASSES I WAS PRIVILEGED TO TAKE WAS ONE OF THE LAST MR. Calhoun taught in historical theology. I had much to learn about the Christian tradition and was fortunate to take Mr. Calhoun's course. He was an extraordinary scholar and teacher who never published. I suspect Mr. Frei had Mr. Calhoun in mind when he later characterized Yale theology as "generous orthodoxy." That was Mr. Calhoun, whose lectures were models of careful presentations of the tradition. When he taught the debates surrounding the Council of Nicea, for example, those who lost would get equal time with those who won. It was from Mr. Calhoun that I learned what was at stake in the early Trinitarian and Christological controversies.

We read primary sources with Mr. Calhoun, but our main assignment was either to write a fifty-page research paper or take a five-hour exam over an important text. I decided to do the latter. Thinking I needed to read Thomas Aquinas, I chose the *Summa Theologica.* I had no idea what I was doing, but I started to read. It took a while to get the hang of it, but before long I was moving from question to question, increasingly intrigued. I had decided not to read secondary literature until I had first read the *Summa.* After completing this task, I read what the neo-scholastics said Thomas was saying and had trouble identifying it with the Thomas I had read. I read Thomas as if he was conducting the kind of intellectual investigation I identified with Wittgenstein, but most of his commentators clearly assumed he had a position. It was only when I went to Notre Dame and met David Burrell that I realized I was not alone in how I had learned to read Thomas.

I was reading Thomas at the same time I was taking Mr. Gustafson's Christian ethics course. I could not help but notice that contemporary Christian ethics, which was dominated at the time by the controversy occasioned by the publication of Joseph Fletcher's *Situation Ethics,* had nothing to say about the virtues. I was also reading philosophical ethics, for example, R. M. Hare's *Freedom and Reason,* which also had little to say about the virtues. Somewhere along the way I discovered Elizabeth Anscombe's essay "Modern Moral Philosophy," and I began to think that there were some connections between what I was learning from Wittgenstein and a focus on the virtues.

These connections between Wittgenstein and Thomas, and between Wittgenstein and Barth, were swirling for me as I was taking one interesting course after another. For example, I had tested out of Jaroslav Pelikan's introductory course in church history by reading Williston Walker's *A History of the Christian Church*. I thought, however, that I should take a course with Mr. Pelikan somewhere along the way. I took his seminar on the history and doctrine of the Eucharist. I learned more about Radbertus than I probably needed to know, but the course left a lasting impression on me. I wrote my paper on John W. Nevin and the School of Theology at Mercersberg, Pennsylvania. I even went to the trouble of following the Nevin-Hodge debate that appeared in the local paper, the *Mercersberg Record*.

I was beginning to have some idea that Christianity might have something to do with worship, which was not obvious to a Methodist from Texas. And even being at Yale was little help, because chapel was not exactly at the center of the school's life. If we went to chapel, it was because one of our teachers happened to be preaching and we were curious about what that person might say in that setting. However, I thought I at least ought to try to understand why Christians had put such stress on the liturgy, so I bought and read Gregory Dix, *The Shape of the Liturgy*. By reading Dix I caught a glimpse of the world into which I would be pulled when I went to Notre Dame to teach.

Almost as important for me was a course I took with Ian Siggins on Luther and Calvin as scriptural exegetes. Mr. Siggins was an Australian who had come to Yale to do his Ph.D. under Mr. Pelikan. I seem to remember that he was a Roman Catholic. We read extensively in Luther's and Calvin's commentaries. I wrote a long paper comparing Luther's and Calvin's reading of the Gospel of John. That turned out to be a wonderful exercise, not only because it made me appreciate so-called "pre-critical exegesis," but also because I learned so much about Christology.

That course prepared me well for Mr. Frei's Christology seminar. He began with the councils, but the primary focus was on Friedrich Schleiermacher, the liberal lives of Jesus, and Barth. I gained a great appreciation of the liberal tradition. I saw that the liberal emphases on the life of Jesus could be interpreted as the rightful refusal to let go of the life of Jesus. Both more "orthodox" Christologies and the Protestant emphasis on justification seemed to give in to the temptation to leave Jesus behind. I think I wrote a paper on H. Richard Niebuhr's Christology in which I argued that the structure of his theology reproduced the habits of liberal Protestant thought.

I am not sure how, but some of us got hold of an early manuscript of Frei's *The Identity of Jesus Christ*. I began to think that there might be connections between Frei's use of analytic philosophy to deal with issues of identity ascription and my inchoate thoughts about the virtues. I remember testing some of those ideas out with Mr. Frei. I was particularly interested in how such a perspective might illumine the connection between Barth's Christology, particularly as developed in *Church Dogmatics* IV.1 and IV.2, and Barth's account of sanctification. I could not believe it, but I was beginning to think that Methodists might be on to something.

Seemingly missing in my Yale education was any determinative engagement with the church fathers. I was introduced to the fathers in Mr. Calhoun's course, and that was not without effect. But I did not take a course in patristics. I was, however, befriended by Rowan Greer. Anne and I had moved to an apartment because the divinity school let you stay in their housing only for a set period. Rowan Greer, who had done his degree in New Testament at Yale and then taught in a "wee" Anglican seminary in Scotland only to return to teach at Yale, lived across the street. People would think us unlikely friends. Rowan was from a different social class, signified by his having gone to Yale as an undergraduate. He was also an Anglican priest. But Rowan seemed to take a liking to me.

Rowan and I talked often, and through those conversations I was given an invaluable introduction to the church fathers. I read Rowan's lectures and many of the texts on which they were based. Theodore of Mopsuestia, particularly his commentary on Hebrews, became a theological companion. From Rowan I learned to distrust the accounts of the debates surrounding the Trinity and Christology that presented the issues largely in philosophical terms. The issues, at least as Rowan presented them, were exegetical. I became increasingly convinced that he was right.

I think I learned from Rowan a lesson I also learned from Mr. Hartt, namely, that theology is not best understood as a "system." I had a hint from the course I had taken with Mr. Frei that narrative might have something to do with theology. The emphasis on character and the virtues I was trying to recover in ethics also suggested that something like a notion of narrative might be useful. I cannot say I knew at the time how to develop these intuitions, but somehow they were beginning to find a home amid the diverse influences on me.

I do not want to leave the impression that everything I studied was of a piece. Mr. Calhoun was concerned that some of us were overly influenced by Barth. Accordingly, he offered a seminar in the work of F. R. Tennant. Tennant, drawing on the work of Bertrand Russell and Alfred North Whitehead, argued that God, world, and the self had equivalent epistemological status. It was a wonderful seminar. I also took a seminar with Mr. Hartt that dealt with the work of Paul Weiss, a philosopher in the American pragmatist tradition who was one of the more lively men I have ever encountered. He often came to the seminar to defend his position.

My time as a divinity school student passed quickly and, outside the unceasing intellectual stimulation, was relatively uneventful — with one exception. Anne and I had spent an evening with Jim and Georgia Childress. Jim and I had entered the divinity school at the same time. He came as a married student from Mount Aire, North Carolina. We shared many of the same courses, both wanted to study Christian ethics at the Ph.D. level, and were equally competitive in general (and in particular on the basketball court) — all of which should have meant that we would not have been close friends, but we were. Anne also liked Georgia, and we enjoyed doing things with them.

One night we had supper with Jim and Georgia. Because we were having such a good time, we had not noticed that a heavy snowstorm was in process. On our way home, as Anne and I were going down the Canner Street hill, a car on its way up the hill swerved into our lane, forcing me to turn my wheel to avoid it. We hit a light pole. I was not seriously hurt, but Anne sustained a blow to the mouth and cut lip.

At the hospital, we were extremely fortunate to have an accomplished surgeon on call. He carefully sutured Anne's lip, making it almost impossible to detect that she had ever been injured. The surgeon was Richard Seltzer. His literary work would mean a great deal to me later, but at the time he was an associate professor of surgery at Yale

Medical School, and he had yet to write any of the reflective works on medicine for which he would become well known.

The wreck intensified Anne's general tendency to blame me for just about anything. And I was pretty sure she was right. After all, I was the one going to school. I was the one doing what I wanted to do. She had to work. All I had to do was study. I had come from a world in which men were supposed to support their wives. I wanted to support my wife, but that had to be delayed if I was to do a Ph.D. Anne seemed to want me to do a Ph.D. At the very least that meant I would not be in a church.

During the years I was in divinity school, I began to notice Anne's disdain for all things Christian. I had attributed her negative attitude to the church as a legitimate reaction to her mother. But it was not long before her hatred of what she took to be Christianity was directed toward me. Accordingly, she took no interest in my developing passion for theology, nor would she consent to accompany me to church at Hamden Plains.

I do not want to leave the wrong impression. At the time, this was not a major problem for me or the marriage. I was too self-absorbed to worry about Anne's attitude toward the church. I did not think her relation to the church mattered one way or another. I suppose I was a bit hurt that she did not seem to care about my work, but I was sympathetic with her dislike of intellectual pretension. I am sure, moreover, that when we got together with my fellow students Anne could not have helped but feel excluded by our insular debates about such matters as Barth versus Brunner.

That we were young was at once an advantage and a disadvantage. Sheer energy will get you through difficulties that should make you think twice. But I did not know how to think twice about our marriage and the antagonism that might be developing. There is no doubt that Anne felt "caught." She had a stake in my future as a theologian, but she had little sympathy for what I increasingly cared about. Neither of us had really thought through, or even knew what it would mean to think through, how to have a life together. Anne had certainly wanted to "get married." At the time, I had seemed not a bad catch. But she seemed to grow increasingly unhappy with her lot. She was beginning to feel that she was not getting to do what she wanted to do, even if it was not clear what that was.

I confess that I did not know what to do to make her life better, other than to do whatever she wanted me to do. On the whole, I did what she wanted me to do, except change my desire to do further academic work. However, as I progressed through the second and third years of the divinity school, such matters seldom intruded into our daily routines. Anne got up and went to work. I got up and went to class. Then in my third year of divinity school, I applied to do Ph.D. work in Christian ethics.

I applied to Yale but thought it unlikely I would get in. Childress would surely get in, and I did not think they would take us both. I thought I might be able to get into Duke or Princeton. My quantitative scores on the GRE surely set a new record for a bottom line. But, I suspect, due to the good office of James Gustafson, I was admitted to Yale Graduate School. I was turned down by Duke.

My PARENTS CAME TO MY GRADUATION FROM THE DIVINITY SCHOOL. AFTER graduation, we went on a trip to Maine and Canada. It was a disaster. Mother talked constantly, driving Anne crazy. Confined to a car, none of us could escape. Mother had the unfortunate habit of reading all the signs we passed on the highway. Before long, Anne began to mock her. Mother was driving me crazy, but I thought Anne was cruel. I was caught in between — a place and a role, it turned out, that I would occupy for the next twenty years.

At the time, however, distance proved salutary. My mother and father returned to Texas, and life in New Haven went on as normal. I had received a fellowship from Yale, so our finances were better. I do not think I noticed any big difference between the work I had done in the divinity school and the work I was doing as a Ph.D. student. I was fortunate to take a course with William Christian on value theory in which we read C. I. Lewis as well as Nicolai Hartmann. Mr. Christian also gave me a reading course on Spinoza's *Ethics*.

Liston Pope, who was a former dean of the divinity school, returned from sabbatical to teach. He was an extraordinary man whose book *Millhands and Preachers* was a classic study of ministerial resistance to the development of labor unions in the South. He combined social gospel passion with Niebuhrian realism. He was also rumored to be an alcoholic. I liked him, and he seemed to like me. He often called to ask me to run the seminar he was teaching in social ethics when he was too "sick" to make it. The seminar was not particularly focused, but it gave me the opportunity to read some of the great texts of political theory: Plato's *Republic*, Aristotle's *Politics*, as well as Machiavelli, Hobbes, Locke, and the Federalist Papers.

I am not sure how it happened, but during this time those of us studying ethics at Yale came to know Charlie Reynolds, who was studying ethics at Harvard. Charlie was from Arkansas, had gone to Perkins, and was destined to be a lifelong friend. He would go on to do more than most of us have to make Christian ethics an identifiable discipline, not only by founding the *Journal of Religious Ethics*, but also by working to make the Society of Christian Ethics responsive to wider intellectual developments. Even then, Charlie had a gift for putting people in contact with one another.

For example, Charlie arranged for students studying ethics at Harvard and Yale to have a colloquy between the institutions. That is how we learned about John Rawls. Charlie was taking Rawls's seminars, in which Rawls was developing what would become *A Theory of Justice*. Along with the students at Harvard, we were reading and rereading Rawls's ever-changing mimeograph versions of the text. Rawls was even kind enough to give those of us from Yale an evening seminar on his work at Harvard. At the time, we did not have a clue, as has recently been discovered, that when Rawls had been an undergraduate at Princeton he had been a Christian.

I was also taking courses with William Miller in which we read Robert Dahl and other contemporary political theorists. William Connolly had begun to criticize Yale "pluralist" theory, but at the time I was unsure what to do with his criticisms. I discovered Ted Lowi's work, as well as that of Robert Paul Wolff. It may seem odd that I was reading so much in political theory, given my interest in the virtues. However, I saw no tension between these interests, which is not to say that I knew what I was doing. I was impressed by Rawls's grand theory; I assumed that Reinhold Niebuhr was largely right; and I thought that somehow Barth was congruent with all of this and more. God knows how I thought I could put all this together.

David Little had come to Yale from Harvard, where he had studied with James Luther Adams. I took some of his courses during the time I was a divinity school student, but his course on the social sciences when I was a Ph.D. student was particularly important. We read Max Weber, Ernst Troeltsch, Émile Durkheim, and Talcott Parsons. It may have been at this time that I first began to read someone named Alasdair MacIntyre, whose work on the philosophy of the social sciences seemed to me to be on target. I suspect Little, however, would have had little sympathy for MacIntyre, or how I have since used what I learned from him.

Of course, I was taking Mr. Gustafson's graduate seminars. Oddly enough, I do not remember what we read in those seminars. What I do remember is that Mr. Gustafson was kind enough to give me a reading course in which I again read Aristotle and Aquinas on the virtues. *Character and the Christian Life* grew out of that reading course. That may not quite be true. *Character and the Christian Life* grew out of everything I had been doing, but Mr. Gustafson's course certainly helped me focus what I needed to do to write my dissertation.

Mr. Gustafson did not direct the dissertation because he went on sabbatical the year I was writing. Instead, Eugene TeSelle served as my director. I had taken Mr. TeSelle's course on nature and grace, in which we read Maurice Blondel, Henri de Lubac, Karl Rahner, and Joseph Marechal. I also was a graduate assistant in his undergraduate course, The Religious Roots of Western Culture. The latter was a wonderful experience, not only because of what I learned in the process, but also because I quickly came to understand that Yale undergraduates in 1967 were not all that interested in theology. On the final exam, for example, one student identified Alcibiades as a minor Hebrew prophet.

Mr. TeSelle was not all that sympathetic with the sources I was using in the dissertation. I was reading Charles Taylor, Stuart Hampshire, and Elizabeth Anscombe to try and develop an account of agency. He was much more impressed with the work on action being done by the phenomenological tradition. I had read Husserl in college and Merleau-Ponty and Sartre in divinity school, but I was too immersed in the analytic tradition to switch horses at that stage of my dissertation.

God only knows what Mr. TeSelle, Mr. Gustafson, Mr. Hartt, and Mr. Pope (my dissertation proposal committee) thought when they let me loose to write the dissertation, but thank God they let me bite off more than anyone should. The very idea that a dissertation would provide an account of both Aristotle and Thomas on practical reason should suggest that no one could possibly treat either adequately. That I was also taking on both Barth and Bultmann should have raised some eyebrows. But they let me do it, and I am damn glad they did. I confess that I can barely bring myself to read the book today, but I still think what I did is largely on the right track.

I do find it interesting that the first sentence of the preface I wrote when the dissertation became a book in 1975 reads, "This book attempts to do Christian ethics in a serious way by providing the means to place rightly the discourse that Christians use about their moral life." Not a well-written sentence, but one that indicates that the primary task of my work even then was to demonstrate the link between the truth of what we say we believe and the shape of the lives we live. "Ethics" has always been my way to pursue that task.

THE LAST SENTENCE OF THE SAME PREFACE READS: "FINALLY, I WOULD LIKE to thank my wife, Anne, for being my wife and Adam's mother." I am not sure if I was truthfully thanking Anne for being my wife, but I know that thanking her for being Adam's mother was heartfelt. She had long wanted to quit work at Connecticut Blue Cross. Sometime during my second year in graduate school, we decided we were financially able to live on my fellowship. Anne wanted to get pregnant, and in this case at least she got what she wanted.

It turned out that Anne loved being pregnant — at least at the beginning. In particular, she loved making maternity outfits. She could sew quite well and made a number of stunning outfits. Just as I did not know what we were doing when we got married, I did not know what we were doing when we had a child, but it seemed like a good thing to do. I began to notice, however, that Anne became increasingly agitated the longer she was pregnant. I think she was frightened.

God only knows how her as-yet-undiagnosed psychological anxiety may have affected the pregnancy, but sometime in the late seventh or early eighth month, a portion of her placenta tore. She had vaginal bleeding, which, of course, frightened us. We had a wonderful doctor named Fiskio. He was the father of Lenore Fiskio, one of Anne's friends from work. Dr. Fiskio met us at St. Rafael's hospital, and thankfully Anne did not go into labor. After a few days, she was sent home to be confined to bed for the duration of the pregnancy. However, only a week or so later Anne went into labor.

After the wreck, we had bought a 403 Peugeot. It was a car the French had designed for Africa. I am sure it was a good car for Africa, but it was not a good car for cold weather. As Anne got ready to return to the hospital, I tried to start the damn car. It would not start. It was late at night. There was only one thing to do — call Rowan across the street. Dressed in his pajamas and covered by an overcoat, Rowan drove us to the hospital. Praise God for Rowan.

Adam John Hauerwas was born on January 26, 1968. I will never forget seeing him for the first time. He had a forceps mark on his forehead. He weighed only four pounds eight ounces, but he was alive and would survive in intensive care. I did not know it at the time, but he would be crucial to my own survival over the next eighteen years. I remember walking back to our apartment after his birth in a snowstorm in shoes that were anything but waterproof. I had to get back to call our parents with the news.

We knew we needed help. Anne's antagonistic relation with her mother meant she preferred my mother to come first to help her recover. Adam was to stay in the hospital for almost a month, but after a few days Anne came home. What a horrible time. She was not able to breast-feed because her episiotomy restricted her movements, and so she could not return to the hospital. I have long wondered if that was not a decisive loss, accounting for her inability to bond with Adam. Even worse, my mother came full of good will and completely lacking in insight about Anne's loss of not being able to have Adam with her. Mother simply failed to understand what it meant that she was able to go to the hospital to see Adam when Anne could not. She even insisted on wearing her nursing outfit to show that she was more than capable of caring for Adam.

I do not know how long Mother stayed, but any time was too long. At first, Anne needed what Mother could do, but the more she healed, the more she resented having Mother there. As usual, I was caught in between. Things only got worse when we were finally able to bring Adam home. Mother tried to not get in Anne's way, but her being in the same room with Anne got in Anne's way. Mother finally left.

Adam had to be fed every four hours, which meant that sleep was a precious commodity. I did the feedings during the night. In the process, Adam began to train me to be a father. I do not know if I wanted to be so trained, but I know that is who I am. Adam and I became preternaturally close because we were bound together in an embrace necessary for survival. That embrace began in New Haven the night he was born.

Years later, after Anne had left and I was to marry Paula, Adam came home from college for the wedding. As we left the airport, I asked how he was doing. He said he was not doing well. I assumed it was because he had wrecked his car, which he had bought with summer earnings. But it was not his car. The reason for his distress, he said, was that my impending marriage to Paula signified the real divorce. He said he knew it sounded strange, but really he and I were the married people who just took care of his mom. By marrying Paula, I was divorcing him.

I said I thought that was right, but that as much as we loved one another we each had to "go on." If I did not go on, then neither could he. Adam has gone on to be a better husband and father than I was able to be. The gift of our friendship, a gift that partly came through terror, is a gift I learned first to receive by feeding him at three in the morning for days on end.

But we were not out of the woods. Anne's mother was still to come. She came, not at all happy that my mother had come first. But on the whole her visit was without incident. Life was returning to "normal." I began to work hard to finish my dissertation. What a blessing and a curse to have my mother's energy. Adam had colic, which turned out to be an allergy to milk. We had to feed him soy milk. Anne, however, simply could not negotiate his crying. I did a lot of walking the floor with him.

By spring, we were taking long strolls with Adam in the pram. We had become close friends with the Barnetts, who lived on the first floor of our building. Hank was in Yale Law School and after law school joined a New Haven firm. He finally became president of Bethlehem Steel. They had two sons, which meant that they could loan us baby stuff, including the pram. Spring in New Haven can be quite wonderful and bright. I was ready for the light.

I was also looking for a job. I now had a family to support. I did not have a clue how to get a job. Now young academics go to professional meetings in their first year of graduate school. I did not know there were such things. I do not know how it happened that Augustana College in Rock Island, Illinois, contacted me for an interview. But sometime late in the spring of 1967, I took a train to Philadelphia, where I met the president of Augustana. He thought it best to check me out before they flew me out to visit the college. I passed that test, so the next thing I knew Anne and I were on a plane to Augustana to be interviewed for a job. My life as a teacher was about to begin.

CHAPTER 4

Teaching

I did not notice the Sixties until 1969. I realize that may seem odd, given the mythic character the Sixties now have for many. Of course those of us studying Christian ethics at Yale were well aware of the civil rights struggle. We followed the war in Vietnam. But I had little sense that we were in a cultural revolution. Drugs and sexual liberation were simply not on my radar screen.

Drugs may have been present in high school and college, but I do not remember ever being offered a joint. In high school, that may have been due to the class characteristics of the student body. In "North Dallas," where the moneyed folk lived, there may have been a drug problem, but I was unaware of any such problem at Pleasant Grove High. Drinking beer and making out were about as far as we went to challenge the morality of the day. That was also true at Southwestern, where the social life was more or less an extension of high school.

I left Yale in 1968. Yale exploded in 1969. I did not know what to make of the explosion or of the alleged revolution associated with Woodstock. The latter seemed to me indulgent. I was from the working class. I wondered where people got the money or the time to do nothing but listen to music and smoke dope. Did they not have to work for a living? I also thought it rather odd to protest the war by getting high and screwing.

In truth, I did not know how to think about the war. David Little introduced us to just-war theory. I cannot remember if he had been influenced by Paul Ramsey. One of my fellow graduate students, Leroy Walters, then a Mennonite, was writing his dissertation on just war.

Accordingly, the question of the war in Vietnam, at least for those of us in the Ph.D. program, was whether the war was just. Mr. Little had developed arguments in support of the war on just-war grounds, which made any easy criticisms of the war difficult.

My graduate training, moreover, meant that I approached the war as an "ethicist." Particularly as represented by Mr. Gustafson, ethicists clarify arguments by suggesting how conceptual entailments might follow from theological commitments. Thus my later characterization of those trained at Yale: we were like the gun fighter portrayed on television who handed out cards embossed with the slogan: "Have gun. Will travel." Our card would read, "Have conceptual tools. Will travel." The conceptual tools we acquired were often imitations of Niebuhr's "method" in *Christ and Culture*. Accordingly, as graduate students at Yale we assumed that the person with the most inclusive typology at the end won.

There was even a joke about the different perspectives of Union, Harvard, and Yale graduate programs in theology and ethics. If you posed a question to graduates of Union, a school in which Reinhold Niebuhr and Paul Tillich set the agenda, they would think for a minute and respond, "The answer is one, two, three, four, five." If you posed the question to graduates of Harvard, a school dominated by James Luther Adams, they would think, start to answer, only to think again, finally saying, "I do not know the answer to that question." If you asked Yale graduates, a school shaped by H. R. Niebuhr, the same question, they would think, start to answer, think again, and finally respond, "I do not know the answer to that question, but if these are your fundamental presuppositions then you have these alternatives; or if these are your presuppositions, then these are your alternatives."

God knows I tried to be a good Yalie, even though it was against my nature. I think I have good analytic abilities, but I am too passionate to be a "bystander." It is not fair to characterize the Yale mode of analysis as the perspective of the bystander, but that is the way it felt to me. And this is the stance I assumed as I left Yale, a stance that shaped how I thought about the war in Vietnam. I took it to be my job to help people develop consistent arguments about the war without betraying any position I might have had on the topic.

My role as an "ethicist" would not survive my early years as a teacher. Given who I am, this is not a role I could have occupied for long in any case. But becoming a teacher in 1968 forced the issue. Even students at Augustana thought it was a time that required you to stand up for what you thought mattered. I thought that clear thinking mattered, but it was soon clear to me that clear thinking meant you also had to have something to think about.

In truth, I had not thought about teaching until the president of Augustana interviewed me in the Philadelphia airport. He asked some general questions designed to discover if I would "do." He then asked me what I would teach. I suddenly realized I was going to be a teacher for the rest of my life. Just as I had gone to divinity school not realizing that you usually go to divinity school to study for the ministry, it had not occurred to me that I was doing a Ph.D. to become a teacher. I have now been teaching for more than forty years, and I am still not sure what it means to be a teacher. But whatever it means, I have reveled in it.

God knows I was lucky to get the job at Augustana. I actually had one other interview, at DePauw University in Greencastle, Indiana. I preferred DePauw to Augustana, not only because Bob King taught there, but because I thought it a better school. It also had a Methodist background, which seemed to make DePauw a more natural fit. But I did not get the job at DePauw. I am not sure how I got the job at Augie, as the school was called, because I was the first non-Lutheran to be hired to teach in the Bible and Christianity Department. They changed the name to the Religion Department in my first year, but the original name gives some idea of the strong Lutheran background that had shaped the school. I was damn lucky to get the job.

Augustana is in Rock Island, Illinois. It is a lovely school not far from the banks of the Mississippi. Swedish Lutherans founded the school, and in many ways it had an impressive intellectual tradition. One of the Swedish kings had given the school his library. Conrad Bergendorff had been the president for many years, bringing a high intellectual standard to the school. A. D. Matson, one of the few Lutheran social gospelers, had taught in the seminary at Augustana, before it moved to Chicago. I felt like the school had a lot going for it.

It did have the disadvantage of being in Rock Island, Illinois. The area was known as the "Quad Cities" because Davenport and Bettendorf, Iowa, were just on the other side of the river, and Rock Island was right next to Moline, Illinois. I had no idea what it would mean to live in the Midwest, and I had never lived in a Mississippi River town. But I soon discovered I liked the Midwest — at least I liked the people of the Midwest. They really are down to earth. I did think, however, that you had probably lived in the Midwest too long when you knew what Basagram does to protect corn from pests.

Anne did not like the Midwest. At least she did not like where we were living. I was to make $8,000 my first year. Everyone else in the department was a Lutheran minister, which meant they received a tax-free housing allowance. I had no ecclesial status and so could not get the tax break. The college did own some small houses we could rent at a reduced rate. I rented one such house that was perched on the cliff just above the college.

Anne had gone to Texas with Adam to visit her parents while I moved us to Augustana. I got to the house before our furniture and worked my butt off to try to make the house as nice as I could before the moving van got there. It was not easy because the house had not been well cared for. The mover got there on a Sunday and was unable to find anyone to help him unload. I offered to be his laborer and was paid accordingly. I arranged the furniture as best I could and left immediately for Texas to pick up Anne and Adam to return to Rock Island. The trip back was tiring because we drove through the night, with Adam sleeping in his crib in the back seat.

Arriving at the house, Anne went mad. She threatened to leave me to return to Texas. I had never seen her so angry or completely out of control. It was as if she was possessed. I remember falling on my knees and begging her to stay, promising I would do everything I could to make things better. I did not realize it, but I believe I was witnessing one of her early psychotic breaks. At the time, I had no idea what a psychotic break was. I do not remember how it happened that she calmed down, but she did finally say she would stay. Her staying meant, however, that it was up to me to make things "all right." God knows I tried, but it was not easy, which was my own damn fault. I simply could not avoid getting in trouble. I did not try to get in trouble, but I had a knack for it.

Teaching

AUGUSTANA WAS AN EXCELLENT LIBERAL ARTS COLLEGE THAT ATTRACTED students who had won an Illinois scholarship. These state scholarships allowed students to attend private schools in the state. They were one of the ways the state of Illinois found to support private education, as well as relieve some of the pressure on student enrollment in state institutions. Accordingly, the students at Augustana were quite good, as I am sure they are today.

The students were, however, mainly white and from the middle and upper-middle class. Many of them came from North Side Chicago, which meant they were city kids who thought of themselves as far too sophisticated for a river town that bordered on Iowa. They were in a generalized way Lutheran, which meant in some vague way that they thought they were Christian. At least one of the missions of Augustana was to reinforce that vagueness. Or as I learned to put it — our task was to give the parents the impression that by sending their daughters to Augustana they would not lose the virginity they had already lost in high school.

I had not been at Augustana long before I was drawn into a controversy about whether the doors of coeds could be shut during the times Augustana males were allowed to visit in the women's dorms. A reporter for the campus newspaper asked me what the new Christian ethicist's view might be about this crucial issue. Drawing on my experience as a Texan, as well as having just come from Yale, I responded, "Well, I guess it's a good way to avoid getting grass stains." I was quoted in the weekly edition of the paper. I later came to understand that such an observation was not well received by the administration.

I made matters worse when the issue was discussed at a faculty meeting. Try to remember that I was twenty-eight. I was in my first year of teaching. If I had had any sense, I would have kept my mouth shut. But when the dean justified the policy of keeping the doors open on the grounds that we had to protect the students from themselves, I could not resist observing that this could also be a rationale for slavery. In truth, I thought the whole issue was stupid. If students could not find alternatives to having their doors shut, they should be condemned for lacking imagination. Even if I was right, however, I should have kept my mouth shut. But wisdom is not a characteristic you associate with twenty-eight-year-olds in their first year of teaching.

I think over the years I have grown in wisdom, but this incident proved to reveal a tendency that continues to characterize my life. I simply lack patience with cant. As a result, I often seem to lack any political sense. My lack of political sense, moreover, makes me vulnerable to those who do have political sense. I am not referring only to that intense politics of envy associated with university faculties and administrations, but with the politics of knowledge itself. I have never been able to discipline what or how I think by what others think important. As a result, I have spent a lifetime being misunderstood by people who think they know what I think, given what they think, but in fact I am trying to change how they think. I am not complaining. It is just the way things are.

It never occurred to me that I might get into trouble by saying what I took to be the truth in a faculty meeting. I simply assumed that if you were smart, if you worked hard, if you cared about your teaching and published, then you would be doing what you were meant to do. Such an ethic was nicely exemplified in the TV program *M*A*S*H*, where being a good surgeon meant that there was nothing they could do to you. Moreover, I thought universities were places where you told one another the truth. That I might offend someone was not something I thought about. I had much to learn.

As it turned out, it was not sex that really got me in trouble; it was race. I had, of course, sympathetically followed the civil rights struggle during my time as a graduate student. Jim Childress had written his dissertation on civil disobedience, so I had learned much from him about the struggle for racial justice, as well as about how to protest against the war. I had also learned a great deal from Joe Hough, a graduate student at Yale several years ahead of me who had written his dissertation on black power. His book *Black Power and White Protestants: A Christian Response to the New Negro Pluralism* was published in 1968 and was fundamentally a Niebuhrian reading of the black power movement that I found extremely persuasive.

There were nineteen African Americans in the student body at Augustana. I had a number of them in the required courses I taught in Bible, as well as in the course I taught called Christian Ethics and Democracy. The latter course was designed to help students make connections between issues in liberal political theory, protests against the war, and the civil rights campaign. We read people like Reinhold Niebuhr, Robert Paul Wolff, William Connolly, and C. B. Macpherson. We also read the "Port Huron Statement" and the "Letter from Birmingham Jail." The idea was to help students see how the latter documents drew on liberal democratic presumptions and were implicated in fundamental questions about the role of the church in society. I thought, given the turmoil of the time, that such a course might be useful to help students think through what they saw happening in the world in which they found themselves.

Midwesterners mistook my Texas accent for a Southern one, so it was assumed I was a Southerner. You might think that the African American students would have distrusted a Southerner. The exact opposite proved to be the case. Though most of the African Americans at Augustana were from inner-city Chicago, many of them had parents or grandparents from the South. It did not take long, therefore, for us to discover that we often shared more in common culturally with one another than with our Midwestern neighbors. Thus I became the unofficial advisor to the unofficial but no less real association of African American students.

It was the time in which calls for black power were in the air. At Augustana, such calls were primarily interpreted as an attempt to re-segregate society. The first thing I ever published was "An Ethical Appraisal of Black Power," which appeared in 1969 in the *Augustana Observer*, the campus newspaper. In the article, I suggested that the negative reaction of white liberals to black power not only exposed shallow and platitudinous sentiments such as "all men are created equal," but also robbed white liberals of their attempt to relieve the guilt of being white by identifying with the civil rights struggle. I then argued that black power was an appropriate democratic strategy of a people to secure greater equality and justice while avoiding anarchy or resorting to "excessive violence." Accordingly, I suggested that the black power movement was a healthy reaction against Martin Luther King's idealism. Black power rightly represented the African Americans' claim that they did not have to represent a higher morality to participate in American society. Nor was it their mission to "save" whites from the prison of their own prejudice. I was particularly hopeful that the black power movement might help white and black alike envision a way of life not determined by middle-class America. I suggested that African Americans' particular experience in America has left them dissatisfied with the "quality of life" in the wider society, which might mean that African Americans might help us all find a better way to live.

I ended the article with two concerns. First, I worried that the black power movement might not accomplish politically what it promised. The rejection of coalition politics by advocates of black power might prove counterproductive, even given the power of African Americans in the urban centers of America. Second, I worried that the movement might want to achieve black identity through political action. This worry was based on the Niebuhrian insight that although the realm of politics is important, it is a poor place to discover the significance of one's life.

It is clear that the way I thought about black power was shaped by how Reinhold Niebuhr had taught me to think. I am deeply grateful for what I learned from him, and from his brother H. Richard. But I think I rightly came to see that there are profound limits, both theologically and politically, to the Niebuhrs. But that I was or was not Niebuhrian was not what got to the folks at Augustana. The problem was my "activism" on behalf of the African American students.

There was no African American on the faculty or in the administration at Augie. My interaction with the African American students made me keenly aware that they needed someone besides me, a white guy, to talk through the challenges of being an African American in a predominately white school. Most of these students were from inner-city Chicago. They had grown up around other African Americans, but at Augustana they had no place to go to escape interaction with whites.

Somehow I pushed a resolution through a committee of the faculty requiring the dean to begin to search for an African American to join the faculty. At Augustana the faculty met once a month as a whole to conduct faculty business. At our monthly meetings I would ask for a progress report from the dean concerning the search for an African American. After a few months, one of the senior members of the faculty, the former dean as well as the chairman of my division, had had enough of me. He rose, explaining that it was hard for schools like Augustana to find African American faculty members. It was difficult, he reported, to attract African Americans from reputable research universities to teach at small schools like Augustana. And, he added, even if they would consider teaching at Augustana, they could command more money than Augustana could pay. Moreover, he concluded, even if those obstacles could be overcome, it would be difficult to fit African Americans into appropriate academic slots.

It was clear that I was to keep my mouth shut, which, of course, I did not do. Instead, I "allowed" that I understood the challenge, but I wanted to point out the racist character of his remarks. He presumed, for example, that only "star-quality" African Americans could be hired at Augustana, but that is to hold African Americans to a standard we did not use for the rest of the faculty. I observed that we were more than willing to hire mediocre white scholars with only master's degrees to teach at Augustana. Why were we unwilling to hire a few mediocre M.A. blacks to teach at Augustana? Why did we have to call research universities? Why not call schools like Prairie View A&M? Needless to say, these comments did not make me popular among certain segments of the faculty.

I suspect, however, that the proverbial straw that broke the camel's back was my participation in a protest organized by the African American students. They wanted a room set aside in the student union for their activities. Their request had been turned down by the administration on the grounds that such a room would suggest segregation. The students decided to demonstrate at the annual festival. I no longer remember what the festival celebrated, but its primary purpose was to show what a harmonious place Augustana was. To demonstrate was, of course, antagonistic, because it challenged the presumption that Augustana was one big happy family. They asked me to go with them.

I am not an activist by nature. I find it hard to be in a crowd of any sort, no matter how deeply I may sympathize with what is being protested or promoted. Images of Nuremberg haunt me. But it did not seem like a big deal, so I readily agreed. Circling a tent with nineteen African Americans is a long way from a Nuremberg rally. I shall never forget walking into the room in which they had gathered before the protest. It was a Saturday morning. I came in carrying Adam. The tension in the room was palpable. But as soon as I walked in, it was like a cloud had lifted. They were not alone. We circled the tent that had been put up for the festival. I seem to remember that they even got their room in the student union. It was not a big deal, but I am sure my being with them was duly noted.

I was not trying to be a pain in the ass, but I must have seemed to some like a problem. I got a clear indication that this might be the case when, in my second year, my chairman, whom I liked a lot, informed me that my position might not be funded in the future. He wanted to assure me that this was strictly a financial matter that did not reflect my teaching or scholarship. But I knew the writing was on the wall and that I had better start looking for a new job. I also thought that if I was unable to find another teaching job, I could always go back to laying brick.

I DO NOT WANT TO LEAVE THE WRONG IMPRESSION. I REALLY LIKED AUGIE and my colleagues. I thought it a great boon that it was impossible to avoid interacting across disciplinary lines. I learned much from my colleague Ross Paulson, who taught intellectual and comparative history. John Hepburn, a sociologist specializing in criminology, and I taught a course together. I loved the folk in the English Department. Augustana even had a Geography Department, which I assumed must be the most boring subject in the modern university curriculum. But I soon learned from a young faculty member that geography had transformed itself through the recognition of the ideological functions of maps. I learned a great deal about oceanography from a friend in geology.

I was happy to be at Augustana. I particularly liked teaching Bible. Every Augustana undergraduate was required to take a one-semester course in Bible. I had no idea how to teach Bible, but I decided that rather than teaching about the Bible, I would teach the Bible. So instead of spending most of the time introducing them to scholarly debates about JEDP — the sources of the Pentateuch — I had them read the text. This was a wonderful opportunity for me because it meant that I, too, had to read the text. I learned a great deal.

I also discovered that I really enjoyed teaching undergraduates, and that undergraduates liked me as a teacher. I had absolutely no pedagogical sense, but I think my enthusiasm for the importance of what I was teaching was infectious. I loved to lecture, but even more I enjoyed the questions that the lectures engendered. I learned later that some of the students had promoted me as the "best professor" my second year of teaching. I had lost by one vote to a physics professor who had long been at Augie. The students running the election were all "my" students, and they seriously considered making me the winner. They told me that, after a long debate, they decided not to do so because they knew that I "would not like it." They were right about that.

They were also right about the war. Only after I began to teach at Augustana did I start to think that the stance I had taken toward the war was a deep mistake. The war was not something just "to think" about. War had never played a large role in my family's life. My father had not been drafted to serve in World War II, nor had any of his brothers. The family was, in general, "patriotic," but no one trusted the politicians, who we believed served the interests of the wealthy classes. My own stance toward war was shaped by the Korean War, which I generally thought was a "good thing."

I still carry in my wallet my history with the Selective Service System. On November 21, 1962, the year I entered Yale Divinity School, I was classified IV-D. In other words, the Dallas draft board assumed that because I was in divinity school I should have a ministerial deferment. I wrote to tell them that I was not going into the ministry, but they did not bother to change my classification until 1967, when I was reclassified II-S, a student deferment. I thought that this classification was also inappropriate, so I wrote again, suggesting that I be reclassified I-A. I received a I-A classification on February 17, 1970. I was finally vulnerable to the draft and would remain so until I was thirty-five. But I never lived in fear of the draft. The students I taught did.

I remember one student in particular. His name was Bill Sampson. At another time and place, Bill could have been a Bill Clinton. He was extremely handsome, had the manners his upper-middle-class background demanded, and was quite smart. He was also the president of the student body. He had taken one of my courses, but the last thing he was interested in was theology. However, as graduation and the draft loomed, he decided to go to divinity school to avoid the draft. He asked me to give him a reading course in modern theology to prepare him. I was glad to do so. He went to Harvard Divinity School, where, he told me, he never had to study because the reading course I gave him taught him enough to get through most of his courses without studying.

Rather than studying theology, he took courses at Harvard on the side, in the hope that after the war he could get into a medical school. He did go to medical school, but during his residency he became attached to a lady who convinced him to come to North Carolina to organize workers. Bill was killed in Greensboro, North Carolina, by the Klan. I have never forgotten him, not only because I was quite fond of Bill, but also because he seemed to me to exemplify what a strange, terrifying, sad, yet wonderful time "the Sixties" names.

I know that the way I now think owes much to what I learned from those who lived through the Sixties. Many of the students I had at the time, people who sought "alternative lifestyles," ended up selling insurance for a living. That they did so is not a bad thing, but it is a bit sad. I have always lived a conventional life, but I would like to think that the radical challenges the Sixties represent have stayed with me.

Of course, it would be a mistake to romanticize that time. The liberations heralded destroyed many. But for me the sheer energy, the willingness of many to put their lives on the line, and the challenge to imagine a different world remain gifts. The way things are is not the way things have to be. That thought began to shape my understanding of what it might mean to be a Christian — namely, Christianity is the ongoing training necessary to see that we are not fated. We can even imagine a world without war. That is a thought that would come later, but I was beginning to think that I needed to think differently about Vietnam.

The more I thought about the challenge presented by Vietnam, the more I began to think that there might be limits to how Reinhold Niebuhr had taught us. I have always stood in awe of Niebuhr. Although I never met him, I have always thought of Niebuhr as the exemplification of sheer intellectual energy. He was one of those people for whom the description "the force of their personality" must have been apt. Accordingly, you cannot help but feel overwhelmed by his work. Moreover, his work contains an unrelenting honesty about our lives that is compelling. Indeed, I suspect that the power of Niebuhr's work, the reason that so many people have found his theological construal of the necessity of violence intrinsic to personal and political human relations so persuasive, is that they rightly sense Niebuhr's passion for truthful speech.

Yet the war in Vietnam, the civil rights struggle, and the counter-cultural protest against "normality" were making me rethink Niebuhr. I was not trying to make Niebuhr or Niebuhrians responsible for the war. My worries went deeper than that. I began to think that Niebuhr had seduced me — and "seduction" is exactly the right word — to assume that the way things are is the way things have to be. In truth, I did not know how to go on if in fact Niebuhr needed to be left behind, but at least I was beginning to think the interest-group liberalism intrinsic to my defense of black power was a mistake.

I HAD BEGUN TO READ IRIS MURDOCH AT YALE, BUT I WAS NOW READING everything of hers I could get my hands on. I have always loved to read novels, so I began to read not only Murdoch's philosophical essays but also her novels. I wrote her to suggest that her essays should be brought together in a book. I even volunteered to select and introduce the book. She wrote a gracious note in return, telling me that she quite appreciated the offer but noting that *The Sovereignty of Good* was soon to appear in print.

I was reading Murdoch, but I also stumbled onto a book that was crucial for how I came to think. The book was entitled *Moral Notions* and written by Julius Kovesi. "Stumbled" is not an accurate description of how I came to read the book. Because issues in philosophical psychology were so important for the work I was doing in my dissertation, I had begun to read the books in the series Studies in Philosophical Psychology. I had learned to keep an eye out for books that would appear, so I ordered Kovesi's book as soon as it appeared in 1967.

Kovesi's critique of G. E. Moore, his account of rules, and his understanding of how descriptions work struck me as being crucial for developing further an ethics of the virtues. I did not realize at the time that Kovesi was developing arguments begun by Philippa Foot, but I thought I saw some connections between Kovesi and Murdoch. Only later did I learn that Foot and Murdoch were close friends and shared deep philosophical convictions. I also thought Kovesi provided an account of language, an account I associated with Wittgenstein, that Murdoch's account of "seeing" needed. I understood that Murdoch was a "Platonist" and disagreed with her just to the extent that her Platonism led her to what I can characterize only as a strange type of mysticism.

Another book that proved decisive for me I discovered by sheer good luck. I had sent my dissertation (at the suggestion of Mr. Gustafson, I think) to a new publisher called Corpus Press. They expressed interest in my book. In order to suggest how my book might fit with their publishing strategy, they sent me one of the first books they had published. It was Herbert McCabe's *What Is Ethics All About*, published in England as *Law, Love, and Language*. Unfortunately, Corpus Press was soon to go out of business, but they had done me a great favor. Between Kovesi and McCabe I thought I saw the way to articulate a richer account of the moral life than that dominating the current philosophical and theological paradigms. I wanted to put William Frankena's *Ethics* out of business.

I do not remember when or how I wrote "Situation Ethics, Moral Notions, and Moral Theology" or "The Significance of Vision: Toward an Esthetic Ethic," but I somehow began to write them at Augie. My first year I taught four courses a semester. My second year we moved to the quarter system, which did not lessen the teaching. Yet somehow I began to write. It did not occur to me that I needed blocks of time to write. Give me thirty minutes here or there, and I could get something done. I am often asked how I have written so much. That is how. I write like I learned to lay brick. You do it because you have to get it done before it rains.

Those early essays are still at the heart of the way I have tried to think over the years. If you want to understand me, those are the essays with which you should start. I have learned much since I wrote those essays, but I could not have done so without what Murdoch, Kovesi, and McCabe taught me. No doubt Alasdair MacIntyre became increasingly important, but I am sure I was able to read him more intelligently because of the work I had done with Murdoch, Kovesi, and McCabe.

I was primarily concerned with questions of how claims Christians make might be falsified. I began to think that such a testing of Christian claims could be done by placing the concrete events of our lives in relation to the story of Jesus. Reinhold Niebuhr was a master of a genre that might be called theological journalism. Whatever doubts I might have had about the content of his journalism, I was sure that he was right to risk a providential reading of history. That is what Hans Frei and George Lindbeck came to describe as the text absorbing the world. This is not, perhaps, the happiest way to put the matter, but without knowing what Mr. Frei and Mr. Lindbeck would say later, I was beginning to develop an account along similar lines.

Because I was beginning to think along these lines, I discovered that the church might be important. I need to be clear. This discovery was first and foremost notional. I do not remember if I even went to church when I was working on my Ph.D. If I did, I went only spasmodically. I discovered that the church might make a difference because I thought you needed a community that spoke the language called Christian if Christians, as I would put it much later, were to perform the faith. Although I did go to church at Augustana, Christianity was for me primarily still an "idea."

To be sure, I thought I was a Christian, but I am not sure what that meant. I had done a Ph.D. in Christian ethics for God's sake. Surely I must be a Christian. But did I need to be a Christian because I had done a Ph.D. in Christian ethics? If I had become convinced that the God Christians worship did not exist, would I have resigned my position? Or is that even the right question? I am not sure what I would have done at Augustana if I had ceased to believe in God, but increasingly I have come to believe that "believing in God" is not a description that helps us know much about what it means to be Christian.

Perhaps even as early as Augustana, I had begun to think that believing in God was not all that interesting. After all, I had drunk deeply at the Barthian well, which means, at the very least, that I had learned not to take my own subjectivity all that seriously, particularly in matters having to do with God. Moreover, as a Barthian you cannot know in which God you believe or disbelieve unless you know that God is the Father, Son, and Holy Spirit. Barthian that I was, however, I also worried that Barth may have given an account of Christian doctrine in which the material conditions necessary to make doctrine intelligible were not accounted for sufficiently.

I think one of the reasons many of us at the time were "happy" to be Christian was the extraordinary witness of the African American church. Christians finally seemed to be on the right side. Moreover, Christian participation in protests against the war seemed to make Christians "relevant." At the time, it seemed morally reasonable to be Christian. That, of course, would soon change. Being a Christian, going to church, would again be a sign of "normality."

At Augustana, I did start to go to church again with some regularity. I am not sure what possessed me to do so. I remember that after we had settled in Rock Island I went to a Methodist church not far from where we lived. I heard a terrible sermon matched by an equally horrible liturgy. I resolved not to make that mistake again. I learned from some of my students that there was a church on campus that was not the official church of the college. It seems students had formed a church and called a pastor. The pastor turned out to be a wonderful man named Richard Swanson (remember, this was the Swedish Lutheran Church). We soon became fast friends.

I had never been around Lutherans. I had, of course, read Luther. My Luther, influenced as I was by Jaroslav Pelikan and Ian Siggins, was much more the Catholic Luther than the Luther who allegedly made "justification by faith" the center of his theology. It never occurred to me, moreover, to think that the Reformation was based on Luther's alleged commitment to freedom of conscience. I was quite critical of Luther's strong distinction between the orders of creation and redemption. However, I found the liturgy (we used the "Green Book") to be not only substantive but beautiful. I began to attend the Sunday worship. In particular, I began to appreciate how important it was to have the Eucharist every Sunday.

Because this was a student enterprise and students made up the congregation, I felt free to bring Adam. He was just beginning to walk, so I could let him loose during the service without his becoming too much of a distraction. Anne no longer regarded herself as a Christian. There was never a question of her coming to church, but she was quite happy for me to take Adam. It was a pattern that Adam and I would follow for many years.

It was not long after we had arrived in Rock Island that Anne began to be sick. By "sick," I mean she was beset by "pains" in her stomach that would not go away. She went from one doctor to another until she finally got a diagnosis she wanted. One doctor thought she had porphyria, an extremely rare enzyme disease whose symptoms involve abdominal pain and psychological manifestations such as depression or anxiety. Anne was quite happy to have her "problem" diagnosed. I was not only sympathetic but supportive. I tried to do everything that might make her life less burdensome.

For some time, Anne had sleep habits that made it quite difficult for her to get up in the morning. Our daily routine was for me to wake up with Adam, to feed and play with him until Anne got up, and then to go to the school. I would then come home as early as possible so that I could take Adam for walks in his stroller. Anne loved Adam, but she found the demands of a child hard to negotiate. Much of the child care fell to me. I have never regretted that it did so. Adam was a delight. Intelligent and curious, he would, of course, get into everything he was not supposed to get into. I must have pushed him in his stroller hundreds of miles. We wore out at least two strollers along the way. We would get to this or that park, and I would let him loose to chase squirrels. Rock Island was populated by a species of black squirrel. They were, if squirrels can be, quite beautiful.

Adam's first word was "bird." We kept his playpen in a room on the back of the house. The room had obviously been a back porch converted into a room by adding windows. It was a wonderful bright space that allowed you to look out into the surrounding trees. Because we were on the Mississippi, we had a great variety of birds come through Rock Island. One morning after breakfast, Adam, who must have been somewhere between one and two, began to point excitedly and say "bd, bd." It took me a minute, but I got it.

Although increasingly difficult, things were not awful with Anne. We enjoyed many joint activities. I learned a great deal from Anne, for example, about art. I am not sure why, but in college I had been quite attracted to the world of art. I even took the Metropolitan course in the history of art. I dutifully paid $4.95 for each of the books you would get monthly in the mail. Anne really had a sense of beauty that enhanced our lives. She could take a few rolls of contact paper and turn a piece of plywood into an abstract design that enhanced our kitchen. I am sure the importance of "seeing" that I was learning from Murdoch seemed significant to me because of how I was being taught to see by Anne.

On the whole, our life seemed normal. Routine is a mode of survival. We made love routinely. We had meals routinely. We routinely went to movies and concerts and played bridge with a group of other young faculty. We did some things that sometimes upset the routine. For example, we got Adam a dog — Pepper — a cockapoo we were never able to train adequately. We made trips "home" to Texas. The relation between Anne's mother and father was a disaster, but we somehow survived our time with them. My mother and father loved Adam. We seemed to be settling into Augustana for the long haul. Life was "pretty good."

Anne even began to take some art courses in the college. She seemed to enjoy learning to draw, but she also found the courses quite stressful, because she desperately wanted to please the instructor. Nothing less than perfection would satisfy her, which meant she was never satisfied. Moreover, her "failure" had to be attributed to something, and I was it. She let me know that she could have dedicated more time to her art if she had not been married to me. I was trying to do everything I could to make her life better, but it seemed the more I did, the more I was part of the problem.

For example, I assumed it was my responsibility to do the housework. Anne was a wonderful cook, and at least for a while she loved to entertain. I always did an additional cleaning before we had guests. I had done all the housework when we were in New Haven, which seemed nothing but fair because she was supporting us. So I simply continued to do the housework after we moved to Rock Island. But no matter how hard I worked to have the house in good shape, what I did was never sufficient to meet her standards.

Anne was smart. She read widely. So it is not surprising that she soon discovered the women's movement. I am not generally considered a "feminist." I certainly have worries about the theological and political presumptions that have informed some forms of feminism. I am not a liberal. But I was quite sympathetic with Anne's feminism. I accepted critiques of "patriarchy." Even more, I thought women were quite right to demand to be seen as something other than an enhancement of the male ego. I had read Margaret Mead. I thought she was right to suggest that anything males can do females can do as well, if not better. Accordingly, the problem for women is what to do with the males whose "manliness" turns out to be necessary to hide their fundamental insecurity. God knows any male has to tire of the constant demand to be "strong." I read with interest Germaine Greer's *The Female Eunuch*. I liked the more radical feminists like Shulamith Firestone even better.

Teaching

I did so because I thought they represented a more fundamental challenge to the status quo than liberal feminism did.

So I was not opposed to Anne's feminism. Yet she blamed me for her decision to get married before she knew that she might have had other alternatives, which she was now discovering in feminism. Of course, the problem was not feminism. The problem was quite simply anger. Anne was angry. There was much, moreover, that she was right to be angry about. But I could not undo what had been done. She may have been mistaken to think she had to marry. She may have been mistaken to have married me. She may have been mistaken to have had a child. But I could not undo what had been done. I could, and I tried, to make what had been done less onerous, but it was a project doomed from the start.

THE LOOMING DISASTER WAS DELAYED. THE DELAY CAME BY WAY OF A PHONE call from someone named Jim Burtchaell, C.S.C, the chair of the Department of Theology at the University of Notre Dame. He explained that he was coming to the Quad Cities to celebrate the wedding of a former student from Notre Dame. Jim Gustafson had given him my name as someone they might consider for a faculty position at Notre Dame. They had offered the position to Jim Childress, but he turned it down and also suggested I might be someone to consider. Burtchaell explained that as long as he was coming to Rock Island anyway, he thought he might use it as an opportunity to have a conversation with me.

I was more than happy to meet with him. I had a three-year contract and had been told it was quite likely it would not be renewed. I was not desperate, but I was intrigued. I had gotten to know a wonderful man from Notre Dame in my last year of doctoral work, which had made me think that Notre Dame might be a good place to be. His name was Charlie Sheedy, and he was a C.S.C. — Congregation of Holy Cross — priest. Charlie had taught moral theology at Notre Dame, as well as served as dean of the college. Charlie, who I was destined to come to love as a close friend, was "the real deal." I figured that any place where someone like Charlie could be dean could not be all bad.

I agreed to meet Burtchaell on a Saturday morning on the steps of

"Old Main," the landmark building at Augustana. Jim Burtchaell, who was also destined to become one of my closest friends, is a stylish and cultured man. I did not know such a person existed. I had read Aquinas's *Summa*, but I knew nothing of Catholicism. I had become friends with Al Jonson, then a Jesuit, who had come to Yale to study ethics under Gustafson. Al was, like most Jesuits, well educated. I had also gotten a hint from being around Al that a priest might live quite well, but that "hint" did not prepare me for the reality that was Jim Burtchaell.

Though it is not quite fair, I sometimes try to describe Burtchaell to those who never knew him by suggesting, "Try to imagine Richelieu." Burtchaell had the bearing of a priest who would be a prince. He was not afraid of power. He wanted power. Power finally destroyed him. But that was still to come. When I met him in Rock Island, I did not have any way to comprehend who he was. My stereotype of Catholic priests did not allow me to imagine that a priest would think it important to know what wine you should drink or what the best restaurants in Chicago might be. I assumed that because he was a priest, he must care about what I cared about. This assumption, at least, was not wrong. It turned out he had done his doctorate in New Testament at Cambridge.

I was an equal shock to Jim. It was a Saturday morning. I dressed as I always dressed: shorts, a shirt with no sleeves, tennis shoes with no socks. Years later Jim told me that when he saw me on the steps of Old Main he prayed: "Dear God, please don't let it be him." But it was me. We went to my office and engaged in an energetic conversation about "ethics." I knew a little about Catholic moral theology because I had taken a seminar from Father Haring during my last year at Yale. I had found much to admire in Father Haring's attempt to make Catholic moral theology more theological, but I did not think he had found a way to integrate his theology and casuistry.

It turned out, however, that Burtchaell was not looking for someone who knew a great deal about Catholic moral theology. He was looking for someone who might provide a quite different way to think about "ethics." I must have convinced him I was someone who might be able to do that, because the week after we met he called to offer me a job at Notre Dame. He explained that I would be replacing a priest who was going on leave and might come back. If he did so, I might have the job for only a year. I needed the job, but I still thought it important for me to be interviewed by the faculty. So I asked if, before I made up my mind, I could come to Notre Dame to meet with some of the faculty. He readily agreed.

I arrived to be interviewed at Notre Dame along with a twelve-inch snowstorm. It was the first week of April. I suspect that for some faculty it was unclear which event was more unwelcome. During a reception, not for me but for a visiting dignitary, I was introduced to Father Ed O'Connor. I had no idea who Father O'Connor was, but it turned out he was an extremely conservative priest. His theological discipline was Mariology, and he later became deeply involved in the Catholic charismatic movement. With my usual lack of thought, I introduced myself by saying, "My name is Stanley Hauerwas. I am from Texas. That is where it takes six syllables to say 'Gawd dammm.' " It had not occurred to me that such a comment might be offensive. Ed had little patience with liberal Catholics, but he always treated me well. I think that he thought I had the disadvantage of being raised Protestant. I was someone that might still be won over to the true church.

I had no idea how to write what is now called a "job-talk." But I did write a paper entitled "Politics, Vision, and the Common Good." I had read Sheldon Wolin's *Politics and Vision*. Drawing on Wolin, I was trying to grope toward an understanding of politics that could serve as an alternative to the interest-group model I had learned at Yale and by reading Niebuhr. It did not occur to me that the ten or so folk to whom I read the paper could not have cared less what I thought about such matters. All they wanted to know was if I could keep Notre Dame undergraduates interested in a subject they had been inoculated against by the instruction they had received in their Catholic high schools. The faculty seemed to think I could do that, so I was offered the job.

I remember that Aidan Kavanaugh, a Benedictine who taught liturgy, asked me how I would teach Protestant moral theology. Aidan, who was destined to be a good friend, had been raised a Baptist in Waco, Texas, only to migrate to being an Anglican, a Catholic, and finally a Benedictine. He was one of the best preachers I have ever heard. I told him I had no idea how to teach Protestant moral theology because I was not Protestant or Catholic when it came to ethics. For example, I argued that Thomas was not a Roman Catholic theologian because that identification only made sense after the Reformation.

There was something right about that response, but such a response was also deeply inadequate, because it hid the ambiguity of my ecclesial status. It was true that I was neither a Protestant nor a Catholic. I did not have to be a Protestant or a Catholic because I had gone to Yale. The sad reality is that, for many of us, where we went to graduate school was more important than our ecclesial identification. I am not sure I would have understood the significance of this fact if I had not been given the opportunity to teach at Notre Dame for fourteen years.

I returned to Rock Island with the news. Anne was quite happy that we were leaving Rock Island. Notre Dame at least sounded like "a better place." I told my immediate superiors at Augustana. One of my friends in the History Department, Tom Treadway, had just been named the new president of Augustana. He kindly offered me the possibility of returning if things at Notre Dame did not work out. I thought, however, that it was time to burn the boats on the beaches. It would either work out at Notre Dame or it would not. There would be no going back.

I shall always be grateful to the people at Augustana for putting up with me. God, I was young. There are some advantages to being young. But there is also an arrogance and self-righteousness that often comes with youth that I suspect clung to me. I was smart, but I had not yet learned to listen. I am not sure how any of us learns to listen, but I suspect for people like me, people who seem "in control," you simply have to be "stopped." At least one of the names for how I was "stopped" turned out to be Anne.

CHAPTER 5

Catholics

Catholicism is a world. The University of Notre Dame is part of that world. I had no way to imagine when I came to Notre Dame in 1970 that Catholicism was a world, or what it might mean for Notre Dame to be part of that world. I thought I was simply getting a job at a better university. Just as it had not occurred to me what it meant to go to a divinity school to explore the truth of Christian beliefs, I really did not *get* what it meant for me to teach at Notre Dame. I did not understand the Catholic difference, which was probably a good thing. If I had understood the Catholic difference, I might have had defenses that would have prevented me from learning from that difference.

I spent the next fourteen years at Notre Dame. I had been trained to be a theologian at Yale. At Notre Dame, I began the slow, agonizing, and happy process that has made me a Christian. I am well aware of the oddness of that claim. Surely I have been a Christian of some sort from my Pleasant Grove beginnings? Probably. But there is no substitute for learning to be a Christian by being in the presence of significant lives made significant by being Christian. I have no doubt, as I hope is evident in the story I have told so far, that such lives were present in my life prior to Notre Dame, but at Notre Dame they got my attention.

"Significance" can, of course, be a misleading description of the lives that got my attention. Significance suggests importance. It suggests lives that make a difference and that demand acknowledgment. But the lives of significance I began to notice were not significant in any of those ways. Rather, they were lives of quiet serenity, capable of attending with love to the everyday without the need to be recognized as "making a difference." Such lives came in all shapes and sizes at Notre Dame. Some of them were called "Father" or "Sister."

Paradigmatic of such a life was Charlie Sheedy. Jim Burtchaell had hired me, but before I arrived at Notre Dame he was appointed provost. Charlie Sheedy became acting chair of the Department of Theology. It was not clear what it meant for Charlie to chair the department. He had formerly been dean of the college, but Charlie did not have an officious bone in his body. David Burrell, who was to become chair of the department, described Charlie as that bit of humanity thrown into the wheels of bureaucracy to bring them to a stop.

I had met Charlie first when he was on sabbatical at Yale, but I had no sense of who he was. We were destined to become unlikely but close friends. Charlie exemplified Catholicism and Notre Dame for me. A priest, an alcoholic, a chain smoker, an avid reader of French novels, a fan of the Chicago Cubs, he defied all stereotypes. Before and after Vatican II, young men going into the priesthood assumed that priests needed to have all the answers worked out. Charlie never assumed he had any answers worked out, but he knew he was a priest.

Some years after I left Notre Dame I met Charlie on a bench in front of the Dome. The Dome, with Mary on the top, is the focal point of the campus. Charlie was retired but living in Corby Hall, the residency for the priests who taught or had other responsibilities connected to the university. Notre Dame had begun the attempt to be regarded as one of the premier research universities in America. Charlie observed that he found such an endeavor "crass," but he was not really that interested in the topic. What he was interested in was learning to die. Thus he asked, "What do you think heaven will be like, Stanley?" God, how I loved him.

Of course Charlie, like Notre Dame, took some getting used to. For example, I could not understand Charlie's "leadership style" as acting chair of the department. He simply did not seem to take his responsibilities seriously. I was an ambitious young academic wanting to get ahead in a department that wanted to get ahead. Charlie led the department as if we had all the time in the world. He did so because he had been there in the beginning, which meant he had no illusions.

The Department of Theology at Notre Dame was created after World War II under the leadership of Father Theodore Hesburgh. Up until that time, it was assumed that what made a Catholic university Catholic was that you taught undergraduates philosophy. Though Notre Dame was a university governed by the fathers of the Holy Cross, they had borrowed the Jesuit presumption that philosophy was the necessary discipline to sustain the Catholic faith. Theology was a subject taught in the seminary for the training of priests. Why would someone who did not intend to become a priest need theology?

However, it soon became apparent that the students coming to Notre Dame did not know enough about being Catholic to sustain being Catholic in America, so a department of theology was created. Father Hesburgh was named chair. He assigned "disciplines" to various members of the Holy Cross order. Because Charlie had a law degree from Catholic University, he got "moral theology." Charlie said he did not know anything about moral theology, but in 1949 he ended up publishing a widely used textbook that bore the title *The Christian Virtues.*

In the preface, Charlie explained why he thought it important to put in print a book "as poor and inadequate as this one doubtless is. The only explanation is that we wanted to teach the virtues; we had no book on them; and so this one was written." He acknowledges that the book depended on the work of Father Benedict Merkelback, O.P. Just as I had done in my dissertation, Charlie was making use of new readings of Thomas for rethinking ethics. The Department of Theology had gone through many transitions by the time I arrived in 1970. The faculty was no longer dominated by members of the Holy Cross order. Even Jesuits were allowed to teach at Notre Dame. One of them was from, of all places, the Netherlands. I had no idea that a Jesuit could come from the Netherlands, much less be a student of Mircea Eliade and specialize in African religions. His name was Frank DeGraeve. He was not only a good friend for me but extremely kind to Anne and Adam. He loved music and art and often joined us on trips to Chicago to see art exhibits at the Chicago Institute for Art. I could not have imagined a person like Frank existing before I came to Notre Dame.

Lay Catholics were also teaching in the department. For example, Bill Storey taught liturgy. I had no idea that liturgy was or could be a proper subject in a university department of theology, but there it was, part of the curriculum. I came to think of liturgists as patristic scholars with a difference, the "difference" being that they thought it mattered how Christians actually worshiped God. Over my years at Notre Dame, I probably learned as much from the liturgists as from my other colleagues in the more conceptual fields.

There was even a lay woman, Josephine Massyngberd Ford, teaching New Testament. Josephine was from England. To say she was an English eccentric would not be a sufficient description to capture the complexity of Josephine. Josephine, a pious and conservative Catholic who had defied her family to become an academic, could have been a character in an Evelyn Waugh novel, but I suspect even Waugh might not have thought such a person actually existed. Josephine not only existed; you could not avoid her reality. For example, I introduced her to Robert Wilken, who had just joined the faculty. Robert expressed his delight in meeting her and asked innocently, "How are you?" Josephine, who at the time thought she had lupus, responded, "I am dying."

The Department of Theology was in the College of Arts and Letters because its primary responsibility was to teach two required courses in theology to every Notre Dame undergraduate. Yet the department also served as a graduate faculty for M.A. and Ph.D. work, as well as the faculty for Moreau Seminary. I had not understood that the department was organized in that way when I joined the faculty, but I came to appreciate the importance of this structure, because it insured that theology gained its intelligibility as a discipline of the church without being any less a university subject.

I do not know if I was the first Protestant hired to teach in the department, but I was certainly among the first. It did not occur to me that some faculty might worry that my teaching theology and ethics to the undergraduates could suggest that it was legitimate to be a Protestant. At the time, I did not think I was either Protestant or Catholic. I discovered who I was in a faculty meeting some years later when we were asked to reflect on how our various backgrounds contributed to our attempt to be a theology department in a Catholic context. The Jesuit, Dominican, Reformed, and Lutheran faculty responded by suggesting how their tradition shaped their understanding of being at Notre Dame. I was silent. I could not say how being a Methodist shaped my understanding of what it meant for me to be at Notre Dame. Then it occurred to me, "I'm not a Methodist. Hell, I went to Yale." Over the years at Notre Dame, I would slowly discover the limits of that ecclesial identification, but not at first.

THE YEAR BEFORE I CAME TO NOTRE DAME, A NUMBER OF STUDENTS HAD been suspended for protesting the war in Vietnam. They had blocked the entrance to the administration building, defying Father Hesburgh's fifteen-minute rule, that is, if they did not disperse fifteen minutes after he had warned them to do so, they would be suspended. He was not kidding. They were suspended but allowed to return the next semester. Many of them were in my class on Christianity and democracy.

What a wonderful time to teach. You certainly had no problem making clear that questions of political obligation were unavoidable if Christians were to be serious about their faith. It was a time when students were more than willing to suggest that you were a fascist pig for even suggesting that the Vietnam War might be just. Many of these students had been influenced by Jim Douglass, the author of *The Non-Violent Cross: A Theology of Revolution and Peace.* Jim had been hired to be a peace witness on campus, but he was soon fired by Father Hesburgh. It did not take long for me to become aware that there was a radical Catholic peace witness, which again challenged my assumptions about "Catholicism."

I was enthralled by Notre Dame. I fell in love with Notre Dame. I could not imagine a better place to be: a beautiful campus, engaging students, a place that thought theology mattered, and most of all an extraordinary faculty. At Notre Dame we actually got to know our colleagues in other disciplines because we had the misfortune of having our offices in the basement of the library. Cramped in small offices without windows, we could not avoid getting to know one another. I thought I was in intellectual heaven. I had never met so many bright and engaging people who often brought to their work perspectives I found fascinating.

Phil Gleason, a historian, introduced me to the German Catholics who settled in St. Louis. They were so theologically and politically conservative that they were radicals in America. I began to see connections between their organic views of society, the liturgical movement begun at Saint John's Abbey by Virgil Michael, and the political presumptions that shaped Leo XIII's *Rerum Novarum*. Ed Goerner's *Peter and Caesar: Political Authority and the Catholic Church* opened my eyes in a similar way. Goerner, who taught political theory in the Department of Government, helped me understand the limits of John Courtney Murray's attempt to reconcile the American democratic project with Catholicism.

I was being reeducated by being introduced to literature I had not known. Through friends in the English Department, I discovered Pietro Di Donato's novel *Christ in Concrete*. I could only wonder how I had missed this haunting account of the hard life Italian bricklayers led in New York City. It was as if I was Theron Ware in Harold Frederick's *The Damnation of Theron Ware*, a book I also discovered at Notre Dame. Like Ware, I was being overwhelmed by the sophistication of a Catholic and European culture. I did not, however, feel overwhelmed. I felt like I was a kid in a candy store.

Assistant professors at Notre Dame were expected to share an office with another assistant professor. I was lucky my first two years at Notre Dame to share an office with Father Jean Laporte, a French priest and patristic scholar. I was lucky because he did not use the office. Jean was promoted and got his own office. That meant I had to share the office with Peri Arnold, a new hire in the Department of Government. Peri was a rotund Jew from North Side Chicago who had done his Ph.D. at the University of Chicago. I remember saying to him as he entered the office, "Arnold, I do not want you here." He responded, "Hauerwas, I do not want to be here." We became fast friends.

Our problem was that we shared too many intellectual interests. We could not stop talking to one another. Peri was not a political theorist, but he had done his work at Chicago, so theory informed the work he did on how different modes of administration shaped the presidency. From Peri I learned not to dismiss Hoover, to appreciate Eisenhower, and to worry about Truman. Peri and I even ended up teaching a course together on ethics and public policy. From Peri, who came from a good socialist background, I learned that even more important than what a social order identifies as a social policy is that which is not so identified.

Peri and his wife, Beverly, also saved my life, not only because I could count on them in emergencies, but because they refused to let Anne's aggressive and often bizarre behavior determine our relationship. Friendship is a complex and fragile business, but friendship between couples can be even more complex. That is particularly true when a marriage is troubled, as my and Anne's marriage was. Peri and Beverly refused to let the pain of our marriage prevent us from being friends.

Of all the people I met in the basement of the library, none proved to be more important than David Burrell, C.S.C. Our offices were not far apart. We could not avoid meeting. My life and his life are now inseparable. I have no idea what David made of me early on. I am sure he must have thought that I was far too self-important, but we discovered that we shared some similar intellectual roots. David had been a Notre Dame undergraduate. He had discerned a call to the priesthood and undergone formation at Moreau Seminary. He then did his S.T.L. at the Gregorian University under Bernard Lonergan. He was among the first C.S.C. priests to be allowed to do a secular Ph.D. He completed his Ph.D. at Yale in philosophy in 1965 and then returned to Notre Dame to teach in the Department of Philosophy. We overlapped at Yale, though we never met there.

David, deeply influenced by Wittgenstein and Heidegger, sought to provide a rereading of Thomas's account of analogy by suggesting how the language we use is our best resource for thinking about issues identified as metaphysical. He argued, contrary to the received view, that Thomas had no theory of analogy. He therefore sought to distinguish Thomas from Duns Scotus and Cajetan by drawing on J. L. Austin's performative account of language. It was extraordinary. It seemed as if David and I had been working on the same problems, reading the same books, drawing similar implications without knowing it. We soon recognized that we shared much in common.

To say that we shared much in common, however, can be a misleading description. We were different. David had a depth of cultural experience I could only imagine. He spoke many languages. He could navigate diverse cultures and places. To be sure, he wore his cultural sophistication lightly, but David's background, education, travels, and range of experiences put him in a different league from me. But God had brought us together, and I can only give thanks for that. I would not be who I have become, nor have written what I have written, without David. I do not think the reverse to be true.

For many around Notre Dame, David seemed to be something of a "flake." How could you take seriously a priest who did yoga exercises? David did not just do yoga, he often did yoga during committee meetings when he got bored. Then there was that little thing with Elena. When David was an undergraduate at Notre Dame he fell in love with an undergraduate at St. Mary's named Elena Maltis. But the call to the priesthood was too strong. David became a priest and Elena a nun in the C.S.C. order. Elena went on to do a Ph.D. and taught theology at St. Mary's.

David and Elena would often be separated by time and space, but when possible they continued to develop their special relationship. For example, they often shared meals and trips. They never betrayed their vows. For Protestants, such an arrangement may seem unthinkable, but for David and Elena it "worked." Catholics, I think, knew that such relations were possible, but it still disqualified David from being taken seriously for higher office at Notre Dame.

David was a member of the Philosophy Department. Through my developing friendship with David, I soon got to know many people in the department. What a department it was. Soon I was part of the reading group that met every other week to carefully study a text. We spent the first year reading Wittgenstein's *Investigations* line by line. The next year we read Jürgen Habermas's *Knowledge and Human Interest*. Under the extraordinary leadership of Ernan MacMullin, a priest and philosopher of science from Ireland, the Notre Dame Philosophy Department was not, as many departments in Catholic universities tended to be, overdetermined by developments on the Continent. Some faculty read Heidegger, but the history of philosophy, analytic philosophy, and the philosophy of science constituted the center of the department.

Particularly important for me was David Solomon. David, a fellow Texan who had done his work at the University of Texas, was one of the philosophers who specialized in ethics. David had written under Edmund Pincoffs. He was, therefore, quite critical of the way ethics was conceived after Henry Sidgwick and climaxing in R. M. Hare. Deeply influenced by Philippa Foot, David began to teach me alternatives to the standard account exemplified by Frankena's *Ethics*. David remembers that he introduced me to Julius Kovesi, but I am sure I had, as I have suggested, read Kovesi while I was still at Augustana. Either way, we both saw in Kovesi a new beginning.

Catholics

Every year, the Philosophy Department, under Ernan's leadership, sponsored a series of lectures on a theme. Philosophers from around the world came to deliver four lectures on the philosophy of science, the philosophy of religion, metaphysics, epistemology, or ethics. These lectures were an ongoing education for me. I got to hear people like Bernard Williams and Philippa Foot. I believe I first met Alasdair MacIntyre when he came to give lectures in that series. Ernan knew quite well that these lectures not only enhanced our discussions at Notre Dame but also served to educate the wider philosophical community about Notre Dame.

Ernan had also discovered that most of the philosophy taught in America, interestingly enough, was taught in Catholic colleges. But often faculty at those colleges did not have the time to "keep up" in the literature. Ernan raised the money to begin a summer institute to bring teachers of philosophy to Notre Dame to attend lectures and seminars by the best philosophers of the day. I had not been at Notre Dame long before the focus for the seminar was ethics. Ernan asked me to give four lectures on some "practical issues." I agreed but had no idea what I was getting myself into.

It turned out that I had to lecture right before R. M. Hare was to give his lectures. Professor Hare had to listen to me, and I in turn listened to him. I had read and reread *The Language of Morals* and *Freedom and Reason* when I was a graduate student. I was intimidated by Hare's presence, but all I knew to do was proceed. I had become quite interested in the discussions surrounding claims that human survival was threatened by overpopulation. In at least one of the lectures, I challenged the utilitarian presumptions that shaped the rhetoric of survival. Professor Hare was kind enough to say he found my lecture "interesting."

One of the benefits of being part of Ernan's summer symposium was the presence of John Score. I had encouraged John to apply to be a participant. He did, was accepted, and came. It was wonderful to be with him again. Anne had always liked John, so during his time in South Bend he often came to the house to share a meal. John loved to eat. Adam was still quite young. John, being John, was quite clear about not knowing how to act around young children, but I think he liked Adam. After all, Adam's middle name was given in honor of him.

I WAS HAPPY TO BE AT NOTRE DAME, BUT MORE IMPORTANTLY ANNE WAS happy to be at Notre Dame. I am not sure why she was happy. It may have been simply because she felt that we were in a more "prestigious" place. I know she certainly enjoyed being around people she regarded as more cultured. In particular, she liked Jim Burtchaell. She liked how he liked her cooking. She also liked David Burrell, who also enjoyed her cooking, but then David would eat anything. Adam often observed that when David was coming to dinner there would be no leftovers.

She also liked South Bend. For the first two years we rented a nice house not far from the campus. Though again I had come ahead to search for a place to live, this time Anne thought I had done well enough. I called by phone to ask if I could see the house and was puzzled by the landlord's hesitation to show it to me. It never occurred to me that he assumed, given my accent, I was African American. His whole body was flooded with relief when I stepped out of the car to see the house. It turned out that he was a lovely man, but then lovely men can turn out to be haunted by racial prejudice.

We had just turned thirty when we arrived in South Bend. In many ways, we were still living like graduate students. At least we were still living with the furniture we had acquired while at Yale. Furnishing our new home was one of the few things we enjoyed doing together. We would explore used furniture stores in search of oak furniture made by Sears in the early part of the twentieth century. We bought tables, chairs, and china cabinets for no more than twenty dollars. I would then spend hours refinishing our purchases. I discovered that I really enjoyed working with wood. I will never forget one cabinet that had been painted on the inside with red buttermilk paint. God knows how many times the thing had been painted. Only with great effort was I able to get it clean. It turned out to be a beautiful piece of furniture — even more important, Anne thought I had done a good job.

Adam was close to two when we moved to South Bend. Anne had begun to enjoy him because it was hard not to enjoy him. He loved to ride in the car with Pepper as we foraged the surrounding area for cheap buys. We always included him in meals when we had guests or went out to eat. Sometimes, as two-year-olds are wont to do, there were "moments," but the older he got the more he enjoyed being included with the "adults." Life seemed good.

Catholics

I did not know what to do about church. I thought I had become a Lutheran by attending the campus church at Augustana. But the Lutheran churches I attended in South Bend were quite different from what I had become used to at Augustana. As far as I could tell, the liturgical tradition they represented had little to do with how I had learned to worship at Augustana. Moreover, it was clear that Adam was not welcome during the liturgy, and I had become so used to having him with me that I did not want to lose his presence. I tried some of the Methodist churches with no better result.

Once classes started, I became aware that David said Mass every Sunday in the pit in Grace Hall. Every residential dorm at Notre Dame had at least one priest who lived with the students and said Mass at least on Sunday and often every day. David was one of the priests in Grace Hall, a high-rise dorm that housed a huge number of students. I realized that this was a perfect opportunity. Adam and I were always present on Sunday mornings when David said Mass for hungover undergraduates. Not only did I get to hear a fine homily, but Adam thought it quite appropriate to join David at the altar as he celebrated. I simply assumed that Adam and I should receive. That is how I became a Catholic at Notre Dame. Of course, only a Protestant could be that kind of Catholic.

There was a great irony that David was one of the priests in Grace Hall. The Grace after which Grace Hall was named was not God's but Joseph P. Grace, of W. R. Grace & Co. — a chemical and shipping company heavily involved in Latin America. His son, J. Peter Grace Jr., had pledged the money to build the dorm but had not given the full amount. The year before I arrived, the building had been finished, and events were planned to celebrate its completion and its dedication. David and his fellow priest and closest friend, John Gerber, were not content to let the celebration occur without some indication that the policies of the W. R. Grace & Co. were anything but good for Central and South America. Accordingly, they arranged for a panel that included Latin American priest-theologians and J. Peter Grace Jr. Mr. Grace was so offended by what the priests said during the panel that he told Father Hesburgh he would not give the rest of the money for Grace Hall until Father Hesburgh apologized. Father Hesburgh thought that what David and John had done was a mistake. In fact, he was livid; but he was equally sure that he was not going to apologize to Mr. Grace. Notre Dame, as far as I know, never received the rest of the money, but Grace Hall remains named after Joseph P. Grace.

RELIGIOUS ORDERS ARE STRANGE AND WONDERFUL BEASTS. I AM NOT SURE that those of us on the "outside" can even begin to understand what makes a religious community work. I also suspect that those on the "inside" often find that they do not know what makes the order religious, or a community. Father Hesburgh and David Burrell are remarkably different people, but they were both members of the C.S.C. They both, moreover, understood their vocations as first to serve God and then Notre Dame. Accordingly, Father Hesburgh, livid though he may have been at David, did not hesitate to approve David as chair of the Theology Department. The appointment was unusual because David was a philosopher. But given David's training, he was well prepared for the task. What a pleasure it was for me to work under him.

The complexity of the relations between members of the congregation was determined by the congregation's role at Notre Dame. Any C.S.C. member could not help but imagine that to be ordained meant you had a position of power at Notre Dame. When I first came to Notre Dame there was a general consensus that there were three candidates waiting in the wings to replace Father Hesburgh: Jim Burtchaell, David Burrell, and Ernie Bartell, who was a priest in the Economics Department. They were known as the "three Bs." Under these conditions, it is remarkable that they were able to maintain civil relations. Bartell and Burrell were even friends, but each had a difficult relation with Burtchaell, whom most regarded as the heir apparent. As it turned out, none of "the Bs" became president of Notre Dame.

But David did become chair of the department, serving from 1971 to 1980. Academically, these were some of the best years of my life. David thought ideas mattered for how a department was put together. Before I knew it, I had been made part of an extraordinary endeavor to rethink what a theology department in a Catholic university might be. David knew that we did not want to be another religious studies department, which meant that every discipline was insufficiently understood if it was not first and foremost a theological discipline. Of course, the historical work in Scripture must be done, but such work could not be an end in itself. Joe Blenkinsopp was as fine a theologian as he was a scholar of the Old Testament. Robert Wilken, who was hired the year after I joined the faculty, was a church historian whose work was increasingly theological.

Under David's leadership we came to understand ourselves not as a Catholic department but as a "theology department in a Catholic context." We probably did not know what we meant by that description, but it sounded good. At the very least, it meant that we were determined to "be Catholic," which meant that we desired to hire Catholics to fill positions when they came available. Burtchaell, much to the displeasure of many Catholic members of the faculty, had begun a campaign as provost to urge all departments at the university to hire Catholics. Anyone unfamiliar with Notre Dame may think its Catholic identity is no less certain than the pope's. But in truth, Burtchaell was right to insist on hiring Catholic faculty if Notre Dame was to avoid drifting into the cultural mainstream.

Of course, the kind of Catholics hired made all the difference. I soon learned that self-hating Catholics were no help. Indeed, I began to find tiresome the Catholic habit of blaming the "hierarchy" or the "clergy" because it had rained on Tuesday. I began to think that Catholics had developed the bad habit of not taking responsibility for the conditions that made them possible. For many Catholics, the church just seems so "there." Moreover, many of the Catholics at Notre Dame had never lived outside the Catholic world. They talked constantly of making the church relevant to the world, but they had little idea what the "world" was like. I kept trying to suggest that we Protestants had long made all the mistakes they seemed desperate to copy.

Some faculty wanted Notre Dame to be the Catholic Yale. I had been to Yale and liked it well enough, but I saw no reason why Notre Dame should try to be what it never could be. I thought it quite enough of a challenge for Notre Dame to be Notre Dame. Following Burrell's lead, I felt like I was part of an exciting intellectual adventure that might avoid the sterile "liberal" and "conservative" alternatives that seemed to shape the theological world.

For example, it was not long after Burrell became chair that we began to think about what it might mean to make an appointment in Judaic Studies. Drawing on the wisdom of Blenkinsopp and Wilken, we thought it a mistake to hire someone who would teach only the historical background necessary to understand Christianity. More important, and challenging, would be the appointment of someone in Judaica who would force us to recognize the continuing challenge Judaism represents for Christians. Although only a beginning for what we imagined, we did make an appointment in Judaica.

I was, of course, in the process of learning about developments in Catholicism that were new to me. I knew my Augustine and Thomas, but I had little idea, for example, who the Catholic modernists might be. I soon found myself reading a dissertation on George Tyrrell, Alfred Loisy, and Friedrich von Hugel that required me to educate myself on this important development in Catholic intellectual life. I came to appreciate Nick Lash's judgment that the modernists were on the whole right, but by the time that was recognized the issues that concentrated their attention were no longer the issues that mattered.

I had read Karl Rahner at Yale, but it now became increasingly important to read his *Investigations*. I thought Rahner's *Hearers of the Word* and, later, his *Foundations* to be too "foundationalist" for me. But I admired and learned much from his more occasional writings. Lonergan also became required reading. I found *Insight* well worth the effort but could never understand the excitement produced by his *Method in Theology*. We spent a faculty retreat discussing that book. I kept wondering: where is Barth when you need him? The answer was that Barth was almost entirely my responsibility.

The Catholics were mainly innocent of Barth's significance. All they had were the easy dismissals without engagement with the *Dogmatics*. I was bound not to let that continue. So I soon found myself teaching a graduate level course in which we read Aristotle, Thomas, Kant, and Barth — in a semester. It was a great course and some terrific dissertations, such as Paul Wadell's *Charity as Friendship with God and Form of the Virtues*, were the result; but I must have been crazy to put students through such a course. However, they were kind, assuming that I knew what I was doing, when in fact I was flying by the seat of my paints. I have taught this course, admittedly in many different narrations, for many years, and it continues to bear good results.

Catholics

BURRELL BECAME CHAIR OF THE DEPARTMENT OF THEOLOGY MY SECOND year at Notre Dame. The priest whom I had replaced decided not to come back, giving me another year. Sometime in that second year, I asked David if I could count on staying at Notre Dame. I have no idea what grounds he had for assuring me that I could stay, but he did.

Not only was I to stay, but David soon asked me to be director of graduate studies. As usual, I had no idea that some faculty might think such an appointment inappropriate. I thoroughly enjoyed working with colleagues and students across the disciplines. Indeed, it gave me the opportunity to learn what was going on in fields that were new to me. Not only had I landed in an intellectually rich environment, but thanks to David I was given a constructive role in the formation of the department. I was, of course, not yet tenured, but Anne and I felt secure enough to decide to buy a house.

We found one just across from the Notre Dame golf course. It was a Dutch Colonial with four bedrooms, a large living and dining room, a small kitchen, and a basement that would flood with every heavy rain or snowmelt. It cost $36,000. Real estate in South Bend was extraordinarily cheap after the closing of the Studebaker plant, but we still did not have sufficient funds to make a down payment. My parents loaned us $2,000, which I paid back by teaching summer school. I ended up teaching summer school for a number of years, not only to supplement my salary, but also because I enjoyed teaching and learning from the women of the diverse religious communities who came to summer school to be, as they would say, "retooled" after Vatican II. I gained a deep respect for these remarkable sisters who labored in the church's vineyard even though the significance of their work was not acknowledged.

The house was a great boon because it gave us something to do. It needed a lot of work. The rooms were covered with wallpaper from the Fifties. It is hard to describe how ugly the wallpaper was. Anne had a wonderful sense of color and design. She was sure she would be able to repaper the walls if I could get the old paper off. There must have been five layers in each room as well as in the hallway and stairwell. I would soak the walls with a solution that allegedly would make it easy to strip the wallpaper from the walls. It never seemed to work, but I refused to be defeated. I kept at it day after day until we were back to the plaster. Stripping the ceilings was absolute hell, but I was a bricklayer.

Anne soon discovered she could not, as she had thought, hang the new wallpaper. Yet she had invested a good amount of money in buying all the tools necessary to do the work. It was the beginning of a pattern that became increasingly recognizable. She would make quite grandiose plans to do something — for example, make drapes for the living and dining rooms — and then not be able to do what she had planned to do. She was not able to accomplish what she had planned because she had such a strong perfectionist streak. Yet her failure to carry through could not be her fault. It had to be someone's fault, and often that someone was me.

I often assumed she was right. I needed to make things work. People could be hired to put up the wallpaper. But that meant it was all the more important for me to do as much of the other work as I could to make the house over in Anne's image. The windows and doors of the house were trimmed with gumwood. It was hard as iron. You could not drive a nail through it. But the wood was quite beautiful once you got the paint or varnish off. So I began systematically stripping all the woodwork in the house.

Anne was happy with the changes we were making in the house and with where we were living. She was even beginning to make friends in the neighborhood. Adam soon became old enough to be put in preschool. It turned out there was a wonderful Montessori school at Little Flower Parish into which we were able to get Adam. One of the requirements was that parents had to volunteer to be present one day a week. Anne enjoyed working at the school, though she soon had antagonistic relations with some of the teachers.

I loved the school and my involvement in the classroom. Reading Maria Montessori's books, moreover, was a real eye opener for me because her "method" seemed to suggest that we learn to think with our hands. Though she had never read Wittgenstein, her educational philosophy could well be understood as drawing out some of the implications of Wittgenstein's understanding of the bodily character of language. At the very least, I owe a great deal to Montessori, because reading her helped me see that Adam's work at the knot board was just that: work. In short, Montessori helped me see Adam not as a potential adult, but as a human being.

We continued the routine begun in Rock Island. Adam and I got up together and had breakfast. I became a great pancake maker. I usually took him to Montessori. I tried to come home early to play with him. We did not live far from Leeper Park, which had a wonderful playground. The Saint Joseph River ran through the park, having just made the "south bend" to flow into Lake Michigan. The St. Joe is one of the few rivers in America to run north. You could rent canoes in the park to paddle with the flow of the river to a farm in Michigan. As Adam grew older, we often made that canoe trip.

When he was still small, I gave him a bath in the evening and put him to bed. But we always spent some time reading books together. At first, of course, I did the reading. But he loved to pick out the words on the page. By the time he was four he was reading. I do not think he remembers a time when he could not read. Friends soon began to observe that Adam and I seemed to have an unusual relationship. I think that was surely the case. We were father and son, but we were also friends. The bond between us would soon be necessary if we were to survive.

On the whole, our early years in South Bend were the best years we had. Adam was flourishing. Anne had friends and enjoyed entertaining as well as being entertained. I loved teaching at Notre Dame. My Catholic colleagues might have found the student body too Catholic, but I loved the extraordinary diversity of the students. After all, we were teaching "the world." I had no idea that so many different kinds of people existed. Just calling the roll at the start of a semester was for me a major challenge. I thought my name was hard to pronounce, but compared to many of my students "Hauerwas" was easy. I began to understand that a "mixed marriage" was one between an Irish and an Italian.

I HAD STARTED TO WRITE AT AUGUSTANA, BUT AT NOTRE DAME I REALLY began to put words on paper. I did not write because I thought you needed to publish to get tenure. I was not that savvy about how these things worked. I probably did need to write to get tenure, but I wrote because I thought I had something to say. It was such an exciting time. I wrote an article for the campus magazine, the *Scholastic,* on the role of the university in a time of turmoil. I tried to provide a defense of disinterest, but what I clearly did not understand was that I should not have been wasting my time writing for a campus publication if I intended to be a successful academic.

Two developments were crucial for giving me the presumption that I might have something to say. First, I had become friends with a fly geneticist named Harvey Bender. Harvey was involved with Logan Center. The center's mission was to provide schooling for the mentally disabled, and it was located across the street from Notre Dame. The center was constantly on the lookout for people to serve on the board who did not have a mentally disabled member of the family. They did so because it was one of the requirements written into their incorporation that members of the community who were not directly connected to the work of the center should be on the board. I have no idea how it came to be, but I was asked to serve on the board.

What an experience it was for me to become part of the world of the mentally disabled. That world, as I suspect it should have, frightened me. I shall never forget the first time I was given a tour of the center. A seven-year-old boy who had Down syndrome jumped in my arms and hugged me. He was too close, right in my face, and would not let go. I carried him as we continued the tour. I had to act like everything was just "fine," but really I was terrified. I soon began to think that learning to live with the mentally disabled might be paradigmatic for learning what it might mean to face God.

The second development, not unconnected with the first, occurred because of an article I had written in 1972 entitled "The Christian Society and the Weak." I wrote the article to articulate theologically how I understood the challenge of learning to be with the mentally disabled. It was published in the *Notre Dame Magazine.* I was cutting the yard (with our old push mower) when Anne called me to the phone. "Sargent Shriver wants to talk with you," she reported excitedly. I thought she must be kidding, but Sargent Shriver was on the phone. He and Mrs. Shriver had read my article and found it "powerful." They were anxious for me to come to Washington, D.C., to take part in a conference they were planning on medical ethics. That is how I became a "medical ethicist."

I had never been around people like the Shrivers. I liked Sarge. I found Mrs. Shriver "a bit much to take." I simply had no idea what it meant to be around people of "power." I soon realized that they assumed their job was to find people to do the work they thought needed doing. The work that needed doing in this case was the care of the mentally disabled. They had been drawn into this work by the existence of Mrs. Shriver's sister. It was good work, and I wanted to be of use. But I found I simply was not cut out to play the game at their level.

The reason I had difficulty was brought home to me one evening when Anne and I had been invited to have dinner with a number of other philosophers and theologians at the Shrivers' home. There were, of course, servants in attendance, but this did not stop some at the dinner from talking about how hard it is to find "good help." I could not forget that the people who had prepared the meal, the people who served the meal, the people who cleaned up after the meal, were my people. I have since enjoyed many meals in which servants were present, but in truth I have never gotten used to being waited on. And I have trouble being around people who have.

In 1973 Mr. and Mrs. Shriver made it possible for me to have a sabbatical at the newly formed Kennedy Center for Bioethics at Georgetown University. The Kennedy Center had been the brainchild of Andre Hellegers. Andre, originally from Holland, was an extraordinary man who understood earlier than most that medicine was facing a moral crisis. The crisis was not that associated with the increasing technological sophistication of medicine, but rather with whether we as a society had the moral presuppositions and practices to sustain medicine as a practice of presence to the ill.

Andre thought it quite important to educate some of us who claimed to be ethicists in the actual work of medicine. Paul Ramsey was among the first to receive this education. Andre brought Paul to Georgetown, with the happy result being Paul's great book *The Patient as Person*. I am in Andre's and the Shrivers' debt for giving me the opportunity to learn firsthand the nature of modern medicine. Like medical students, we rotated through the different departments in the hospital.

I was fascinated by the way physicians learn to see their patients, because I thought they often exemplified the way practical reason is supposed to work. It turns out, just as Ramsey argued in *The Patient as Person*, that doctors treat patients — not diseases. Moreover, every patient is different, requiring doctors to attend to the concrete particular. It occurred to me that the way we train doctors might be a model for moral training. I have often wished that we could train those going into the ministry not unlike how doctors are trained.

I began to think it a mistaken idea that medicine had much to learn from ethics. The reverse more likely is true. The practice of medicine is a moral practice from beginning to end. Physicians must be trained to see and care for their patients in a manner such that all other judgments are irrelevant. I take this training to be one of the most strenuous moral commitments one could imagine. Physicians must acquire the virtues to sustain their commitment to be present to the ill even when there is not much they can do to make those for whom they care better.

Too often it is assumed that medical ethics is, or should be, primarily about what doctors do. But far more important is what kind of people we should be to be patient patients. I fear that patients who are no longer patient in the face of illness and death cannot help but bring expectations to medicine that are corrupting.

I did not put *Suffering Presence* together until 1985, but those essays reflect what I learned during my time at the Kennedy Center. The way medical ethics came to be conceived means that I am not a medical ethicist, but I believe that some of the writing I have done that is allegedly medical ethics, particularly *Naming the Silences,* is among my best work. That someone like Brian Volck — a Catholic, a doctor who often practices on reservations in the Southwest, and a poet — finds what I have written about medicine helpful is extremely gratifying.

I hope my work in a book like *Naming the Silences* exemplifies what I can describe only as the importance of having a novelist's eye. We are complex creatures constituted by contradictions we refuse to acknowledge. The novelist must help us see our complexity without providing comforting explanations. We must be taught to see our pain and the pain we cause in others without trying to excuse ourselves by offering explanations.

I think "ethics" depends on developing the eye of the novelist. If my work is compelling, I suspect it is so to the degree I am able to write like a novelist. If I have a novelist's eye, it is not accidental. I have, after all, spent many years reading novels. Reading novels will not necessarily make one better able to see without illusion, but it can help. My ability so to see, moreover, depends on how I have come to understand what it means to be Christian. I fear that much of the Christianity that surrounds us assumes our task is to save appearances by protecting God from Job-like anguish. But if God is the God of Jesus Christ, then God does not need our protection. What God demands is not protection, but truth.

I was beginning to develop a different way of "doing" ethics. I had learned from Wittgenstein and Kovesi that description is everything. But to sustain truthful descriptions requires agents habituated by the virtues necessary to avoid the lies unleashed by our desire to avoid suffering the suffering of others. Descriptions, moreover, are not just "there" but interconnected. The interconnection is called "a story." Such a story must be told, tested, and retold countless times if we are to approach the truth.

To approach "ethics" in this way depended on my dissatisfaction with the focus on decision and choice that dominated — and continues to dominate — ethical theory. Influenced by Iris Murdoch's claim that choices are what you do when everything else has been lost, I became increasingly convinced that what we do is not what destroys us. Rather, our fate rests on how we describe what we do. Indeed, we do not know what we have done until we get the descriptions right. I think I was beginning to see more clearly some of the implications correlative to my attempt to recover the significance of the virtues.

I think also at work was my increasing realization that it is a mistake to think Christian ethics can be divorced from theology. I realize that many who want to maintain the independence of Christian ethics would protest that "divorce" is too strong a word. But too often it accurately describes how ethics is done. Love or justice or some other fundamental principle is identified as *the* source of the moral life. God and the church might be assumed as background beliefs that may be needed to sustain the intelligibility of the fundamental principle or principles, but they are seldom thought to be vital to how our lives are morally constituted.

Too many people, I fear, become "ethicists" because they do not like theology. I have always been a strong supporter of the Society of Christian Ethics, but the very existence of such a society can be a temptation to separate theology from ethics. I suspect that one of the reasons some of my colleagues in ethics find me hard to take is due to my unrelenting claim that God matters. Not just any God, moreover, but the God that has shown up in the life, death, and resurrection of Jesus Christ.

I began to think that the separation of Christian ethics, or moral theology, from theology proper was a reflection of the presuppositions of a liberal social order. The distinction between theology and ethics legitimated the public-private distinction that is the heart of the liberal project to domesticate strong convictions and, in particular, strong religious convictions. So the work I was doing in political theory, philosophical ethics, and the care of the mentally disabled seemed inextricably connected. That is what I thought I had to say, and I was determined to say it.

The other development that made all the difference for how I was learning to think began quite innocently. I thought it might be a good idea to find the guy named John Howard Yoder who had written that pamphlet on Barth I had read just as I was leaving Yale. Goshen was not far from South Bend, so one Saturday I put Adam in the car and drove out to Goshen, assuming that this must be where the Associated Mennonite Biblical Seminary was located. It turned out that the seminary was in Elkhart. But in Goshen I did go into College Church and discovered a display of pamphlets, some of which had been written by Yoder. There was one on Barth, another on Reinhold Niebuhr, and still another on capital punishment. I seem to remember that they each cost a dime. I had the money, so I bought them.

I drove back to South Bend and devoured what Yoder had written. I was stunned. I could not avoid recognizing that this guy had extraordinary analytical power. He wrote clearly and powerfully. I was overwhelmed. I also assumed that he had to be wrong. After all, he was a Mennonite. Mennonites were pacifists, and pacifism had to be a mistake. But I was intrigued. I discovered you could call Elkhart, Indiana. I even discovered you could call Yoder at the seminary in Elkhart. So I called and made an appointment to come to see him. I had no idea that a trip to Elkhart, Indiana, was going to change my life.

The Associated Mennonite Biblical Seminary is an appropriately modest collection of buildings on the south side of Elkhart, Indiana. John occupied an equally modest office in one of those buildings. I have no idea what John made of me. I did allow that I found his writing profoundly challenging. I suspect he must have assumed that I brought

Catholics

all the prejudices and stereotypes about Mennonites characteristic of someone educated at Yale — stereotypes that placed him in a "Christ against Culture" position. In short, he may well have thought that, however our conversation developed, I would assume that he bore the burden of proof.

John Yoder was tall, and many people reported that they thought of him as severe. There is no question that he could be quite intimidating. I probably should have been intimidated, but I was not. I did, however, find him hard to talk to. John had little use for casual chatter. I would ask him a question, and, as was his habit, he would answer using as few words as possible. John never tried to use charm to convince you to be an advocate of Christian nonviolence. Charm and John Howard Yoder were antithetical.

I did my best to make conversation, but it was not easy. I finally resorted to the academic game — "So, what are you working on now?" John said he was not producing much that he thought might interest me. I noticed, however, a shelf of mimeographed materials and, assuming they might be something he had written, asked if I might read them. I left with a stack of his work about a foot high. I had also found in the seminary bookstore a copy of *The Christian Witness to the State,* which had been published by the Faith and Life Press in Newton, Kansas, in 1964.

I returned to South Bend and began to read. I discovered in the mimeographs a book entitled *The Politics of Jesus.* I met John in the summer of 1970. *The Politics of Jesus* would be published in 1972 by Eerdmans. I do not think reading the book had the same effect on me that Kant reports reading Hume had on him. After all, reading Barth as I had was preparation for encountering Yoder; but I recognized that Yoder's book was not just another position one might consider. Stanley Fish reports that when he teaches Milton there comes a moment when an undergraduate expresses admiration for Milton's poetry, giving Stanley the opportunity to observe, "Milton does not want your admiration. He wants your soul." Yoder did not want my soul, but he made clear that Jesus did. This was not going to be easy.

I began to read John's essays published in the *Mennonite Quarterly Review* as well as some of the pamphlets produced by the Concern Group. The latter was a group of young Mennonites receiving education in Europe. They were united by a desire to recover the radical character of the radical reformation. I was particularly struck by Yoder's Concern pamphlet "Peace without Eschatology?" I began to understand that "pacifism" is not a position that you might adopt after you get your Christology straight. Yoder forced me to recognize that nonviolence is not a recommendation, an ideal, that Jesus suggested we might try to live up to. Rather, nonviolence is constitutive of God's refusal to redeem coercively. The crucifixion is "the politics of Jesus."

The Original Revolution, a collection of John's essays, was published in 1971. The collection not only included "Peace without Eschatology?" but also the title essay, "The Original Revolution." I had presumed that an account of the virtues necessarily entails a politics. Reading Yoder's understanding of the church made me think that I might have discovered what such a politics entails. I do not think it is accidental that MacIntyre's *Against the Self-Images of the Age* was also published in 1971. Thus began my strange project, as some people have described it, of suggesting how Yoder's account of the church might satisfy some of the aporias in MacIntyre's work.

It was not long before I was given the opportunity to "go public," that is, to expose what I was learning from Yoder. Sometime before I had arrived at Notre Dame, the departments of theology from Notre Dame and Valparaiso, a Lutheran school, had started a yearly get-together, on the grounds that it was a good ecumenical idea. It was my first year at Notre Dame, but Sheedy asked me to give the paper when our faculties met. Given all I had read of Yoder's, I decided to write a paper on his work.

I began by noting that I was a Methodist with a doubtful theological background, since it goes without saying that a Methodist has a doubtful theological background. I noted further that I was representing the most Catholic department of theology in the nation, speaking to a bunch of Lutheran theologians, to argue that the Anabaptists had been right all along. I then suggested that I hoped to show, by directing attention to Yoder's work, how much Lutherans and Catholics had in common; that is, when all was said and done, they both assumed it was a good idea to kill the Anabaptists. Of course, that is exactly what happened, both historically and in response to my paper. The Lutherans and the Catholics joined in a common effort to show why, if you are to act responsibly, you will need to be ready to kill.

I was beginning to understand that this was not going to be easy. Indeed, I was to learn how patient Yoder was in his willingness to respond to misshapen critiques by those who had not read him but assumed they knew what he must think. At the time I gave the paper at the Valparaiso–Notre Dame event, I was not able to bring myself to say that I was a pacifist. That came a year later. I had leaned on David, suggesting that we ought to appoint Yoder to the faculty. Some arrangement had been worked out for John to begin teaching at Notre Dame. John, with his usual insistence on having a clear assignment, was to teach peace studies. As a result, other members of the faculty were beginning to know John. Robert Wilken and I were talking on our way to a faculty meeting, and Robert, at that time a Lutheran, was asking me what I made of this guy Yoder. I confessed that I was impressed, then hesitated, only to blurt out, "In fact, I'm a pacifist."

God knows what led me to say that, but ever since I have worked to understand what I said. Learning what it means to be nonviolent or, as I would prefer, to live peaceably begins with coming to terms with the resistance that such a declaration elicits. For example, I had a hell of a time trying to get the paper I had written on Yoder published. Every journal I sent the article to rejected it, not because of what I said about Yoder, but because of what Yoder said. One journal editor refused the article on the grounds that Yoder's reading of Scripture was pre-Bultmannian.

It simply did not occur to me that being identified with Yoder might be a bad "career move." I was ambitious. I wanted to make a difference. I was writing as fast as I could. I had not learned to write well. I thought the ideas mattered — not the writing. Burrell forced me to recognize that what I had to say could not be separated from how I said it. I slowly became a better writer by writing. I still find it painful, however, to read some of my early work.

I had revised my dissertation and was trying to get it published. Burtchaell said I should let Notre Dame Press look at it. They sent it to Martin Marty, who thought it "ten years ahead of its time." Because it was so, he told the press the book would not sell well, so Notre Dame would not take it. Gustafson told me that Trinity University Press in

San Antonio was beginning a new monograph series in religion. I submitted the book to them, and they accepted it for publication. I owe John Hayes, who was then teaching at Trinity, and Lois Boyd, the director of the press, a great debt for publishing a book by an unknown.

I had also written a series of essays that I thought might be brought together to make a more or less coherent book. I called the book *Vision and Virtue: Essays in Christian Ethical Reflection.* I did not have any sense about the politics of publishing. I thought what was important was to just get the stuff out there. There was a small press in South Bend called Fides Press. They had an office across the street from the Notre Dame library. I crossed the street with my little manuscript, hoping they might be willing to publish my essays. *Vision and Virtue* was published by Fides Press in 1974. *Character and the Christian Life* was published by Trinity University Press in 1975.

In 1974, I was promoted to associate professor with tenure. As usual, I paid little attention to the process. I suspect Notre Dame had not yet developed the tenure review process that now dominates research universities. I assume I must have been run through some university procedures, but I certainly had little sense that I might be in any trouble. I remember David telling me I had received tenure. He reported that the only worries about me were that some faculty thought I had come up a year too soon and that I needed to be more careful with my language.

Being careful with my language meant that I should not, as I was wont to do, use profanity. I had continued to talk like a bricklayer. There were certain words that I knew how to use and that were, not surprisingly, offensive to people at a place like Notre Dame. I also used a wide range of other words that people might have thought offensive. I used those words because that is the way I had learned to speak. I confess that I often found the middle-class and upper-middle-class etiquette that dominated university life oppressive. I certainly was not above sometimes using words that I knew would offend precisely because I knew they would offend. It took an article some years later in *Lingua Franca,* in which I was described as "the Foul Mouth Theologian," to make me quit using the most offensive words. I simply became tired of and bored with having that aspect of my life made into such a "big deal."

Catholics

I have the reputation for being the perennial "outsider." There is some truth to that characterization. I am the working-class kid in the world of the university. I am the radical Christian challenging an accommodated church. The list could go on, with each description an invitation to self-deception. In truth, I have no desire to be the "outsider," the critic, the dissident. I want a home. I want to play a constructive role. That is what I thought I had found at Notre Dame. It turned out, however, that I would learn that Christians have no home.

CHAPTER 6

Surviving

"Artists need freedom. We cannot be held to the standards by which other people live. So you cannot object if I have sex with Tom Fern." I had no idea what was going on. I assumed Anne could not be serious, though there was no hint in her speech that she was only considering a theoretical possibility. But I found it hard to imagine that she meant what she said. I knew Tom and his wife well. I could not imagine Tom might want a relationship with Anne.

Tom was an artist and taught in the Department of Art at Notre Dame. Anne was taking one of his courses. She had not slept well for several days. Indeed, she may not have slept at all. But her sleep habits were often irregular. She was obsessed by an art project that was assigned in the class. She stayed awake, compulsively drawing and redrawing what I can describe only as bizarre images. She was desperate to please Tom Fern. I was frightened by her behavior and speech, but I had no idea what might be going on. I had not experienced or seen anyone in the midst of a psychotic break.

I received a call from Tom. I have no doubt he found it difficult to call me and did so only because he thought he had no choice. He reported that Anne had come to his office, talked wildly, and made some quite inappropriate suggestions about what she would like to do with Tom. As much as I would have liked to do so, I could not avoid recognizing that something was desperately wrong. It was in the middle of the afternoon. I rushed home with no idea what to do. Anne was acting even more bizarre. She was lying immobile on the couch in the living room, waiting, she told me, for a message from God that would save the planet.

I gathered up Adam and took him to Peri and Beverly Arnold. Peri and Beverly did not yet have children, but they knew Adam well, and he knew them. I explained that something strange was going on with Anne. I said I had no idea how long they would need to care for Adam. They told me not to worry. I rushed home. Our family physician was a wonderful man named Roland Chamblee. Roland, a native of South Bend, had been one of the first African Americans to graduate from Notre Dame. I called him and described as best I could what was happening. Roland said it sounded like she might be having a schizophrenic episode. He gave me the name of a psychiatrist for whom he had a high regard and who he thought might be willing to help.

I called Dr. Shriner and described what was happening with Anne. He said he needed to see her, but he would do so only if I could get her to the hospital. I began to try to reason with her. She told me she was trying to save Adam from me because Adam was afraid of me. It seems that our problem was that we were spirits imprisoned by our bodies. Originally we had all been one, but God had sent some spirits down to Earth to rescue those of us imprisoned in our bodies. But on the way back, the ladder had broken, and some of the chosen ones had become trapped on Earth.

Anne had been sent to rescue the spirits. Adam was one of the spirits capable of being rescued. But as long as I was in the way, she could not rescue him. My problem was that I was too bodily. What I needed to recognize is that our bodies are full of holes and if we just drink enough water our bodies will melt away.

Anne was well read. She had read R. D. Laing. She knew that mental illness was nothing more than a mad society projecting its madness on those who in reality were sane. I was put in the odd position of having to argue that American society in 1975 was sane. She had heard me dissect America too often not to be able to play back my critiques in support of her understanding of the world. I was desperate. How could I convince her that she needed to see the doctor?

I finally realized that I would get nowhere if I tried to convince her she was out of touch with reality. She was quite fond of Richard Bondi, one of my graduate students, so I suggested that we call Richard to come to the house to wait for the message from God while we went to see Dr. Shriner. She wanted to share her insights with Richard, so she agreed for him to come to the house. By this time it was two in the morning. I phoned Richard. Of course, I was not able to explain to Richard what was happening, but he came over. He graciously received the instructions from Anne necessary for him to be capable of receiving a message from God to save the planet.

I called Dr. Shriner, who said he would meet us at the hospital. I got Anne in the car. The hospital was only a short distance, so we arrived before Dr. Shriner. Once there, we were put in a room isolating us from other patients. Anne became increasingly agitated and angry. By the time Dr. Shriner arrived I was in complete despair. Once Dr. Shriner was present, Anne tried to help him see that I was the crazy one she was trying to save. But I was stubborn. I was possessed by the evil spirits. I would not listen. She repeated again and again the story in which she played such a decisive role for the redemption of the world. Dr. Shriner said little. I kept trying to reason with her.

Finally Dr. Shriner said, "I see you have had some extremely important insights." She readily agreed. He observed, "Right now you are having trouble communicating them." He went on to observe that she must, moreover, be tired because she had not slept for some time and she had been given such onerous responsibilities. Anne again agreed. He then asked if she would like him to give her something to help her sleep. He explained that to do so she would need to stay in the hospital. She signed the consent form, looking at me with anger I shall never forget.

She was taken to the psych unit. I was not yet familiar with the range of antipsychotics that, out of necessity, I would soon know all too well, but I assume that Dr. Shriner had prescribed Haldol. By the time I left, she had gone to sleep. Dr. Shriner said it was far too early to try to make a diagnosis. She had clearly had a psychotic break, but it could be the result of a number of factors. We would just have to wait and see how she did. That is what we did for the next ten years.

ANNE STAYED IN THE HOSPITAL FOR AT LEAST A WEEK. PSYCH UNITS ARE crazy places. She soon made friends with other people on the ward. They were able to bond quickly because they shared the common experience of being misunderstood. I remember, for example, that Anne was outraged because she was not allowed to have a cigarette lighter. Nonetheless, I was expected to supply her with cartons of cigarettes, which she could then share with her newfound friends. I was desperate to please her, so I did whatever she asked.

It took me a long time to see that I would never be able to please her. I could never please her because my very existence was the problem. As she saw it, I had hospitalized her against her will. That she had signed the consent papers never registered with her. She assumed that I had gone to court to have her committed. I certainly would have gone to court to have her committed, but that was not the way it had worked. But the only thing that counted for Anne was her account of what had happened. Her problem was quite simply that I had the power to declare her crazy. The solution for her was for me not to exist.

Yet she could not live without me and survive. She needed me. Indeed, she not only needed me, but I suspect that, in as much as she could, she loved me. Moreover, she loved Adam. She loved her home. "Normality" beckoned, pulling her back into life. She was released, and we returned home. Dr. Shriner was hesitant to put her on any ongoing medication because he was not sure how to diagnose what had happened to her. He thought she might be manic-depressive (the label of the time), but he did not want to put her on Lithium. He was concerned not only about the side effects but also about her compliance with taking the medication continuously, as she would need to do.

The return to "normality" did not last long. The mania soon returned. I was not yet good at recognizing what was happening. For some time, our sexual relations had been infrequent. Suddenly all Anne wanted to do was make love. I certainly did not think that a bad thing. Not only did she want to make love, but she showed a renewed interest in being "religious." Again I did not think that a bad thing. God, how desperately we want the world to be all right.

But the world was not all right. Before I knew it, she had given all our money away. Even though Anne had never been happy with my involvement with Logan Center, she had given all we had, and we did not have that much, to the center. I received a call from the director. He told me that Anne had come to the center and given them a check. Something did not seem quite right about how she was behaving, so he called me. I collected the check and called Dr. Shriner.

Surviving

He had seen Anne several times after her break, and he thought she seemed to be doing well. But it now seemed clear, he said, that she was a manic-depressive and needed to be on Lithium. I knew there was no way I could get her to return to the hospital. I was, moreover, quite sympathetic with her resistance to the psych ward. Fortunately, she liked Dr. Shriner. Somehow I got her to see him at his office. He convinced her to take the Haldol again. We returned home, and she promptly went to sleep. The next day we returned to Dr. Shriner. He explained to Anne the chemistry of manic-depression and why Lithium was the medication of choice. She agreed to begin taking Lithium.

Lithium did not, as it does for some, give Anne the shakes, but it did result in her gaining weight. She now had to have her blood tested every month to make sure that her Lithium level was not too high. She also began to see Dr. Shriner every week, to start, and then every two weeks. She insisted that I come with her because I was the problem — not her. I was happy to go, though it did little to help the dynamics of our relationship.

Early on, I remember seeing Dr. Shriner without Anne present. I think he had suggested that it would be good for us to meet. He asked why we had never had another child. In fact, Anne and I had never considered the possibility. I suspect that neither of us was confident enough in our relationship to have more children. I am possessed by my mother's energy, but I think I sensed my limits.

WE HAD ENTERED THE WORLD OF THE MENTALLY ILL. IN TRUTH, AS I LOOKED back on our life together, that world had been present all along. I just did not know how to see it. I have no doubt that bipolar illness has genetic and chemical predispositions, but I suspect that not everyone who is so predisposed becomes bipolar. Anne's mother clearly had some of the behavioral habits associated with the illness, habits she passed on to Anne. Double-bind games seem to play a determinative role: I will love you if you are perfect; but you are not perfect, so I cannot love you.

I have wondered how this demand to be perfect is connected to schemes of grandiosity to which those suffering from bipolar illness are also subject. Anne would often make elaborate plans she could not accomplish. We had, for example, a room full of cloth she had bought when she thought she would create a new fashion line. Unable to fulfill her ambitions, she would then blame others, usually me, for making it impossible for her to fulfill her ambitions. When she was in a manic episode, she often imagined that she had been chosen to play the role of a savior. Such a role may have been a desperate gesture indicating that she was indeed worthy of being loved.

The emotional habits that are so often associated with bipolar illness are learned early. Anne's mother, a deeply troubled woman, dominated Anne's life. Indeed Anne's first dramatic episode occurred on the first anniversary of her mother's death. Her mother died in 1974. Anne "went crazy" in 1975. That she did so, I believe, had everything to do with the circumstances surrounding her mother's death.

When I was in graduate school, Mrs. Harley called me to report that Anne's father had betrayed her numerous times. I was not to tell Anne, but I refused that request. Anne received the news calmly, and we went on with our lives. Her mother and father, good middle-class people, continued to keep up appearances. But Mrs. Harley was determined to punish Mr. Harley. She was going to make him pay. The way she found to do that was to die of heart failure in her mid-fifties.

Anne went to San Antonio for the funeral. I offered to go with her, but she insisted that I stay home and take care of Adam. I am sure that while Anne was in San Antonio she had a psychotic break. Returning, she reported that she had gone several nights without sleep in order to go through her mother's effects. She told me she had discovered that her mother was sending her messages through the patterns on the wallpaper in her mother's bedroom. She also told me that she was sexually attracted to one of her uncles and fantasized performing fellatio with him. I thought all of this was quite strange, but I had no idea what to make of it. I simply wanted life to return to normal. It did for a while.

Manic-depression is an illness. It is something that happens to you. But you can survive only if you are willing to take responsibility for what is happening to you. God knows, that is difficult. Anne was never able to take responsibility for what was happening to her. It was too easy to blame me. And I was sympathetic with her. I tried to remember that she was in pain. It was often hard to remember her pain because I was the subject of her anger. She was unbelievably cruel. That cruelty is what finally exhausted me.

Surviving

Just negotiating the everyday with someone who is mentally ill takes a hell of a lot of energy. You are never sure whom you are dealing with from one minute to the next. They may seem "normal" but actually be occupying an entirely different world. The longer Anne was ill, the better she got at disguising the fantasy world in which she was often living. But it was not easy for her. She often reminded me of the joke about the manic-depressive wife who greets her husband one evening wearing a seductive dress. Her husband responds by asking her if she has taken her Lithium. Everyone seems permanently captured in a no-win game.

Anne would have three or four episodes a year. I could usually tell two or three weeks in advance when an episode might be coming. Her behavior would change, but I could also notice subtle changes in the muscles around her mouth. I had to be careful, however, because I learned that if she picked up signals from me indicating that I thought an episode might be imminent, it could make a psychotic break more likely. On the other hand, if I waited too long to suggest that she needed to take an antipsychotic, then the episode might be deeper and last longer. Moreover, I could not be sure she was always taking her Lithium. She missed her highs, so sometimes she would only pretend to take her medication.

Episodes would come in diverse and colorful forms. I knew we were in trouble, for example, when she began to read Robert Graves's *The White Goddess*. I wanted to tell her not to read further, because I knew it would trigger an episode in which she would become "the white goddess," which is exactly what happened. The Egyptian *Book of the Dead* was also a problem. Once she began to read Plato, having become fixated for a time on Ernan McMullin, a priest and philosopher whose specialty had nothing to do with Plato. Anne, however, was sure that he had to be a Platonist and wrote him a long letter about Plato that contained some suggestions about the necessity of sexually consummating their relationship. Such a consummation was necessary, of course, on Platonic grounds.

I never got used to these episodes. It was as if each time she died a little death. I had no idea who this was, even though she was my wife and the mother of Adam. In the early years, before I was completely exhausted, I would mourn every time she became manic. At the same time, I was trying to get her to take Haldol. It was never easy. Often it would take days before she would come down. She would go days with little sleep. I remember being startled one night by terrible screams. She had not slept for several days. She thought she was covered by bugs that were eating her alive. I was supposed to brush them off, which of course I did. My heart went out to her.

I could hardly blame her for not wanting to take the antipsychotic. The side effects were no fun. She would go through a period called "agitated depression" that was terrible for her, and us. She could not stay still. Up and down, up and down, to do this or that, but not able to do anything. During these times you could not forget that as hard as this might be for Adam and me it was harder for her.

Adam soon had to learn that when his mother was sick he could not be a child. He had to tell her he was not the son of God. He had to tell her she was not receiving secret messages on the radio. He had to tell her she needed to take her medication. At such times, he had to become an adult. It was not easy for him or for her. She often found it hard to forgive him for telling her what she needed to do. The older Adam became, the more difficult she had identifying with him. We are all fixated on our own needs, but when we are ill such a fixation threatens to be without limit.

As the illness developed, Anne increasingly heard voices that she thought we also should be able to hear. I have no doubt she heard voices and that sometimes she was frightened by what she heard. It did no good to say to her, "Do not listen to those voices." She simply could not shut them out. No matter how much you are tempted to say to someone suffering from mental illness, "Damn it, get a hold on yourself," you must recognize that what it means for the mentally ill to be ill is that they cannot "get a hold on themselves."

Quite understandably, Anne was desperate for others not to know she was ill. She feared that if others knew, they would treat her as if she was ill, and that would only make it more likely that she would be ill. She insisted, therefore, that I not tell anyone of her illness. Of course, given the way the illness manifested itself, many people knew she was ill, or at least that something was wrong. But I tried as best I could to honor her desire for others not to know about her illness.

The world that mental illness creates is lonely enough, but not to

Surviving

be able to share what you are going through with friends makes that world almost unbearable. David Burrell was in Bangladesh the first time Anne became seriously ill. He was teaching in the order's seminary there. It was his way to escape for a period from the wealth and power of Notre Dame. He was, after all, a priest. But that meant I did not have him to talk to. Burtchaell was some help. But on the whole, Adam and I tried to handle things on our own.

Adam could never be sure what he would find at home, which meant that he could not be sure if he should invite friends over. He did invite friends over, but sometimes Anne could be quite abrupt with them. I suspect they seldom noticed what was going on, but Adam and I did. As a result, Adam and I spent a great deal of time together. During the summers, after I finished teaching, we would swim in the lake at Notre Dame, we would ride our bikes all over South Bend, and we would toss the Frisbee endlessly. Of course, Adam played Little League, which meant we spent hours throwing the baseball back and forth.

We also had some lovely times with Rowan Greer. Rowan's family owned a vacation house at Northport on Lake Michigan. Rowan and his brother had inherited the place, and Rowan had begun to go there every summer to keep the house in good shape. On the way, he would come to visit us in South Bend, and we would sometimes visit him in Northport. Several of the times we did so Anne was emerging from an episode. Rowan, being Rowan, always provided the hospitality we needed to have some sense that life was "normal." Buying "pickled bologna" at the local store in Northport may not seem like a big deal, but Adam and I just loved being with a friend who knew how to let us "be."

The only difficulty with this arrangement was that Anne tended to "fall in love" with men who were "refined," because as such they bore no resemblance to me. Rowan certainly is a person of class in the best sense of that word. So for a time, Anne thought she was in love with Rowan. This was still fairly early in the game, and so she was not yet, as she would be later, prepared to act on her predilections. Rowan, I am sure, never caught a hint of her infatuation, but when we were with Rowan I could sense the stress Anne felt.

My mother and father were desperate to help, but any help they tried only made matters worse. They came to visit the summer after

Anne's first episodes. For some reason, they thought Adam, who at that time was six, might like a carving set. My father whittled, and I am sure my mother thought it would be good if he taught Adam how to whittle. You simply do not give a six-year-old a sharp knife, but mother did. Adam promptly cut his thumb. We had to take him to the hospital to get the required stitches. Anne, not without reason, was livid. Once again, trying desperately to maintain some semblance of peace, I found myself caught between Anne and my mother. It was not easy.

Adam did get to spend time with his grandparents in Arkansas. I had agreed to teach a summer school course at the University of Saint Thomas in Houston. We drove to Houston and on the way dropped Adam off in Mena for ten days. Mother and Daddy drove him to Houston before I finished teaching. I had one more class that morning. I suggested to them that they might like to see Rothko Chapel while they waited for me to finish. I told them that the chapel had Rothko's dark, huge paintings, which he had finished just before he ended his life. After I finished teaching, we gathered for lunch. I asked Mother what she thought of the chapel. She allowed that it was nice and then asked, "But where were the paintings?" I found the question deeply sad, indicating as it does the different worlds we had come to inhabit. That difference only intensified when Anne ridiculed the ignorance my mother displayed.

Our life did not stop with Anne's illness. Though things were never "normal," I continued to do what I habitually had done. I went to Notre Dame to teach my classes. I interacted with other faculty. I began to direct dissertations. I traveled to give lectures at universities, colleges, and conferences when I was invited to do so. We needed the money, so I was glad to receive such invitations. But I lived in fear that Anne might have an episode while I was gone. Adam was still too young to deal with that on his own. I tried never to be gone more than a night.

I liked to lecture, and people seemed to think I was good at it. Moreover, many of these lectures became essays that I eventually collected into books. Increasingly, I found myself writing in response to an invitation to give a lecture on some specific topic. I found it fruitful to try to address the assigned topic without connecting it to some larger "project" of my own. Indeed, by working this way I was training my-self, even if unconsciously, to think in a way different from how I had been trained at Yale.

I have no idea whence it came, but I think one of my strengths as a "thinker" and lecturer is my sense of humor. I seem to be funny. I love to laugh, and I love to laugh with people. I do not necessarily try to be funny, but I would like to think that my gift with "one-liners" is correla-tive with how I think. To learn to see the world and ourselves through the eyes of the gospel makes the world profoundly comic. Put differ-ently, if you are a Christian, you have nothing to lose, so you might as well tell the truth. Such a truth often surprises and delights us. Such surprise and delight is, I hope, the source of what some people find enjoyable about my lectures.

I love to entertain. I have never identified profundity with being dull or dry. Teaching, after all, is a form of entertainment. I used to joke that my lectures are really a Johnny Carson routine interrupted by a five-minute commercial for theology. That is not really how I teach, because in fact it is all a commercial for theology. But I have worked hard to teach in a manner that will be compelling for students. I simply have never been able to enter a classroom or to give a lecture without "giving it my all."

I have a passion to communicate. One form that passion has taken is correspondence. Notre Dame provided the faculty with a secretarial pool, and we could use the phone system to dictate letters. I am one of the least mechanical people in the world, but I learned how to use the dictation system. I was beginning to get letters from people I had never met but who had read something I had written. They wrote to ask criti-cal questions or to tell me that I was wrong about something. I made it a habit to write back.

This habit of correspondence, which I developed at Notre Dame, has continued. I have always regarded the letters I receive as sheer gift, and the time I take to respond as my ministry, to the extent I have one. I still rely on dictation, and it usually takes me about an hour a day to keep up with my correspondence. Some of my closest friendships have begun in this way. In fact, I regard writing as a way to discover friends I did not know I had. Writing an essay or a book is like putting a letter in a bottle and casting it into the ocean. You never know where it may wash up. Often there is no one there, but sometimes, and it can be years later, someone comes along and reads with understanding what you have written. I have been fortunate that so many people have read what I have written and been intrigued enough to raise questions about it.

People often express amazement that I have written so much. Friends ask me how I did it while negotiating Anne's illness and raising Adam. I am not sure. But I know that it has everything to do with being first and foremost a reader. I have always been able to write because I read. Anne's illness meant that reading became all the more important to me. After supper, and after Adam had gone to bed, Anne would simply withdraw. Sometimes she would work on some project. Sometimes she would go to bed. All that was left for me to do was read.

I read philosophy and theology, but I devoured novels. I would read systematically through one author's work. For example, I would decide at the start of a summer to read all of Jane Austen, the next summer George Eliot, then Conrad or Updike. David Solomon was perhaps an even more avid reader. He often gave me wonderful suggestions of books to read. Indeed, I owe him a great debt for introducing me to Anthony Trollope. I once asked David if he had read all of Trollope. He said, "Oh, no. You never know when there will be a dark day when you'll need one of his novels you have not yet read. So you should save a few of his novels for such a day. After all, he wrote only forty-seven." I am not sure if I have read them all. I might have saved a few.

THROUGH MY WRITING, AND WITHOUT QUITE REALIZING IT, I WAS BEGINNING to stake out a quite distinctive position. I was not trying to be "creative." And I do not think theologians should try, as some philosophers do, to have "a position." "Positions" can give the impression that our task is to represent something "new." I believe that through the cross and resurrection of Jesus of Nazareth we live in a new age, but that is why theologians do not have a position. Rather, our task is to help the church know what it has been given. But I was beginning to sense that I had quite a particular take on that "given."

Fearing immodesty, I hesitate to make such a claim. But then I have never trusted modesty because I suspect that the attempt to be modest is betrayed by the very fact that it must be attempted. I do not know how to evaluate the significance of what I have written, but I have learned from others, often those who hate what I have done, that what I think is different. Still, it took time for me to recognize this difference.

Although I began to sense this difference at Notre Dame, I think it was at Duke that I began to recognize the significance of the difference. That recognition came through teaching. One of my primary responsibilities at Duke was to teach the core course in Christian ethics. The course would often have more than a hundred master's students. I would lecture several times a week, but small seminar-style sessions led by teaching assistants from the doctoral program were a weekly requirement. I met every week with the teaching assistants to think about these sessions, and I would ask them to tell me of any difficulties the students might be having "getting" what I was trying to do. Inevitably, they would tell me that some students grasped immediately the argument that shaped the course, but for others what I was trying to do seemed incomprehensible. I remember clearly that in one of these sessions a doctoral student named David Stubbs stated the problem quite simply: in my course the students were confronted by "a wholly different Christianity."

I think this is an apt description of my work, but I also think that the "wholly different Christianity" I represent is in deep continuity with Christianity past and present that is found in the everyday lives of Christian people. You do not get to make Christianity up, and I have no desire to be original. If I represent a wholly different Christianity, I do so only because I have found a way to help us recognize as Christians what extraordinary things we say when we worship God.

I do not desire to be creative, but I am an eclectic thinker. Drawing on diverse influences, I have articulated a Christianity that many people, including me, find compelling and that some, including me, find frightening. I am sometimes introduced or described as "prophetic." I usually respond to that suggestion by noting that no one making a full professor's salary in a major university can be prophetic. But I do think the very existence of the church is prophetic. I have drawn on a strange brew of Catholic and Anabaptist resources to articulate an understanding of what it means to be Christian that for many people rings true. Only at Notre Dame — where I was surrounded by people like David Burrell, David Solomon, and John Yoder — could I have begun to craft an account of Christianity that for many people would seem so compelling and beautiful.

What many people find hard to understand, or at least what strikes them as unusual, is how I combine what I hope is a profound commitment to fundamental Christian convictions with a socially radical ethic. At bottom, the convictions involve the claim that Jesus is both fully God and fully human. If he is not fully both, then we Christians are clearly idolaters. A socially radical ethic follows from this theological conviction because our worship of Jesus is itself a politics through which a world is created that would not exist if Jesus were not raised from the dead. Basic to such politics is the refusal of a violence that many assume is a "given" for any responsible account of the world.

I discovered that I had to write to explore this set of convictions. I continue to do so. My writing is exploratory because I have no idea what I believe until I force myself to say it. For me, writing turns out to be my way of believing. That my writing has taken primarily the form of essays is not only because of the exploratory character of my work, but also because, given my other responsibilities, essays have always seemed "doable." *Truthfulness and Tragedy* (1977) and *A Community of Character* (1981), both collections of essays I wrote while at Notre Dame, are books that can be read as my attempt to develop the conceptual tools that resulted in *The Peaceable Kingdom* (1983). I was finally able to write a book, I suspect, because of what I had learned through writing more occasionally.

I suspect it is all "there" in *The Peaceable Kingdom*. Most of what I have said since, I said there. But if so, then everything remains to be done, insofar as everything is projected toward the future. What I had discovered in my teaching and writing at Notre Dame is the difference it makes when you refuse to ignore the eschatological character of the gospel, a discovery that Barth made in the second edition of his commentary on Romans and that Yoder made as he wrote pamphlets for display in the back of Mennonite churches. Barth's discovery, bound as it was by the possibilities of European Christianity in 1921, awaited and required rediscovery. And Yoder helped me see that God has freed the church from its cultural captivity to the world that, after all, the church had helped create. In *The Peaceable Kingdom*, I tried to think through what this freedom might entail. In doing so, I reframed how Christians should think about our "political responsibilities," our willingness to have children, our understanding of marriage, our regard of death and our care of one another through the agency of medicine, and our understanding of medicine itself. I reframed all of our questions about these topics by stressing that any answers we might offer entail an understanding of the contingent character of our existence.

To say that our lives are contingent is to say that they are out of our control. Being "out of control" is the central image that runs through *The Peaceable Kingdom* and much of my work. Certainly that image described my marriage to Anne, but I do not think this image is autobiographical. In fact, I think the image came to me because of the influence of Yoder, who taught me to think that following Jesus means you cannot anticipate or ensure results. Learning to live out of control, learning to live without trying to force contingency into conformity because of our desperate need for security, I take to be a resource for discovering alternatives that would otherwise not be present.

In this sense, the notion of being out of control is one that stands as an alternative to Niebuhrian realism. The problem with "realism" is that it can shut down the imagination. These were theological lessons I was learning from Yoder. Unfortunately, I did not think them applicable to my life with Anne. Her illness was all too real.

I DO THINK, HOWEVER, THAT LEARNING TO LIVE WITH ANNE MEANT THAT I was forced to grow up. I am not sure, even now, that I know what it means to be grown up. But something was happening that meant I was beginning to mature as a theologian. I may even have begun to be a Christian. David Burrell no longer lived in Grace Hall and therefore was not saying a Mass Adam and I could attend. Adam was older, moreover, and I thought it important that we participate in something more like a church. The main church on the campus of Notre Dame was Sacred Heart. They had a wonderful Mass every Sunday. It just seemed like a natural place for us to go. We would ride our bicycles over in rain, sleet, snow, and sunshine to be present at Mass. For some years, we may have been the most constant communicants at Sacred Heart. We particularly loved Christmas and Holy Week.

I never had to make Adam go to church. Mass at Sacred Heart was a feast for the senses. He seemed to love every minute, even before he could understand the sermon. He, of course, recognized and knew well many of the priests who celebrated at Mass, and that made him feel at home. It did not occur to me that there might be a problem with our receiving communion. I assumed we were welcome, and we were never refused. Notre Dame was officially a site for liturgical study and innovation. I thought Adam and I were part of the innovation.

I will never forget a Mass we attended at Moreau Seminary, which sits across from the university. The occasion was the ordination of some of the seminarians I had taught. Anne had known some of these young men, and they had invited the whole family. She was just emerging from an episode and was a bit more congenial about such matters, so she came. When the time for reception came, Adam and I stood up to enter the procession toward the altar, but Anne jerked Adam down and would not let him go to the altar. It was not a place to begin an argument. I returned from receiving communion. There were giant tears running down Adam's cheeks. I resolved that he would never again be denied. He knew what he had missed.

We continued for a number of years to go to Sacred Heart. I am not sure how many years we had been at Notre Dame when I began to think that I was more Catholic than Protestant. I thought it was dishonest for me to teach Catholics, to be supported by Catholics, to worship with Catholics, and not to be Catholic. I came to the conclusion that it was time to explore what it might mean for me to become Catholic. To think about becoming a Catholic at Notre Dame, however, is tricky. It could so easily be understood as a grasp for power. Young men called into the priesthood while students at Notre Dame face the same challenge: Do they really want to be priests, or someday the president of Notre Dame? I do not think I was looking for power. I think I was looking for a home.

I talked to David about my becoming Catholic, but he quite rightly thought he was the wrong person to help me discern if I really wanted to take that step. He sent me to John Gerber, C.S.C., who was David's best friend in the order. At the time, John was the priest in charge of Sacred Heart. He said he would be willing to give me instruction, but he was not sure what that might mean. He assumed that I already knew what a Catholic needs to know to be Catholic. It is true that I had thought about Mary and had come to believe that she was the Mother of God. I had thought about the pope and could acknowledge that the bishop of Rome was the office of unity. I had thought about contraception, and I was pretty sure the Catholics were wrong about that one. But I still felt that I had much to learn.

Before I took the next steps, I thought I should tell Anne. She exploded. She told me that my becoming Catholic would be the last straw, that if I went any further along those lines the marriage would be over. I was desperately doing everything I could to sustain the marriage. I thought that when we married I had made a promise I should keep. I was afraid of divorce, particularly what it might mean for Adam. I was, I am sure, also afraid of failure. I may have been so unsure about being Catholic that I was looking for a reason to abandon the plan. After all, how could I be so influenced by John Howard Yoder and be a Catholic? Given Anne's reaction, I did not pursue becoming Catholic.

I AM NOT SURE IF IT WAS THE INFLUENCE OF YODER OR NOT, IT MAY HAVE JUST been the lingering influence of Protestant nostalgia, but I began to think that Adam and I needed to be part of a congregation. Those of us who worshiped at Sacred Heart knew one another, but we never had to do any work to sustain ourselves as a congregation. Catholics have a well-developed account of the church as hierarchy but little understanding of the congregation. So Adam and I began to look for another place to worship. For a year we went to an African American Catholic church. We liked it well enough, but we were not really part of the parish. Moreover, I became tired of how the choir dominated worship.

Then I encountered John Smith in a bathroom. John was attending a meeting of the South Bend district of Methodist clergy at which I was speaking. No doubt I was giving one of my stump speeches about it being time for the church to be the church. At a break I found myself using a urinal next to this guy with a bushy beard. He asked me where I went to church. I told him, "Here and there," to which he responded, "You certainly do not live up to what you preach." I thought, "This guy has got to be all right."

I discovered that John had returned to northern Indiana from California to serve in the Methodist ministry. He was originally from Indiana but had married a woman from California and had been in the ministry there. However, the marriage had failed. He had remarried and returned to Indiana. As a divorced returnee, John had been given the shit-end of the conference. He was the pastor at Broadway United Methodist Church in what had become one of the worst areas of South Bend. It had been a neighborhood where machinists who worked at the Studebaker plant had lived, but after the plant closed it had slowly become an impoverished African American neighborhood.

Broadway had originally been Evangelical United Brethren. The EUBS, as they were called, were German Methodists who had fairly recently been absorbed into United Methodism. John had been appointed to Broadway with the hope that he could save it. After all, the building, built by Germans, was solid. By the time John had become the minister at Broadway, the church was named after the street and the congregation numbered no more than sixty. John, however, was not deterred by size and had begun a ministry to the neighborhood by providing daycare to children and stocking a food pantry. This ministry to the neighborhood was called the Broadway Christian Parish.

After my encounter with John, I did not show up immediately in his church. But one Sunday Adam and I went to the African American Catholic church we had been attending only to discover that it was closed because of a choir trip. We decided to try Broadway. The building had been designed to hold several hundred people. There may have been thirty in attendance. John preached a wonderful sermon. He even made clear that if we were doing things right we should have the Eucharist, but since that was as yet not the custom at Broadway we would have to wait. I was impressed.

Adam and I started attending every Sunday. John, it turned out, had gone to Yale Divinity School and been well schooled. We became increasingly involved in the ministries of the congregation. After about six months, I told John that I would like to join the church. He asked me about my formal church membership. I confessed that I had no idea. I was not sure I had been a member of a church after I left Texas. He said that was an indication of what a sorry churchman I must be. He then told me that, before he would let me join the church, I would need to come to a class he was beginning for people like me. I dutifully and gladly did so for a year.

Surviving

I was received into the church on Easter in 1980. Broadway, under John's guidance, had started having a full Holy Week. Accordingly, we gathered at four on Easter morning, had the fire, sang the psalms, had the full rendition of salvation history, and celebrated the resurrection. I thought I had died and gone to heaven. This was not only a wonderful liturgical community. This was a wonderful community period. The congregation was filled with extraordinary ordinary people.

Conrad Damion, for example, taught high school in one of South Bend's not-well-integrated schools. He simply refused to give up on the students he taught. He also refused to give up on the neighborhood. He had bought a house not far from the church. No matter how many times his home was broken into, he refused to move. He was, moreover, a committed Methodist who worked hard and long to make the larger denomination aware of what it might be to be a church that cared about justice and peace. Conrad was crucial for helping us see the essential connections between our Eucharistic practice and our commitment not only to feed but to eat with the poor.

John had long made clear that he wanted the church to celebrate Eucharist every Sunday. He usually ended every sermon suggesting how, if we could move to the altar, the Eucharist would confirm the word. I had become chair of the worship commission. We organized a congregational study of the church's Eucharistic practice across our history. We paid particular attention to Wesley's understanding of constant communion. After we had studied and prayed, the worship commission brought to the board the suggestion that we move to weekly Eucharist.

The board discussed the motion quite favorably. John had worked for years to reach this moment. I then suggested that we vote. At that moment, John, who had been quiet during our discussion, suddenly declared, "You will not vote on this issue." I thought he had gone bonkers. This is what he wanted. He explained, however, that the Eucharist is about the unity of the church. If a majority vote determined the matter, then that unity would be betrayed. He noted that some people in the church might not be ready to make this move. He would call a meeting, inviting those who might have reservations to come and express their worries about moving to Eucharist every Sunday. If they strongly dissented, we would have to wait.

He called the meeting. Some people expressed concerns, but everyone present said they would be willing to try weekly Eucharist. We began the practice. It did not take long before we could not remember not having the Eucharist every Sunday. A young man named Gary Camp and his mother always led the way to the table. Gary was moderately mentally disabled, and his mother was quite elderly. Because Gary was hard of hearing they always sat on the front pew. When time came to gather at the altar, Gary would deliberately and slowly lead his mother to the rail. The church would hold its collective breath until they made it. We would then join them. If Gary and his mother were absent, you could feel the church wondering if we could have Eucharist, because the whole church was not present. Of course, we did celebrate Eucharist without them, but their absence was palpable, and we made sure to take the Eucharist to them when they were absent, and to anyone else who had to miss the service.

Conrad was chair of our outreach commission. During the early years of the Reagan administration, unemployment was horrific in South Bend. People were going hungry. We had a food bank and gave food to those in need. But Conrad suggested that we needed to be more intentional in feeding the hungry. He explained that just as we had learned how important it was for us to be fed by God, so we should try to feed the hungry in our neighborhood. He told us that the meals we would prepare would not be Eucharist, but they would witness to what the Eucharist had made us. We were being consumed by what we consumed.

This was a major challenge for the church. We had grown to seventy or eighty members, but we were still what many would consider a struggling church. Nonetheless, we decided to do what Conrad suggested. We divided the church into five teams, each with the responsibility to prepare a meal for the neighborhood each Sunday after Eucharist. We discovered that we could get food from government storehouses, particularly cheese. Some grocery stores and restaurants in South Bend were also quite generous, giving us their leftovers. The team responsible for that Sunday would come early to cook the meal to be served after church.

It did not take long before we had a large and steady group of people to feed. I was not a great cook, but I was pretty good at slicing and washing up. Adam joined in with no hesitation. Seldom did any of those we fed come to church with us, but there was a bag lady who did begin to join us. She prayed quite wonderfully that God would see fit to help us help her. We were a bunch of liberals who were not used to asking God for help with our own lives. She taught us how to pray.

Early one Sunday morning, a young man burst violently into a Sunday school session we were having prior to worship. He was obviously high on something. He asked what we were doing. We explained that we were reading a portion of Scripture in preparation for the sermon. Without missing a beat, he calmed down and entered the room. He picked up a Bible and joined right in. We tried to get him to stay for worship and the meal but were unsuccessful.

Adam loved Broadway and jumped right into the various activities, but he had not been confirmed. He was now thirteen. We had a number of children in the church who were old enough to be confirmed. John believed that one of his most important duties was preparing children through confirmation. The process took a year and involved the study of Scripture and church history. John and the candidates made a covenant with one another four times during the year. John suggested to them that just as Israel's covenant had to be renewed so did their covenant with God, the church, and with one another. It was his way of stressing the importance of their decision to be a member of the church.

The last covenant was right before Holy Week. At breakfast, on a morning of the week before Holy Week, Adam told me that as much as the church meant to him he just did not think he could make this last commitment. His mother was in a rather dramatic and seemingly unending episode. He explained that life at that moment just seemed too hard. He simply did not see how he could take on any more responsibility. I did not try to convince him otherwise. All I said was that he needed to talk to John. With his permission, I said, I would call John to see if he could meet with Adam before Holy Week.

I called John while Adam was in school and set up an appointment. Early on the Saturday morning before Palm Sunday, I took Adam to see John. While they talked, I went to a coffee shop. I had no idea how the conversation might go. Anne never came to church, but John knew that she was ill and that she could be a difficult person. I returned a couple of hours later. Adam got in the car and explained that he had decided to make his final commitment. He said that John had listened sympathetically, observing that he often felt like Adam. He just could not do everything people expected of him. Moreover, he told Adam not to worry about disappointing me. Rather, John said, Adam had to recognize that he could not be a Christian alone. By becoming a member of the church, he was asking for and receiving help. By learning to receive, he would be able to give.

Thank God for a wise pastor. That Easter Adam became a member of the church. It was a wonderful Holy Week and Easter. It may have seemed a far cry from the high drama of Easter Mass at Sacred Heart, but Adam and I are Christians because of the people at Sacred Heart and Broadway who welcomed us into their lives and made us participants in the drama of our salvation. There is no denying my ambiguous ecclesial identity, but I cannot help but believe that there is a profound unity between those Catholics at Notre Dame and that modest group of people gathered at Broadway United Methodist Church on Easter morning. Without those communities, Adam and I would not have survived.

It was in Sacred Heart and Broadway United Methodist that Adam and I discovered not only that we were friends, but that we had friends who saved us from being friends only of one another. During the years that Anne's illness dominated our lives, I discovered the gift of friendship. Indeed, I discovered I had a gift for friendship. I love and trust people. My love and trust may at times be unwise, but I prefer the risk. I am not stupid. I do not like fools or pretension. But I love interesting, complex, and even difficult people. Thank God, they often love me.

What it means for me to be a Christian and to be a friend has become so intertwined that I cannot untangle one from the other, nor do I wish to. Given Aristotle's and Aquinas's influence, I had thought about friendship as integral to an emphasis on the virtues, but increasingly friendship was becoming for me an existential necessity. I had learned much from Aristotle's account of character friendship, but I knew his account could not be the last word because I found myself becoming friends with those called mentally disabled.

How could I have anticipated, moreover, a friend like David Burrell?

David and I were not equals, as Aristotle would have us be. He was smarter, better educated, a Catholic priest, a member of a religious order, and from a "better class of people" than I was. But we became fast friends. We did so, I think, because we shared not only a common love of Wittgenstein, but, as Wittgenstein taught, common judgments. Even after what has now been almost forty years, David and I can be apart for a year or more at a time and still pick up the conversation we have always had without missing a beat. "Conversation" is but a description of our common commitment to keep one another honest as best we can.

I do not think that questions concerning the truth of Christian convictions can be isolated from what is necessary to sustain friendships that are truthful. I am not suggesting that Christians can be friends only with other Christians. Some of my most cherished friendships are with non-Christians. Rather, I am suggesting that if what it means to be a Christian is compelling and true, then such truthfulness will be manifest and tested through friendship.

Friendships are complex, but some are more so than others. A wonderful graduate student at Notre Dame, Mary Jo Weaver, became a good friend, not only for me and Adam but for Anne. Mary Jo came from pre–Vatican II Catholicism. She would become a prominent academic in the Department of Religious Studies at the University of Indiana. She was a wonderful presence in our family because she was willing to be present even when Anne was crazy and cruel. Mary Jo was a student, and friendships with students are always complex. But she was not one of my students. She was writing her dissertation on Philo under Jean Laporte. The complexity of our friendship had less to do with the fact that she was a student than with our unacknowledged feeling that, if it had been possible, the two of us might have loved one another.

Mary Jo graduated and began her academic career at the Pontifical College Josephinum, a seminary in Ohio under the administrative control of the pope. The German Catholics had arranged for the seminary to be a papal institution in order to avoid being under the control of the local bishop, who was Irish. Mary Jo arranged for me to lecture at the Josephinum. I was not a success, but I did get to sleep in the bed of the papal delegate to America. Mary Jo and I continued to stay in touch for a while after she went to Indiana, but I think she found it increasingly difficult to enter the pain that was the family Hauerwas.

Robert Wilken and Joe Blenkinsopp were good friends. I remember once visiting Robert. I was not able to stay long because, even though Adam was asleep, I did not want to leave him alone with Anne. I did not explain why I had to leave early, but Robert simply said, "I understand, but I miss you." It was a lovely gift. Robert, at the time a Missouri Synod Lutheran, made available to me the benefits of Catholic Lutheranism that he had learned in St. Louis, as well as an appreciation for what the divinity school at the University of Chicago had to offer. Joe and I often tried to kill one another on the tennis court. He also taught me how Protestant interpretations of the Old Testament were shaped by anti-Catholic polemics — that is, Protestants turned Second Temple Judaism into priest-ridden legalism so that Jesus could be Luther. I also was befriended by people across the university. The dean of the law school, Tom Shaffer, took me in, so to speak. Tom was a Baptist from Wyoming who, by marrying a Catholic, became a Catholic with the breadth of soul befitting someone from the West. He and Nancy had seven children. Tom loved the law, but he never forgot that the law exists to serve people. I loved to teach with Tom because his approach to things was just an angle off. Like me, he increasingly came under Yoder's influence.

I think I was one of John Yoder's closest friends. I have no idea what that meant. Many people, on encountering Yoder, found him intimidating and even arrogant. I just thought he was shy. There is no question that John had a "big brain." I often observe that I have known two really "big brain" people: Yoder and Alasdair MacIntyre. I have never known any other people quite like them. I have no idea how it may be connected to intelligence, but Alasdair is, and John was, a bit awkward in personal relationships. I never let that get in the way of my relationship with them. Alasdair has a wonderful sense of humor, and so did John. He in particular enjoyed being joshed.

Even to this day, I am not quite sure what John made of me. Once we were making presentations to the incoming class of graduate students at Notre Dame. I went first and described how I became committed to nonviolence by reading John. John, who often presented himself as having no "field," described himself as a representative of Anabaptist forebearers, noting that he had been hired by Notre Dame to teach courses on the ethics of war and nonviolence. He said that, as far as he knew, after thirty years of representing Christian nonviolence he had convinced only one person. I think he was referring to me, and I could tell he felt some ambiguity about that achievement. But I loved John Yoder. I think he loved me.

I also loved Paul Ramsey. I spent one summer soon after I came to Notre Dame reading and rereading everything Paul wrote. I took extensive notes, thinking I might actually write a book on his thought. I decided not to do that, but I learned a great deal about how to think about abortion, medicine, and war. I first met Paul when I was a student at Yale. Gustafson had arranged for us to have a seminar with Paul, who gave each of us a copy of *Christian Ethics and the Sit-In.* It was, as he put it, "a book that fell stillborn off the press," leaving him with more copies than he knew what to do with. So he gave each of us a copy, a gift for which I will be ever grateful, believing as I do that it is one of his more important books.

I suspect that few people appreciate how deeply Paul Ramsey's work has shaped the way I think. I dedicated *Against the Nations* to Paul and John Yoder because, as I note in the preface to that book, I do not think I would have understood the significance of Yoder's arguments if I had not learned from Paul how to think of just war as a political ethic. But Paul was not only an intellectual influence — he befriended me, even though during my Notre Dame years we usually saw one another only at the yearly meeting of the Society of Christian Ethics.

As we came to know one another through the meetings of the Society, Paul took a liking to me for some reason. Maybe it was our common Mississippi roots. Paul was generously gregarious. He loved people and argument. Like Anne, Paul's wife, Effie, suffered from mental illness. He was willing to talk quite candidly with me about how he had learned to both care for and be with her. I admired and learned from the faithful way he carried on. Paul never felt sorry for himself.

I gained another wonderful friend because some Catholics at Notre Dame worried that I had become the "moral theologian" at Notre Dame. They felt, quite rightly, that they needed a Catholic moral theologian. Catholic moral theology is a club. I certainly was not a member of that club. No matter how sympathetically I might present Catholic moral theology, I was not a Catholic. Moreover, if Catholicism, as I suggest, is a world, then there needed to be someone from that world to train priests. I had never heard anyone's confession.

Where better to find such a person than Ireland? Thus Enda Mc-Donagh came into my and Adam's life. Enda, the great lover of all things beautiful, became our gateway not only to Ireland but to an extraordinarily rich understanding of Catholicism. Enda was so deeply Catholic that he never had to think about being Catholic. He had come from the belly of the beast, having done a Ph.D. in canon law. But he knew moral theology far too well to continue the isolation of that discipline from the rest of theology. Adam and I often picked Enda up to go to Mass at Sacred Heart. He thought it quite wonderful to be picked up by Protestants to go to Mass.

Through friends like these I survived and Adam survived. But the stress of the everyday was always "there." By chance I discovered a way to deal with stress. I began to run. A year after Anne's first dramatic episode, I was giving lectures at Viterbo College, now a university, in La Crosse, Wisconsin. The college was run by the Franciscan Sisters of Perpetual Adoration and named after the Italian city that had given the Franciscan Sisters a relic of St. Francis. I had taught several of the sisters in summer school, and they were kind enough to invite me to give lectures at their annual meeting.

These lovely and amazing women represented for me the complex and extraordinary world named Catholicism. For over a century, they had lived out the name of their order: they had sustained unceasing prayer before the Eucharist. There were always two sisters in prayer before the Eucharist at any one time in case one of them went to sleep. Anxious to make sure that I and Father Maly, an Old Testament scholar from the seminary in Cincinnati who was also giving lectures, were properly entertained, the sisters gave us a tour of La Crosse. The "tour" included a stop at the monastery of the Benedictine Sisters of the Perpetual Rosary.

The Benedictine sister who greeted us was one of six left. I thought she was quite beautiful and serene. She was in her late sixties but the youngest of the six. Unlike their Franciscan counterparts, they did not live up to their name. They were no longer able, she told us, to sustain saying the perpetual rosary. Indeed, most of her time, she reported, consisted in caring for her older sisters. They sustained themselves by baking the altar bread for the churches in the area. As we got up to leave, this sister reached across the low wall separating us, grasped Father Maly's hand, and said, "Oh! Father, please pray for vocations. I know many young people want to go into the world to make the world more just and peaceful, but God needs our prayers. So please pray for vocations."

I suspect that the Benedictine Sisters of the Perpetual Rosary no longer exist. I suspect that the Franciscan Sisters of Perpetual Adoration are now smaller in number than when I was there. I am convinced that we are poorer for the loss of such women. They sustained, often with little reward or recognition, Catholic education and hospitals. Even more, they prayed because they quite rightly understood that God needs our prayers.

I had brought my tennis racquet with me to Viterbo, hoping I might find someone who would like to play tennis. I had no luck. I felt a need to get some exercise. I had not thought a lot about it, but I was over-weight. It occurred to me that people were beginning to jog. I thought I would give it a try. I set out in my tennis shoes, not realizing that they were not the kind of shoes made for running. But it did not matter, because I soon discovered that I could not run far without being com-pletely out of breath. I resolved that I needed to do something about my body.

I came home determined to get in shape. I went to Sears and bought a pair of running shoes that *Runner's World* would soon rate as the worst shoe ever made for running. But they felt fine to me. I began to run late in the evening. I gradually increased my distance. I bought a better pair of shoes. I discovered the faculty locker room in the new athletic center at Notre Dame. I began to run every day at noon. I lost weight and felt better physically. Running, moreover, proved to be a wonderful exer-cise in friendship. It was not long before some of my graduate students were running with me. Charlie Pinches in particular helped me think through many an article while we ran together.

Notre Dame's official name is Notre Dame du Lac, and I came to love running around the lakes after which Notre Dame was named. The story goes that Father Sorin, the French priest who founded Notre Dame, arrived in winter. Snow and ice covered the lakes so thoroughly that he thought there was one lake rather than two. They discovered two lakes only in the spring thaw. By then it was too late to correct the grammar. There are two lakes, and I never tired of running around both of them. During the spring, the redbuds and dogwoods were spectacular. In the summer, I ran while Adam swam.

There was also a wonderful run behind St. Mary's College. St. Mary's was established by the Sisters of the Holy Cross to provide education for women. Like Notre Dame, they owned great stretches of undeveloped property. I often ran a trail along the St. Joseph River. I loved to see the rabbits, groundhogs, fox, and deer I inevitably encountered. I even enjoyed the occasional skunk, as long as she went one way and I went the other.

Anne became increasingly ill. The more ill she became, the farther I ran. I would often run five to seven miles a day. I would run no matter how hot or cold it might be. I would run no matter how hard it might be raining or snowing. I once ran when the wind-chill factor was forty-seven below zero. I was determined that Adam would survive. I was determined that I would survive. I ran, and somehow we survived.

CHAPTER 7

Enduring

I was determined that Adam and I would survive. But survival was not easy, and running was not enough. Over the years, I have made myself available to people who have found themselves living with someone who is mentally ill. I have done so because I know the feelings of abandonment, loneliness, and helplessness that accompany this discovery. The world comes crashing in on you. You hope things will get better with this or that medication, but too often such hopes are unrealistic. When you live with someone who is seriously mentally ill, you cannot live without hope, but you certainly need to learn to live without expectations. You cannot predict what the next five minutes may bring.

My best advice for those who find that they must learn to live with someone who is seriously mentally ill is that their first duty is to survive. If you do not survive, no one will survive. Trying to survive is not selfish. You must strive to survive if you are to sustain any hope that life can go on. I try to remember, moreover, that not every person suffering bipolar illness is as ill or as angry as Anne was. It was the anger, not the illness, at least insofar as those can be distinguished, that finally exhausted me.

I continued to try to do anything I could to make Anne's life better, but one of the survival lessons I learned was that often whatever I did to make her life "better" only made things worse. I have been gifted, as I suspect my mother was gifted, with energy. I was able, therefore, to teach, lecture, write, raise Adam, and somehow negotiate life with Anne on a daily basis. Energy, however, can be a blessing and a curse, both for the one possessed and those who must endure her. I sometimes wonder if in fact it was my ability to keep things together that destroyed Anne. If I had not proved to be up to the task, she might have been forced to take more responsibility for her life. If I had walked out rather than endure one more verbal assault, she might have decided that blaming me was a dead end. But for good or ill, I had the energy to keep it going.

I have no idea why I kept trying. After you have endured one episode after another, you lose sight of the person you once said you loved. I was married to Anne, but I had no idea what that meant. She often made it quite clear that she did not think of us as husband and wife. She often thought she was in love with other people. That meant, she explained, that if she slept with me it would be adultery. From time to time, she would encourage me to have an affair, because she was not about to "make love" with me. Her principles were too high to allow that.

Although "married," I effectively became celibate. There are few worse places to be. Every once in a while, Anne would suggest that we go to bed together. But that suggestion often indicated that she was, or soon would be, in an episode. Perpetually horny though I may have been, I found it hard to "take advantage" of her when she was "not herself." I am not sure such language makes sense of the circumstances, but I could not avoid the reality these descriptions name.

I imagined and hoped that someone might try to seduce me. But that never happened. I do not know what signals I might have been sending out, but I must not have appeared to be available. I also knew myself fairly well. And I did not want to bear the guilt of an affair. I could not see the end of the road, but I knew that end would only be worse if I proved unfaithful. What an absolute and total mess.

Of course I missed sex, but even more I missed just being touched. Anne insisted that I sleep in the guest bedroom, so she rarely touched me. I not only missed being touched but longed for some expression of tenderness, even something as simple as a heartfelt, "How was your day?" But the pain that possessed Anne's life did not allow her to reach out to me in that way. And she increasingly had difficulty reaching out to Adam.

I sometimes wonder if the marriage could have been saved if she had said, "I know this is hard. Thank you for hanging in there with me." But she never said that. Anger possessed her life, and I was the target. I sometimes thought that she had trouble seeing me as a human being. I do not mean to suggest that the abuse was constant, but when she exploded, and the explosions became increasingly frequent, her cruelty seemed without limit.

ADAM AND I HAD ONE ANOTHER. JIM BURTCHAELL ONCE SUGGESTED THAT IT might be a good idea to send Adam to a prep school. The thought had never crossed my mind. If you come from the working class, the idea that a child might be sent away to school is not in the cards. To send a child away to school from my perspective was equivalent to abandonment. Yet it was not just class presumption that caused me to say to Jim, "I cannot send Adam away. I need him."

Of course in truth, we needed one another. But I think perhaps I needed Adam even more than he needed me. We learned to depend on one another. Despite the complexities of this dependency, I do not think it was destructive. We quite simply enjoyed being together. One year the annual meeting of the American Academy of Religion was in New York City. I think Adam was eight. We saved up box tops on a cereal we ate for breakfast to win a plane ticket so that he could go with me. We saved enough and flew to New York. Adam came to listen to me give my paper, which was on the future of Christian ethics. Some people seemed to think it quite odd that I would bring my son to the meeting, but it felt right to me.

We had a wonderful time. We took a bus tour of the city and did the sorts of things all good tourists should do. Richard Neuhaus invited us to come to supper. It was a lovely occasion, at which Adam got to meet Paul Ramsey and some other notable folks. Richard was still a Lutheran and invited us to join him on Sunday morning at a Mass. We did so. The Mass took place in a tenement building with about twenty people present. Richard preached a thirty-minute sermon. Adam loved it. Whatever differences Richard and I had over the years, and they are many, I will always be grateful to him for that moment.

For the trip, Adam had brought a book his mother had given him. On Sunday morning when we got to Richard's, Adam remembered that he had left it in the hotel room. We had already checked out. The incident marked the fear in which we lived. We were both afraid of what it would mean if his mother discovered that he had lost the book. Running can come in handy. I put on my shorts and ran back to central Manhattan and recovered the book. We returned to South Bend quite happy.

Adam and I loved to canoe down the Saint Joe. Once we even took Alfred Kazin with us. He was teaching at Notre Dame for a semester. Adam and I had dinner with him at Peri and Beverly Arnold's. We told him of our plans the next day to canoe the Saint Joe, and he asked to come along. He insisted that we pretend we were the first explorers to have come to the area, so we had to be on the lookout for the Indians who no doubt would want to kill us. Needless to say it was quite a trip.

Adam loved people like Kazin. He was not the least intimidated by adults. Given his mother's illness, most of Adam's interactions, other than in school, were with adults. He listened to and could participate in adult conversations. It never occurred to me to "dumb down" anything I said to Adam. Some years later, Adam remarked that he never had a childhood. That is not quite true. He has forgotten much. But it is true that he had to assume adult responsibilities and that he was raised primarily in the company of my friends. It was increasingly the case that many of those friends were graduate students.

Joe Gower was one of these students. He was doing a Ph.D. in American Catholicism but took several of my seminars. Joe once told me that he talked to Adam the way he talked with his fellow students. It was not a surprising remark. Graduate students were becoming an increasing part of my life at Notre Dame. It was a natural development that they also were becoming an important part of my life with Adam. As soon as I began at Notre Dame, I had taught graduate level seminars. After I received tenure, I began to direct dissertations. I do not remember thinking it important or even wanting to direct dissertations, but as it turned out this task has been at the center of my life ever since.

I THINK, OR AT LEAST HOPE, THAT WHATEVER THE FINAL VERDICT MAY BE ON "my work," I will be understood first and foremost as a teacher. I may not have set out to be a teacher, but the good people who claimed me as such have enriched my life and Adam's life in ways we could not have imagined. And if in fact I have proved to be a good teacher, it is because they taught me how to teach. Of course, students come in all shapes and sizes, which makes it difficult to generalize, but I think I can say that every student whose dissertation I have directed I count as a friend.

I try to remember that every student is different. I let them determine what kind of relationship they want with me. When I began at Notre Dame, I was not that much older than the students I directed. I do not know if I projected the appropriate "professional distance." I do not remember even thinking I should do so. I simply assumed that we were engaged in a common endeavor. The only thing that mattered was believing that what we were doing mattered. If I have been a good teacher, if I have, as I believe I have, directed some wonderful dissertations, it is due to what a compelling subject I have been given to teach.

I have never tried to recruit students or to make them *my* students. They simply show up full of surprises. For example, one of my first students at Notre Dame was a young Catholic layman from Texas named John Popiden. I do not remember how John got to Notre Dame, but he wrote a dissertation on the effort to reform prisons in early America. He compared the Quaker attempt to reform the Philadelphia prisons with the attempt in New York to organize prisons in terms set by the Enlightenment. I have no idea how John got the idea for such a dissertation. I have no idea why I thought I was competent to direct it, but I did. As a result, what Michel Foucault would later teach us about prisons did not come as a complete surprise.

I did recruit one graduate student. Bonnie Raine had come to Notre Dame to do a Ph.D. in pastoral theology. I did not think much of that program, but Bonnie had done course work and finished her exams and was ready to write her dissertation. She was having trouble finding a topic. Bonnie worked at the Logan Center as a social worker for the Protective Service Board, which served as guardian for the mentally disabled who had been abandoned. I served on the board and often went with Bonnie to visit those for whom we had responsibility. Bonnie had a remarkable touch, quite literally, with the mentally disabled. At my suggestion, she wrote a good dissertation that used Barth's Christology to make sense of care for the mentally disabled. Carol Descoteaux, C.S.C., would later build on Bonnie's dissertation and write one of the first dissertations on Jean Vanier's L'Arche movement, as well as on developments in base communities in Brazil, to explore how chronic suffering should be understood theologically.

Some dissertations were the result of courses I taught. Paul Wadell's dissertation on charity as friendship and Simon Harak's dissertation on the role of the passions in the formation of character were the result of a seminar I taught on Aquinas. I loved it when students like Richard Bondi or Charlie Pinches would use what they learned from seminars in philosophy, history, and political theory to enrich how we should think theologically. Richard was one of the first to challenge the Kantian presumption that "special relations" required peculiar justification because they failed to be "disinterested." The arguments Charlie develops in his book *Theology and Action*, which was published in 2002, were first developed in his dissertation on description in 1984.

I loved working with these wonderful students. That I had such good students, that I had such good colleagues, that I had a good church, that I had such good friends, that I had Adam meant that I never felt sorry for myself. At least I do not remember feeling sorry for myself. I thought that what Anne, Adam, and I were going through was hard. But I also thought that the only thing to do was to keep going. I had been given a job to do — I was a theologian.

I AM SOMETIMES ASKED HOW MY LIFE WITH ANNE MIGHT HAVE INFLUENCED my work as a theologian. The truthful answer is that I simply do not know. Some people thought the title of my book *Truthfulness and Tragedy* must in some way have been autobiographical, but I did not regard our situation as a tragedy. Pathos, not tragedy, is a more appropriate description of our life together. If anything, what I learned from living with Anne was how to live when you are not in control of your life. Living a life out of control may have influenced my theological insights, but it strikes me as self-indulgent to make too much of the relationship between my life with Anne and Adam and the way I learned to do theology.

It may seem odd, given my stress on narrative as the necessary grammar of Christian convictions, that I want to disassociate my own story from how I do theology. It may seem even odder that I am making this argument in a theological memoir. But the emphasis on narrative is not an invitation to use whatever we take to be our "experience"

Enduring

to test or determine the meaning of the language of the faith. Rather, claims for the significance of narrative entail a robust set of metaphysical claims required by our conviction that God creates ex nihilo.

If we existed by necessity, we would not need a story — and creation is a story — to say what is. A theory could do that work. The point is simple, but as so often is the case, simplicity is not easily captured conceptually. I had argued in *The Peaceable Kingdom* that the stress on narrative was not only an observation about the significance of stories for determining our lives, but also a robust metaphysical claim. Stories are important, but that our lives can be and finally must be narrated is a confirmation, a witness, to the contingent character of all that is. "All that is," of course, is a metaphysical expression suggesting the unavoidability of separating claims about how we best live from an understanding of the way things are.

Unlike David Burrell, Robert Jenson, and John Milbank, I do not have a natural metaphysical mind. Even so, I think it a mistake, in fact a metaphysical mistake, to believe that you have to get your metaphysics straight before you can do theology. I do metaphysics. But to avoid metaphysical reductionism, I try to do metaphysics by way of indirection, something I learned from Barth. Thus my task as a theologian is first and foremost to make the connections necessary to articulate clearly what it means to say that what we believe is true. Those connections entail metaphysical claims, but that they do so is not an invitation to make metaphysics an end in itself. My worry about metaphysics is but one aspect of my concern about any attempt to provide a shorthand account of what we believe as Christians.

In *Preface to Theology*, John Yoder comments on attempts to distinguish between the kernel and husk of the gospel in order to avoid eschatological claims at the heart of the New Testament. Yoder observes that if all the New Testament means when it speaks of the New Jerusalem is that "God is love," then we do not have anything to say that the world has not already heard. Yoder describes a number of variations on this theme to suggest that the problem with generalizations that attempt to avoid the eschatological character of God's purposes in history is that the gospel so understood has no duration, time, space, or body. Fulfillment understood as timeless fulfillment, according to Yoder, is good Platonism, but not true to the Bible.

In the Bible, Yoder argues, the eternal is not atemporal. Rather, in the Bible the eternal, in Yoder's words, "is not less like time, but more like time. It is like time to a higher degree. The kingdom is not immaterial, but is more like reality than reality is." Yoder argues that if cross and resurrection are real events, then the fulfillment and culmination of God's purposes must be really historic. The God of the Bible is therefore not timeless. Just as Origen and Tertullian insisted that the Logos was with God from eternity, so we cannot conceive of an atemporal God. We can conceive of a hypertemporal God, that is, a God who is more temporal than we are, "who is ahead of us and behind us, before us, above us in several directions, and who has more the character of timeliness and meaningfulness in movement rather than less."

My claim, so offensive to some, that the first task of the church is to make the world the world, not to make the world more just, is a correlative of this theological metaphysics. The world simply cannot be narrated — the world cannot have a story — unless a people exist who make the world the world. That is an eschatological claim that presupposes we know there was a beginning only because we have seen the end. That something had to start it all is not what Christians mean by creation. Creation is not "back there," though there is a "back there" character to creation. Rather, creation names God's continuing action, God's unrelenting desire for us to want to be loved by that love manifest in Christ's life, death, and resurrection.

To speak of narrative as the necessary grammar of Christian convictions is to name this eschatological character of existence. It is also a metaphysical claim that I am confident found a place in my work because of my encounter with the person and work of John Howard Yoder, not because of my "experience." Of course my encounter with Yoder was itself an "experience," which is why such matters are complex. George Eliot captures this complexity well in *Adam Bede*. Commenting on Arthur's betrayal of Hetty, Eliot observes, "Our deeds determine us as much as we determine our deeds; and until we know what has been or will be the peculiar combination of outward and inward facts, which constitute a man's critical actions, we will be better not to think ourselves wise about his character." I certainly do not want to think myself

Enduring

wise about my own character; for, as Eliot observes, "there is a terrible coercion in our deeds which may turn the honest man into a deceiver, and then reconcile him to the change."

What so often makes us liars is not what we do, but the justifications we offer for what we do. Our justifications become the way we try to defeat the contingencies of our lives by telling ourselves consoling stories that suggest we have done as well as was possible. I cannot pretend that I have avoided deceit in this memoir. But I have at least had a check on the lies I might tell. Being Christian means that I must try to make sense of my life in the light of the gospel, and so I do not get to determine the truthfulness of my story. Rather, those who live according to the gospel will be the ones to determine where I have been truthful and where I have deceived myself.

"In the light of the gospel" names for me the discovery that my life depends on learning to worship God. The worship of God does not come naturally to me, as it seems to for some. I live most of my life as if God does not exist. Yet I know I would not have survived without the prayers of friends who have learned to pray the prayers of the church. My life depends on learning to worship God with those who have made it possible for me to go on. Through worship, the world learns the truth that is required for our being truthful about ourselves and one another.

Most people do not have to become a theologian to become a Christian, but I probably did. Of course, being a theologian can be a liability for being a Christian. You cannot help but be tempted to be a "professional believer" because you get paid for believing in God. As a result, you cannot afford to call into question what you say you believe. I do not think I have ever given in to this temptation. After all, I was drawn into the world of the church because I did not want to live a lie.

I pray that continues to be true — that is, I am a Christian because I believe that by so being I have a better chance of living truthfully. I hesitate to put the question of truth in terms of "beliefs." I have come to think that the challenge confronting Christians is not that we do not believe what we say, though that can be a problem, but that what we say we believe does not seem to make any difference for either the church or the world. Stated differently, my early concerns about the truth of Christian convictions were political — not epistemological. Once I realized this, I began to emphasize the necessity of the church's materiality as the precondition for being able to articulate the difference God makes for knowing the way things are.

Despite what so many of my critics started to say, my growing emphasis on the political character of the church, an emphasis that owed much to John Yoder, did not make me an irrationalist, nor a sectarian. Though I utilized Yoder's critique of Constantinianism, that is, the accommodation of the church to the established order, I probably did not make clear that at least some developments identified later as Constantinian can be understood as attempts to instantiate the politics of Jesus. However, insofar as such attempts failed, they exposed the deepest problem with Constantinianism: in the name of being politically responsible, the church became politically invisible. It is as an attempt to remedy this invisibility that my work began to unfold. Ironically, Christians had created a politics that identified what it meant to be Christian with the holding of certain "beliefs" that were then described as "private." Under Yoder's influence, I came to understand that the politics of Jesus was a public affair, with cosmic consequences.

Alasdair MacIntyre has been no less important for my life and work than Yoder. Alasdair and I became unlikely friends. I think we first met when Alasdair gave a week of lectures in the Philosophy Department at Notre Dame. He seems drawn to people who do not quite fit in. I do not know if that is why he took a liking to me, but for reasons completely mysterious to me he seemed to like me. Of course, Alasdair, just by being Alasdair, intimidates me. What do you do or say around one of the smartest people in the world who seems not to have forgotten a single word of anything he has ever read?

I was a student of Alasdair's work before we met at Notre Dame. I had learned much from his early essays in the philosophy of social science and action theory. *Against the Self-Images of the Age* had taught me how capitalism and liberal politics were inseparable. *A Short History of Ethics* had shaped my understanding of the limits of contemporary ethical theory. Perhaps equally important was Alasdair's refusal to separate social, political, and ethical theory from their historical setting. I thought that the way he worked, the form of his thought, was as important as the particular judgments he made about this or that figure or issue.

Then in 1981 he published *After Virtue*. I like to think that this book changed the world. At least it changed the world in which I worked. Prior to reading *After Virtue* I had developed an account of the virtues. I had made suggestions about the necessity of narrative for the work of practical reason and for our ability to render our lives coherent. I had written about how a new morality rooted in narrative and the virtues entailed a critique of liberal political practice and politics. But it was only the clarity of the arguments in *After Virtue* that made it possible for me to write a book like *The Peaceable Kingdom*.

Many people assume that Alasdair and I overlapped at Notre Dame, but I left Notre Dame the year before he joined the faculty. We were colleagues only some years later at Duke. Alasdair, however, was often at Notre Dame during my last years there. During one of his visits he proposed that we edit a series of books that might offer fresh perspectives on ethics. I was more than happy to join him in this effort. Notre Dame and our good friend Jim Langford, then editor of Notre Dame Press, agreed to publish the series. We called it Revisions. In 1983, we edited a volume by that title to define the kind of books we wanted to publish. I am quite proud of the books we published. One of the first was Jeff Stout's *The Flight from Authority*. The series did what it was intended to do, that is, unleash and legitimate a way to do ethics that offered an alternative to the analytic sterility of the dominant paradigm exemplified by William Frankena's *Ethics*.

Some people find it hard to see how the influence of both Yoder and MacIntyre on my work can be commensurable. It would be foolish to deny the tensions my use of them creates in my work, but I think they are fruitful tensions. Yoder seldom thought he needed philosophy for his theological claims. Yet I think philosophy is necessary for theology to be done well. Without the kind of philosophical work that MacIntyre represents, theology threatens to be an esoteric discipline available only to those on the inside. Alasdair (and Aristotle) provided me with the conceptual tools necessary to show that knowledge of God and what it means to be human are inseparable.

Notre Dame continued to be for me everything I needed it to be in order to think about these matters, but that would soon change. In 1979, I was promoted to full professor. I was being considered for promotion at the same time I received an invitation to assume the Kennedy Chair of Bioethics at the Kennedy Center at Georgetown University. Jim Childress had occupied the chair for a number of years, but he had decided to return to the University of Virginia. I was interviewed and offered the chair. At the time, I was still making less than $30,000 a year. The chair carried a salary of $35,000 as well as a supplement to help buy a house, and the teaching load was less than at Notre Dame. It was an attractive offer but also created great difficulty for me. I am hopeless when confronted with the necessity of negotiating such things.

I went to David Burrell with the offer. He was about as hopeless as I was in knowing how to respond. He sent me to the dean of the college, a philosopher I knew and liked. He simply told me that they did not want me to leave and sent me to the provost, a mathematician from South Africa named Tim O'Meara. I assumed that Notre Dame could not match the offer I had from the Kennedy Center. I did not care about having a chair, but the money was enticing. The provost asked what I wanted to do. I said I would like to stay, but I had a difficult family situation and I needed the money. He said, "I will give you thirty six." I said, "I will take it."

He then explained that people in theology had been underpaid for years, but it was our own damn fault. He suggested that we must not think that our work is unimportant because we never asked for more. It had never occurred to me to think like that. It still does not occur to me to think like that. But I was glad I was able to stay. For the first time, we were not under financial constraints.

I was now a full professor and settled in the Theology Department at Notre Dame. David, however, had been chair for nine years. Enough was enough. He did not seek to be reappointed. Little known to us in the department, there was a concern in the university that the department was "too Protestant." During David's tenure as chair, we had appointed a young man in theology. He was one of Schubert Ogden's students. He became a good friend, though we disagreed about everything. However, his willingness to gore Catholic sacred cows in the classroom — "Of course, Jesus had brothers" — meant that Father Hesburgh got calls from alumni wondering what was going on at Notre Dame in the Theology Department. Perhaps just as problematic, the department denied tenure to a young C.S.C. priest. He was, moreover, a good friend of Father Malloy, who would become president of Notre Dame after Father Hesburgh.

All of this stood in the background of the search for a new chair. I assume a search committee was appointed, but I do not know who was on it. We soon were told that our new chair, the first non-C.S.C. chair of the department, would be Richard McBrien, a priest who had headed an institute for lay education at Boston College. Richard had written a huge book simply entitled *Catholicism*. Insofar as the book had a consistent theological perspective, it could be characterized as a popularization of Karl Rahner. In the interest of re-Catholicizing the Department of Theology, the university had hired a Catholic liberal.

I was about to confront another side of the Catholic world. I had known vaguely that this other side existed but largely had been able to avoid it because of David's extraordinary, capacious theological vision. Robert Wilken and Joe Blenkinsopp often complained that David had no idea how to throw a party or attend to day-to-day administration. No doubt they were right about the first but perhaps wrong about the second. I think David was a better administrator than they allowed. From my perspective, David's main weakness was his ability to make silk purses out of sow's ears; that is, he often was able to see "strengths" in people who were decidedly mediocre. In any case, it was clear to all three of us and to many others that David cared about the right things.

Dick McBrien, however, often seemed to care primarily about Dick McBrien. In particular, he cared about being the talking head on television who confirmed that the Vatican was made up of reactionary conservatives. He had actually written an article in which he said that if he had not become a Roman Catholic priest he would have most liked to be a U.S. senator. There is nothing wrong with wanting to be a priest or a senator, but it was difficult for me to understand how the ambition to be one or the other could exist in the same person. But then, I really did not understand Irish Catholicism, particularly as it sometimes became a parody of itself in the cities of the Northeast.

Dick was "political." I thought I was "political," but I was a rank amateur compared to Dick. I simply did not understand how manipulations by the chair could so quickly turn the direction of the department. I need to be clear. Dick was always kind to me. Early on, he told me I was the one person in the department he did not want to lose. But he then explained that under Burrell's leadership we had tried to be a nondenominational department of theology that could compete with Yale, Harvard, and Union. But that was a mistake. Instead, he said, we should be denominationally Catholic and competing with schools such as Boston College and Marquette.

I was absolutely dumbfounded. I responded by observing that Protestants are denominations. Catholics are the church. He did not get the point, which was crucial for understanding what we had been trying to do before he arrived. That is, we knew that only Catholicism could sustain a theology department that included faculty who represented other forms of Christianity as well as Judaism and who sought to do history and theology in a manner that exposed the pain of our disunity and the possibilities of unity. That Catholics should think of themselves as a denomination confirmed that Catholicism in America had become a form of Protestantism.

Dick, quite understandably for a theologian of his generation, assumed that theology was primarily a weapon to be used to fight battles between Catholic conservatives and liberals after Vatican II. We had tried to be a department that avoided those battles. We did so because we thought that too often the way battle lines were drawn between Catholic conservatives and liberals was intellectually uninteresting. Those battles represented and reproduced the insular character of Catholicism. Ironically, Catholic liberals who wanted to be "open to the world" had often never lived in "the world." As a result, they had a more positive view of the world than they did of the church. But the liberals were right to think that the fortress mentality of some Catholic conservatives betrayed the spirit of John XXIII.

During Burrell's tenure as chair, faculty retreats always involved reading and discussing a serious work of theology. Dick immediately changed that agenda, suggesting that the focus of retreats ought to be on how the department was to be organized. As we discussed the changes that Dick was enacting, Ed Malloy, who at least at the time was one of Dick's allies, observed that what was happening was simple. He explained that under Burrell a certain group of people had been in power. They were being replaced, and a new group of people would now be in power. Given my political naiveté, I had assumed that Monk, as he was known, would be on David's side, since they were both C.S.C.

Enduring

priests. I was clearly wrong. It had not occurred to me that there would be tensions between the different generations in the order.

As far as I could tell, McBrien's deepest passion was to Americanize Rome. He wanted the American church to be more democratic. There is much to be said for making the church more democratic, but, to continue the analogy, Dick's way of going about things made it appear that his true interest was in being the first president of Roman Catholicism in America. In fact, the takeover of the department was anything but democratic. For example, it was not long before Dick told me that I was too "articulate" in faculty meetings. As a result, I intimidated some faculty who would otherwise like to speak. Therefore, he suggested, I should seldom say anything. Dick had almost no sense of irony.

Dick also told me that I was intellectually too "high powered" to be "wasted" on Notre Dame's undergraduates, so I should offer courses only at the graduate level. I had always thought that a Catholic should teach the first course in moral theology in the seminary, but it had never occurred to me that I should not teach undergraduates. I loved teaching undergraduates. I hated to give them up. I did continue to teach at the undergraduate level, but I did so as faculty in a new program in the College of Arts and Letters. The program was designed to expose undergraduates to the "classics" of the Western intellectual tradition. I enjoyed teaching in that program because it gave me an opportunity to engage the thought of people like Galileo, Lyell, and Darwin. I loved teaching the classics, but I missed teaching theology at the undergraduate level. I missed it because I often found that the challenge of trying to interest undergraduates in theology was a good way to discover how exciting it is to be a Christian.

FATHER HESBURGH AND OTHERS AT NOTRE DAME HAD SOMEHOW ORCHEStrated the appointment of Dick McBrien as chair of the Theology Department, and Dick was killing a dream. Granted, we in the department had not done the political work we should have done to help people like Father Hesburgh understand the dream. Our dream was to avoid the choice between being a department of religious studies and being a denominationally confessional department. This dream depended on people, Protestant and Catholic, who shared an emerging set of judgments and a vision about the future of the church. God knows we did not see our way clearly, but what we did see continues to animate my life.

Part of the agony for me was what this meant for David. Paul VI had asked Father Hesburgh to set up an ecumenical center in the Holy Land. Father Hesburgh had asked David to go to Jerusalem to head up the center, which had originally been planned for Notre Dame. It seemed like a good thing for David to do after being chair. David was, therefore, not at Notre Dame during the first year of McBrien's take-over. After he returned, David carried on in good spirits, but I found it hard to watch him marginalized the way he was.

During this time I discovered my inability to work for people I do not respect. I will break my ass for what I think is right. When asked, I have been willing to take on tasks and teach courses that have not enhanced my "career." I have never regarded this as unselfishness. I have simply assumed that this is what you do if you care about building for the future. I have always been willing to put off my "own work" to do things that need to be done for the good of a common enterprise. But I just cannot work for people I do not respect. And I do not respect people I cannot trust.

I am sure I was a complete puzzle to Dick. He once offered to take Anne and me out to dinner. I said OK, but then I went for a run. What I did next may have been because I had been reading Trollope. I went to see Dick. I told him I was not being truthful when I indicated that I would share a meal with him. The truth was that I did not trust him, and I did not approve of how he led the department. For us to be seen in public sharing a meal would be disingenuous and false. He could count on me to be as good a citizen as I could in the department, but it was asking too much for me to pretend to be his friend. That was the last serious conversation the two of us had.

In the meantime, the department was being stocked with new appointments to ensure that we were appropriately Catholic. I tried to keep out of the way. I was now a Protestant. I had always told John Yoder that he was far too quiet in faculty meetings. I pointed out to him that he was a tenured full professor who had responsibilities in the department. If he stayed quiet on the presumption that he was first and foremost a guest in the department, he only confirmed the stereotype that Mennonites think they have to withdraw from the world. "Damn it," I would say, "you have power in the department, John, and you need to use it." I think I had been right when David was chair. Yoder's posture as a silent guest, however, proved prophetic with regard to the new regime.

That I was unhappy was no secret. I complained to the dean of the college. But it was clear that the sweeping changes in the department were being dictated from on high. Jim Burtchaell had not been provost for several years, and even though he had returned to the department, there was little he could do. It was not clear why Father Hesburgh had decided Burtchaell should step down as provost. At the time, it was assumed that Burtchaell had simply angered too many of the faculty because of what they took to be his arrogance and because of his emphasis on hiring Catholics. It turned out, I learned only later, that there were other serious issues involved for which Jim paid dearly — that is, it was impossible for him to remain at Notre Dame. He remains a good and dear friend.

Someone had the idea that the best thing for me would be to get away from Notre Dame. The university had started a London program. I was offered the opportunity to teach in London. There was one small problem — Anne. She was not against going to England. Dr. Shriner had just died. She did not like her new shrink very much. Going to London might help us get better care. We would be gone only six months, so hopefully the episodes could be controlled. Adam had just begun high school. It was a good time for him to go to school in London. We went.

Once in London, Anne became fixated on how much Notre Dame was spending on the flats in which we lived. We did live in a wonderful location right off Kensington Gardens. Our tube stop was Bayswater. Anne worried constantly about money. She could not believe, moreover, that she had to shop for food everyday. We made contact with a Harley Street psychiatrist who would keep track of her blood levels. She was not happy, but she stayed relatively sane. I think Anne was afraid of having an episode in unfamiliar surroundings. It was as if you could feel her desperately struggling not to indulge in a high.

We made an anxiety-filled trip to Paris I shall not forget. Anne wanted to go to Paris to see the museums, but once we were there she found the city confusing and threatening. She was fearful that we would get lost, which of course we did. We saw the main museums, but after two days she refused to leave the hotel. I was sure she was going into an episode, but somehow we got her back to London. I still find it emotionally difficult to remember such times, when we were living on a razor's edge of chaos.

Adam loved London. He went to school at Holland Park, a laborite school established to show that a state school could be as good as Eton. That proved not to be the case, but it was a wonderful school where the children of the empire were educated. Adam played endless games of Dungeons and Dragons with friends from India, Pakistan, and Southeast Asia. He quickly learned to use the tube so that he and his friends could go anywhere they liked in London.

He was taking a course in sociology that dealt with Marx. He wanted to visit Marx's grave in Highgate. We took the Northern Line early on a Saturday morning, sharing seats with a punk family on their way to see one of their child's grandparents before enjoying being with friends for the weekend. Only in London would a couple with pink spiked hair, appropriately pierced and chained, be taking their kid in a stroller to visit her grandparents.

We got to Highgate and discovered that it was the anniversary of Marx's birthday. The Communist Party had gathered to begin a parade. Banners and speakers were everywhere. There may have been more police present than Communists. It was a rally that one would never see in America. We even got to hear a lively debate between a Leninist and a Marxist about who had really betrayed the revolution. Adam and I loved England.

We thought we should try to go to a Methodist church. We found one some distance beyond Portobello Road. For a month, we walked an hour each way to go to church with the Methodists. The church was described as a "people's church," which meant that it was mainly black. We liked the people but hated the liturgy. The Sunday that we sang "God is like a magic penny, you lose him and he comes rolling back," I told Adam we were not coming back.

We began to attend St. James, Piccadilly. St. James is a Wren church in the center of the West End. Donald Reeves was the priest. At the time, I had no idea who he was or that some people considered him quite controversial. I admired his intelligence and the energy he brought to St. James. The West End was populated with musicians, artists, and actors, and Reeves knew how to make use of them in the liturgy. Sometimes at noon he would preach to the passing throng from the outside pulpit built into St. James's side. He organized a continuing lecture series on faith and politics, which meant I got to hear Tony Benn and Shirley Williams. I later heard a distinguished canon of Westminster Abbey describe St. James and Donald as "trendy," but if that is the case it is a "trend" to be followed.

I even got to preach at St. James. The text was Luke 24:13-49. I seldom got the chance to preach. I relished the opportunity not only to preach at St. James but to preach on the Emmaus road exchange. I believe that sermons should be arguments, and I argued that Jesus' presence in the bread and wine means that his appearance is no longer necessary. Thinking through that sermon was the beginning of the process that finally led me to write *Unleashing the Scriptures* ten years later. Donald called the sermon "bracing."

I am a hopeless Anglophile. While we were in England, I read all the Trollope I could. Bus trips around England for our Notre Dame students were organized for almost every weekend, making it possible to see the world about which Trollope wrote. I taught a course on the Church of England because I thought Catholics from Notre Dame would benefit from learning about a form of Christianity that shaped the world in which they now found themselves. Bill Cavanaugh, who would later become one of my doctoral students at Duke, was a student in several of the courses I taught in the London program. I remember he was quite taken with Eliot's *Adam Bede.*

England also gave me the opportunity to learn better the English intellectual world. I got Steven Sykes, who at that time was in Durham, to give a lecture to all the students in the Notre Dame program. Nicholas Lash, whom I had first met when he came to Notre Dame to lecture, also gave a lecture in the same series. In return, I gave a lecture at Cambridge. After the lecture, I expressed puzzlement that there were not more questions. He suspected that, given my Texas accent, some of the students and faculty were unsure what I had said.

The Blenkinsopps were on sabbatical in Oxford. They kindly invited us to visit. We accepted, and it was during our visit that I met Herbert McCabe for the first time. Herbert was in his cups, so I did not have a chance to have the conversation I would have liked to have had, but I was thrilled to meet him. Subsequently, I had a return trip to Oxford and had an opportunity to talk with him and Fergus Kerr at Blackfriars. I loved the world I was coming to know.

We also went to Ireland. Enda had returned to Maynooth to teach in the seminary. He invited me to give a week's worth of lectures. Everything was magical. I loved getting up at night to put a peat brick in the fire. It was the beginning of Advent. I went to Mass at six in the morning, with six hundred seminarians filling the largest choir church in Europe. What must have seemed old hat to them was for me extraordinary. I sat with the sisters in the few back pews that faced the altar. I suspect that almost none of the students understood my lectures. Most of them had never heard of Reinhold Niebuhr.

ENGLAND HAD BEEN A WONDERFUL BREAK. I HAD BEEN ABLE TO GET AWAY from the everyday politics of the department. I returned assuming that life in South Bend and at Notre Dame was a given, regardless of how difficult it had become. There was a slight suggestion, however, that I might have another option. Before I had left for England, I had received a letter from a divinity school student at Duke named Michael Cartwright. He had written to explore the possibility of studying with me at Notre Dame. He had obviously read much of my work and, as a good Methodist, wanted to explore further some suggestions he saw there about the relations between the virtues and sanctification. He was also from Arkansas.

I wrote to tell him that I would love to have him as a student, but that he needed to know things were changing at Notre Dame. Those changes meant that I could not ensure him that I would continue to teach at Notre Dame. Michael shared my letter with Tommy Langford. Tommy asked if he might show it to Dennis Campbell, who had recently become dean of the divinity school at Duke. Dennis called me in England to see if I would be open to visiting Duke after we returned, to explore the possibility of coming to Duke. Dennis explained that Waldo

Enduring

Beech, who had long taught Christian ethics in the divinity school, was soon to retire. It might be possible that I could be appointed as Waldo's replacement in anticipation of his retirement. I said I would certainly be open to a visit.

As tempting as Dennis's phone call was, I found it hard to imagine leaving Notre Dame. I was wedded to the university. I liked South Bend, even if I was tired of the "lake-effect" snow and the gray winters. I cared so deeply about the university and about Broadway United Methodist Church that I just could not get my head around the idea that I could live and teach somewhere else. After all, McBrien would not be chair of the department forever. I was even beginning to explore with the dean the possibility of transferring to another department. I was also concerned about trying to move Anne.

That Enda had returned to Ireland, however, occasioned the final and decisive event that made it possible for me to think about leaving Notre Dame. Enda had been directing the dissertation of a young Sister of Saint Joseph named Patricia Schoelles. She had been a student in one of my summer courses. I had encouraged her to do further work in theology. She was a wonderful student who, like many women in religious orders, underestimated her intellectual strengths. She applied to do Ph.D. work and was subsequently admitted. She was Enda's assistant during much of his time at Notre Dame.

She was writing a dissertation on discipleship as a social ethic in which she utilized the work of Dietrich Bonhoeffer and Johannes Metz. When Enda decided to return to Ireland, he asked me, with Pat's approval, if I would become her director. I was more than happy to act in that capacity. I was quite pleased with the work she did in the dissertation. It was one of the first important studies of Metz in America; and utilizing some of the best recent scholarship, she also had offered a good account of discipleship in the New Testament.

I signed off on the dissertation. It was, in my judgment, ready for review by the committee. The director of graduate studies, Eugene Ulrich, noted that because of Enda's absence we were a reader short. He asked if Richard McBrien could be a reader. I agreed, assuming that whatever our battles in the department might be, he would not let them carry over into evaluating a student's work. Moreover, the dissertation was in ecclesiology, and Dick, if you accepted the overdetermined forms of disciplinary divisions spawned in Catholicism, described himself as an ecclesiologist. I assumed that everything would go well.

Before long, I received a call from Pat, who had returned to Rochester, New York, to teach in the Sisters of Saint Joseph's college. She reported that she had received a phone call from McBrien. He told her that he had to fail her dissertation because it represented an ecclesiology incompatible with Catholicism. He explained that her account of discipleship as a social ethic would require the church to withdraw from the world. Such a withdrawal was not consistent with the Catholic commitment to social responsibility. Pat replied, "But I am a nun." Dick did not get the point.

I could not believe Dick had failed a dissertation for what seemed to me ideological reasons. He was attributing a position to Pat that she did not hold, nor was it an obvious implication of the argument she was making. Rather, Dick was reading her dissertation in light of terms he had picked up from debates that my and Yoder's work was occasioning. Thus his judgment that her dissertation was "sectarian." Ironically, such terms were developed by Protestant liberal theologians. If you want to know where Protestant liberal theology went to die, you need to look no further than the work of some Catholic theologians.

Pat was livid. She was almost at the point of saying, "The hell with it. I don't need a Ph.D. that much." I was not exactly pleased, but I knew I could not let my anger at Dick determine the advice I needed to give Pat. So I calmed her down and asked for time to think about it. It occurred to me that we needed the authority of Rahner. After all, Metz had been a Rahner student. I remembered that Rahner had published an article in *Theological Studies* in the early 1960s suggesting that Vatican II represented the discovery that the church was now the church of diaspora. I suggested to Pat that she reframe the last chapter of her dissertation by suggesting how the theme of discipleship expressed what Rahner had gestured toward by calling attention to the diasporic character of the church after Vatican II.

Pat rewrote the last chapter along those lines. What could Dick do but accept her revision? But for me that was the last straw. I was not about to stay at a school where my graduate students would be subjected to such political whim. Dennis had called again to see if I was still open to visiting Duke. I was. Anne was also willing to consider a move. She even decided that she would like to come with me for the interview.

I went to Duke for an interview. It was the fall of 1983. I assumed I would be offered the job. I gave a presentation to the faculty and administrative staff about my work and my next projects. *The Peaceable Kingdom* had been published the previous spring. *Against the Nations* and *Suffering Presence* were in production and would soon appear. It did not occur to me that some of the faculty might find me threatening or not a "good fit." Only years later, after I married Paula Gilbert, who at the time was the director of admissions, did I learn that a dinner had been arranged in which Paula had been assigned the task of judging whether my language could pass muster in a mixed crowd. My reputation had preceded me. They were afraid I might say certain four-letter words. My reputation was deserved, and I easily could have done so. But by the luck of the draw on that night, I did not. Soon after Anne and I returned from Durham, Dennis called to tell me that the faculty had voted to invite me to join their ranks.

I DID NOT UNDERSTAND WHAT I WAS GETTING MYSELF INTO. IT MAY SOUND absurd, but it did not occur to me to give any thought to what it would mean to join a divinity school faculty. I had been at Notre Dame for fourteen years. I was in a department of theology in the university. I assumed that things would be pretty much the same at Duke. During the interview, I had met with the dean of the graduate school and the provost. I assumed I would have the same interactions in the university at Duke as I did at Notre Dame. The idea that most of my teaching would now be for those going into the ministry simply did not cross my mind.

Nor had I really taken in that I was returning to a Protestant world. I had not realized that all those years at Notre Dame had given me deeply Catholic habits. For example, I simply assumed that *Commonweal* and *America* were more important to read than the *Christian Century*. I was surprised to discover after arriving at Duke that the library did not take *Benedictine Way*. I was going to a Methodist church in South Bend, but I had lost contact with whatever reality "Protestant" names.

I had no idea who Dennis Campbell was. He had been a few years behind me at Yale, but I did not remember having known him when we were students. After finishing seminary at Yale he had done his Ph.D. at Duke. I assumed that he had been influenced by Robert Cushman and, therefore, shared my commitment to understand Methodism as a form of evangelical Catholicism. I thought, therefore, that I was being recruited by someone committed to the reform of the Methodist church I had first caught a glimpse of through John Score. I would come to regret these assumptions.

I suspect that at one time Dennis may have had an ambition to make Duke Divinity School a place committed to the reform of Methodism by providing serious theological formation for those entering the ministry. But it turned out that Dennis was not unlike Dick McBrien. He was ambitious, but it was not clear that his talent befitted his ambition. He wanted to be dean, but it did not seem he wanted to be dean for any reason but to be dean. I simply found it hard to understand anyone who so ordered his life.

Of course, in fairness, it is also true that Dennis had no idea what he was getting in me. I am not sure what he had read of mine, but I do not think he had comprehended the radical character of how I had come to think. I told him I was a "pacifist" and that this made all the difference. I do not think he took that in. I suspect he had a more or less Niebuhrian presumption that pacifists were OK as long as they stayed out of the way of the people who had to run the world. The constitutive interrelation of Christology and nonviolence I had learned from Yoder was an unknown thought for Dennis. Like so many liberal and conservative Protestant theologians, he had little appreciation for how Yoder had taught me to think eschatologically. Put differently, he could not imagine what it might mean to say that Christians live in a different time than those who do not share our faith.

When Dennis called to tell me that the faculty had voted to offer me the position, he asked if I was ready to commit to coming to Duke. If I was prepared to give a preliminary "yes," he said, then the next step was for a dossier to be prepared for submission to the provost and the university appointment, promotion, and tenure committee. Anne had enjoyed being the center of attention when we came to Duke. She agreed that this university process could begin.

The appointment and tenure process, it turned out, took over two months. The arduous process associated with appointment, promotion, and tenure committees had not been in place long at Duke. I would come to serve on Duke's APT committee for more than eight years and gain a high regard for the work of this committee. At that point, however, the time it took for the university to evaluate my dossier was difficult to negotiate on my end. I had written McBrien to inform him that I was in discussion with Duke. I am sure he was pleased. That was not the problem. The problem was that after we came back from Duke, Anne fell in love with Jim Burtchaell.

She had gotten quite good at hiding her fantasies and obsessions from me. I did not know, therefore, that she had been watching his apartment at Notre Dame. I had no idea that she was in effect stalking him. She even went so far as to break into his apartment several times in the hope that he would arrive and they would go to bed together. It was like some scene from an absurdist play. But it was not a play. It was a reality I could not avoid.

Jim discovered what was happening when a maid, who had discovered Anne in Jim's apartment, asked Jim if it was — as Anne maintained — all right for her to be in his quarters. Jim got in touch with me to tell me what was happening. I confronted Anne, who insisted that Jim was desperately in love with her. She was only doing what he wanted. Jim came to the house to tell Anne that he was not in love with her, nor did he want to go to bed with her. She listened, walked out, and refused to believe him.

I finally got the call from Dennis telling me that he could officially offer me the job. My salary would be a few thousand dollars higher than at Notre Dame. I was not thinking about the money. I was trying to decide if, in the circumstances, I could leave Notre Dame. By this time, Adam was a sophomore in high school, and he was absolutely wonderful. He had followed my battles in the department. He did not particularly want to move, but he would be entering his junior year and thought this a much better time to move than if he was a rising senior. Moving Anne, however, was an obstacle.

There were few people at Notre Dame with whom I could talk about the decision to stay or leave. I talked with David, Jim, and David Solomon. But what could anyone say? I had a good offer from a good school. The situation in the department was not going to change anytime soon. I was not looking for a counteroffer from Notre Dame. If I was going to leave Notre Dame, this was as good an opportunity as I was going to have. I had been given a week to come to a final decision.

I think I was finally able to accept the position because of the church. After I had come back from the interview at Duke, I told the folks at Broadway about my situation at Notre Dame and that I might receive an offer from Duke. I asked them to pray for us. I then told them that I would do what they told me to do. God knows whether I was serious or not. After I received the call and letter officially offering me the position, I told the church that I now had to make up my mind, and my mind was in their hands. We prayed for guidance. They told me that after much discussion they thought it a good thing for me to go to Duke because there I would be in more direct service to the Methodist Church. They would let me go, however, only if I taught students at Duke what I had learned by being at Broadway. I have tried to keep that promise.

Anne was still not well. I had to make the decision without her. "Do whatever you want," she said. What I wanted was for her to love me. What I wanted was for us to have a life together. What I wanted was for Adam to have a mother. What I wanted was something that might be called "normality." If I thought staying at Notre Dame would have made any of those things possible, I would have stayed at Notre Dame. I called Dennis to tell him I was coming to Duke.

I then rode my bike to see David. I cried as I made my way. After his return from Israel, David lived in two rooms in a house that served as a meeting and worship space for the married graduate students at Notre Dame. He was their chaplain. David was not surprised by my decision and said he thought it was the right one. He observed that we had had a good run and it was probably a good thing now to be scattered. Besides, he said, we would not lose touch with one another. At the time I worried that we might lose touch. I knew David well. His loyalties were to God, the church, the order, and Notre Dame. Given his developing Islamic commitments, I knew that he would be all over the world. But he was right. We have never lost touch.

The next day I told John Yoder. John's office, which like all the single offices in the basement of the library was small, always threatened to be overwhelmed by paper. He seldom threw anything away. He assumed that both sides of any scrap of paper should be used. I made my way into the office, clearing off the chair in the hope that I might be able to sit down. After all the years John and I had been colleagues and friends, I had no idea what John made of me or our relationship. I told him I was leaving. He told me he would miss me, and his eyes misted. He even gave me a hug when I left the office. I had not anticipated that he would respond that way, but neither was I surprised.

Not long before I left Notre Dame, Ed O'Connor, whom I had met when I was originally interviewed, knocked on the door of my office, an extremely cramped space in the engineering building. I had moved to that office for my last two years at Notre Dame because it had a window. Ed, though a conservative Catholic, had more or less supported the changes McBrien had brought to the department. He asked me if he could come in to discuss a serious matter. I invited him in. He let me know that I had upset him with a comment I had made in a faculty meeting in response to an announcement that an exhibit of Murillo drawings of the Immaculate Conception was coming to Notre Dame. I had gone to an exhibition of Murillo's paintings at the Royal Academy when I was in London. Having seen one painting of the Immaculate Conception too many, I blurted out, "If you have seen one Immaculate Conception you have seen them all." Ed had come to my office to tell me that he found that comment disrespectful. He wanted to know what I had against the Immaculate Conception.

I was genuinely sorry I had offended him. I apologized without reservation. I told him the background of my remark, but then explained that I simply had not thought that much about the Immaculate Conception. I said I probably had the general Protestant prejudice against the doctrine. I did not understand why the Immaculate Conception was a necessary extrapolation of Scripture or required by Christology. Ed responded by telling me that the doctrine was not Christological but anthropological. I had no idea what he meant.

Ed explained that to understand what he meant you needed to be deeply Catholic. I acknowledged that I simply was not Catholic, despite my fourteen years at Notre Dame. I then told him that I appreciated the hospitality he had shown me over the years and that I was particularly grateful he was willing to confront me about my remark concerning the Immaculate Conception. That he came to me directly to call me to task indicated that he thought it still possible I was capable of recognizing the truth.

Some years later I was back at Notre Dame to lecture in one of David Solomon's summer institutes on medical ethics. I got up early to take a run. I was running by Sacred Heart on my way to the lakes. Suddenly there was Ed coming around the corner, no doubt headed to an early Mass. He was genuinely happy to see me. He even smiled. I told him how good it was to see him. In return, he said he missed me, observing in a regretful tone that "there were no longer people like me at Notre Dame." I am not sure what he meant, but I received his comment as a gift. To know that Ed O'Connor exists, to know that David Burrell exists, to know that the Sisters of the Holy Cross exist, to know that Enda McDonagh exists, to have been made part of their world — all this was a gift for which I will be forever grateful.

Enduring

CHAPTER 8

Beginnings and an Ending

I had made the decision to come to Duke during one of Anne's episodes and without her consent. After our visit to Duke, she had at first been favorably inclined to a move, but after falling in love with Burtchaell she wanted to stay at Notre Dame. Then Haldol did its work. As she emerged from the episode, she began to think that coming to Duke was "a good idea." She began to make plans to come to Durham. We put our house on the market. It sold readily. I wanted her to take some ownership of the decision to move to Durham. I also thought it important to show that I trusted her. We agreed that she would go to Durham without me to buy a house. I could not have cared less about what she bought as long as she was pleased with her decision.

Having bought a house, she returned to South Bend and we prepared to move. There was just one problem. Her obsession with Jim Burtchaell returned. She was having another episode. She told me that Adam and I should go to Duke, but she had to stay in South Bend to marry Jim. Jim again met with us and assured her that he was not in love with her and had no intention of marrying her. She was clearly unconvinced, but she did agree to take her medication. Emerging from this episode, she agreed to come to Durham and seemed even to look forward to the move.

We moved to Durham in early summer, in the hope that we could settle in before school started. Moving is hell, but the movers actually showed up on time in South Bend and Durham. Anne was absorbed in the details of moving into a new house. I did whatever she asked me to do. I did not particularly like the house she had bought. The rooms were dark and too small. But I am largely indifferent about such matters. Such indifference was partly motivated by my attempt to avoid conflicts with Anne. It is also one form my own self-involvement takes, namely, as long as you let me get on with my work, you can do pretty much what you like.

The summer we moved to Durham I turned forty-four. I did not even notice I was forty-four. I did not even notice I was still a young man. I had no plans for the future other than for Adam to go to college and for me to get through the next day. When you live with someone who is mentally ill, getting through the next day is a big deal. I had no idea, nor had I tried to imagine, how joining the faculty at Duke might change my life.

It had not occurred to me that I would need to get used to the contrast between Durham and South Bend and between Duke and Notre Dame. For example, though I thought of myself as a Southerner, I had never lived in the South. I had never lived amid pine trees. It took me some time to get over feeling claustrophobic. I am a Texan. In Texas, trees do not block the sky. Texans call it the "big sky" for a reason. To be sure, Indiana was not Texas, but in Indiana the tallest thing next to the highway was corn. Driving at night in North Carolina, the tall pines on each side of the road blocking all light made me feel as if I was in a dark tunnel. I was not sure I was going to survive. I had all the tunnels I could handle.

I had also never lived around Southerners. We were recipients of the famed Southern hospitality. The faculty of the divinity school made us welcome, often inviting us over for meals. I have no idea if anyone suspected that we were a troubled family, but I am sure it was hard to miss. At one dinner the host told Anne that she could not smoke. Anne refused to stay in the house and sat in the car until the end of the meal. But these were Southerners. They may have had suspicions that something was wrong, but they would have never let it show.

There is no question that these were kind people. I confess, however, that over the years I have come to the judgment that Southern civility is one of the most calculated forms of cruelty. I do not know if Methodists learned it from Southerners or vice versa. But Methodists and Southerners alike have turned passive-aggressive behavior into an art form. At least from my perspective, that makes Southern Methodism especially problematic.

Beginnings and an Ending

Texans have many faults, but usually we do not try to control you by being nice. Tell us what you want. We will either give it to you or kill you. That is not the way you negotiate life in the South. Courtesy forbids direct speech. There is a great deal to be said for courtesy, but like any virtue isolated from other virtues, it can become distorted. In particular, courtesy can become an extraordinarily subtle form of manipulation favoring those in power.

Duke University and Duke Divinity School were Southern. Duke was a "new" university, as universities go in America. The Duke we currently know had really only begun in the 1920s. The university was built by hiring impressive people to do what had made them impressive. As a result, the faculty had never had the benefit of the basement of the Notre Dame library, that is, there was not much faculty interaction between departments — or even in departments or the professional schools.

The divinity school had been defined by two major developments that it took me some time to understand. Robert Cushman had served as dean for thirteen years. He was an estimable man who never doubted his intellectual judgments. In truth, he was often right, but his autocratic way of doing business, born perhaps from his upbringing in New England, began to try the patience of the faculty. He was finally forced to retire, with bitterness on all sides. Though that battle had taken place more than ten years before I arrived, some of my colleagues still bore the scars of that time.

The other decisive event that had shaped the school was the involvement of some faculty in protests against segregation. The divinity school, much to its credit, had been one of the first schools at Duke to admit African Americans. No doubt, that decision was controversial. Even more controversial, however, was the arrest of three members of the faculty for participating in a sit-in in Chapel Hill. Everyone on the faculty, as far as I could tell, thought integration was a "good idea." The issue was the means to achieve that goal. Some of the faculty did not consider it appropriate for professors from Duke to engage in demonstrations. Civil people just do not do that sort of thing.

Of course, I knew none of this when I joined the faculty. It took some time to discover this history because it was not "talked about." Whatever the tensions from past battles, they were hidden. "Courtesy" ruled the day. I did not set out to offend my new colleagues, but I suspect that some of them found my more direct style a bit hard to take. But having been around the philosophy department at Notre Dame, I simply assumed that a university was constituted by people who had strong views that were to be defended against all comers.

In the transition from Notre Dame to Duke, people made all the difference. And people, of course, defy the generalizations I have used so far to characterize the South and Duke. In particular, there was Stuart Henry. I had originally met Stuart at Yale when he was doing research for the book he would write on Lyman Beecher. We had come to know one another at Yale because Stuart and John Score were close friends. During John's long sojourn at Duke, he and Stuart, then a young professor teaching American church history, enjoyed sharing meals, art exhibits, and concerts in one another's company. Soon after our arrival in Durham, Stuart made it his business to befriend us.

Stuart Henry was from Concord, North Carolina. He had gone to Davidson College and Louisville Presbyterian Seminary. He then served a church for many years in Meridian, Mississippi. He loved his people, but the racism finally drove him away. He came to Duke Divinity School to do his Ph.D. under Shelton Smith, who had come from Yale to put Duke Divinity School on the map. He was among the first scholars to develop the field of American church history. Stuart wanted to write on Faulkner. Smith made him write his dissertation on Whitfield.

Stuart was a Calvinist. The world was dark. But poor Stuart was condemned to live with Methodists, who seemed to think that there was no darkness at all. Stuart had fallen in love when he was a seminarian, but the young lady had married someone else. Stuart was a Southern gentleman. You could never betray your love, so he remained a classic Southern gentleman bachelor. He did so quite happily. He wore dark suits, white shirts, and a dark tie — every day.

There were no flies on Stuart. He missed little. He figured out quite soon that not all was right with Anne. He became an unfailing friend, not only for me but also for Adam. That we were such close friends puzzled many of our friends. I was the blunt Texan. Stuart was the epitome of the cultured South. But Stuart and I shared, in quite different ways, a passion for telling it like it is. I think it no accident that we loved one another.

My first year at Duke was the year he retired — an event about which he was anything but happy. Stuart loved his students and hated giving them up. It turned out that I would also come to love one of those students. Her name was Paula Gilbert. She had graduated from the divinity school, entered the Ph.D. program in American church history, and written her dissertation on Georgia Harkness. When I came to Duke, she was the director of admissions in the divinity school. I thought she was a strikingly beautiful woman. I could not help but register her existence. But given the way I had learned to live, "registering her existence" was all I could do.

ADAM AND I COULD NOT FIND A CHURCH. BROADWAY HAD SPOILED US. ADAM had developed a good ear for spotting bad theology when he heard it in sermons. He was also liturgically sophisticated. We tried the Methodist churches, but neither of us thought we could survive them. During the two years Adam and I shared in Durham, we usually ended up going to the Chapel of the Cross, an Episcopal church in Chapel Hill. Before Adam left for college, we began to attend a Methodist church that we thought had some promise because it was a "start-up."

There was no Broadway United Methodist in Durham, but there were the Durham Bulls. We knew the Bulls before the movie *Bull Durham*. The Bulls were a single-A farm team of Atlanta. They played in the historic Durham Bulls Stadium. You knew it was historic because the field announcer never said the field's name without using the word "historic." Adam was doing well in school, even if his natural abilities allowed him to get away with bad study habits, which meant that we had plenty of time to watch the Durham Bulls play. Soon Adam and I were going to every home game. It was cheap, fun, and we loved the company. Before long we were part of a group of guys who always expected one another to be there, first-base side just up from the boxes and the more expensive seats.

The second summer was particularly memorable. Ronnie Gant was playing second. Jeff Blouser was our shortstop. David Justice briefly came through in right. We even got to see Barry Bonds. He played center field for the Lynchberg Pirates. At the time, he was just a splinter, but I saw him hit a home run over the Brame building in right field that must have gone five hundred feet. He played center field like a gazelle.

Baseball and theology were inseparable for me even before I moved to Durham. At Duke I discovered that this was also true for one of my new colleagues — Geoffrey Wainwright. Geoffrey had come to Duke from Union Theological Seminary in New York a year before I arrived. Perhaps Geoffrey's most notable virtue, as an Englishman who loves cricket above all else, is his love of baseball. In my first years at Duke, we often attended games together. We even once traveled to Winston-Salem, hoping that the Bulls could clinch a playoff berth by defeating the Cub farm team. Gant made an error that allowed Winston-Salem to win, but he would go on to play left field for the Braves. Proving that baseball and theology are inseparable, Geoffrey not only became my friend and companion at baseball games but began to teach me that theologians can never forget that the bottom line is the worship of God.

Adam not only loved going to the games but soon began to work for the Bulls. He enjoyed vending drinks, peanuts, and hot dogs. He was, moreover, damn good at it. It became one of his summer jobs. I loved to watch him kid people. For example, he loved to shout out "sushi, get your sushi here," and this was before baseball became a yuppie sport. Adam became one of the characters that fans look forward to seeing at the games. In South Bend we had a river. In Durham we had baseball — and lemurs.

During one of my runs, I discovered the lemur colony in Duke Forest. Lemurs are wonderful primates from Madagascar. An anthropologist from Duke who was doing research on Madagascar discovered that these animals were threatened with extinction. Determined to save them, he established a colony of lemurs in part of the vast forest Mr. Duke had given to the university. You cannot help but be captivated by the various and colorful species of lemurs. The colony has now become famous, requiring controlled visits, but when we came to Durham you could simply walk around the enclosures. It was often unclear who was watching whom, given lemur curiosity. It became one of Adam's and my favorite things to do.

I was not officially employed at Duke until late August. I needed to be on the payroll in order to get Duke medical insurance. That meant we had to wait for over a month before we could look for a doctor for Anne. I was not too worried, because Anne seemed in fairly good shape, and we would not have to wait long. She stayed in the house most of the time because of the heat of a North Carolina summer. She was concerned that if she perspired too much her Lithium level might be affected. That she was concerned about her Lithium level meant that she recognized something was not quite right. At the same time, however, she denied that she had a problem. Still living out the patterns that had long defined our lives, she was convinced that her only problem was me.

Two days before the start of Adam's school and my first semester of teaching at Duke, Anne went crazy. I was desperate. I was now technically covered by Duke's medical insurance, but we had not yet found a doctor. As usual, Anne was not sleeping. She was, moreover, convinced she needed to return to South Bend to save Jim. It seems he was possessed by demons and only Anne could exorcise them. What absolutely horrible timing.

A few weeks earlier, a young resident in psychiatry had called me to explore the possibility of taking courses with me. His name was Keith Meador. I told him that I would welcome him into any courses I might teach. Then it occurred to me that it might be good to explain my situation to him. I did so, and he gave me his phone number just in case I needed him. With Anne deep in another episode, I called him and explained the situation. He went to his supervisor, Dr. Loosen, to see if he would be willing to see Anne. He was willing to see her, but he explained that first I had to get her to admit herself to the affective disorders ward in the hospital.

I took Adam to begin his first day in school. I returned to the house, having no idea how I could get Anne to go with me to the hospital. She was adamant that she did not need any help. After trying for an hour or more to "reason" with her, I put my hands on her shoulders, shook her, and told her that I was going to get her to the hospital whether she wanted to go or not. I had never used physical force before, but for some reason it worked. She suddenly became calm and agreed to go with me.

I was unfamiliar with Duke Hospital. It was no fun trying to find an admitting station with someone in a manic episode. Nor was it any fun trying to prove that I really was a Duke employee when all my paperwork was still being processed. Somehow I managed to negotiate the "system" and finally arrived in Dr. Loosen's office. Anne's anger returned. She attacked me for committing her. She made fun of Dr. Loosen's slight Germanic accent. He was finally able to convince her to stay overnight because, as he explained to her, he needed to have a better understanding of her biology.

She began receiving an antipsychotic medication that brought her down. It was as if we were reliving her first hospitalization. She was angry that I had the power to have her committed. What could I say? I did have the power, though I had never actually used it. She continued to maintain that I was her jailer. It was clear that any hope of our beginning a more "normal life" was gone. This was the way it was going to be.

ANNE'S FIRST DRAMATIC EPISODE OCCURRED IN 1974, SOON AFTER I RE-ceived tenure at Notre Dame. I have no idea if there is any relation between the two events, but I have wondered about how they might be related. Tenure is at least the symbol of a security she may have thought freed her in an odd way from being dependent on me. I have no idea how many psychotic episodes we had lived through by 1984, when we moved to Durham. All I know is that she became quite clever at hiding from me the fantasy world in which she often lived.

I am not sure what kept me going. I had long given up any hope that she would "get better." I did hope that we might find a way to control the frequency of the episodes, or at least I hoped that she might want that to happen. But she continued to think she was ill because she was married to me. In her mind, she would be well only when I was no longer part of the equation. She could not help but see whatever I did as diminishment. God knows I tried to get out of the way, but how to do that was not clear.

I was in pain, but I could see no alternatives. One of the reasons I could see no alternatives was, interestingly enough, rather self-interested. I worried that if I found a way to "escape" from the marriage, I might lose the critical edge that seemed to make my work compelling. I wondered if my pain was necessary to avoid the superficial character of so much contemporary theological ethics.

But first and foremost, I always thought about Adam. Later, when he was in college, he became angry at me for letting Anne abuse us.

Beginnings and an Ending

His anger was well placed. But at the time, I saw no alternatives. Even more, I hoped that Adam, as he grew older, would be glad that his parents had stayed married, no matter how difficult living in such a family had been.

Though I had little hope that Anne would get better, I continued to think it might be possible for her to take some ownership of our life together. Thus I continued to thank her in the prefaces of my books. I knew that if she read anything, she would read the preface. In *Suffering Presence*, a book published in 1986, I said: "As always I owe Anne and Adam everything, for they literally make my life possible. They suffer my presence day in and day out, not, I might add, without being a bit impatient with my considerable shortcomings but also with love. With their presence I am gifted beyond measure." That was not entirely false. But it was not true that Anne suffered my presence with love.

I wrote the preface to *Suffering Presence* in 1985. That was the last time I would write something to try to seduce Anne into loving me. In 1988, I wrote in the preface of *Christian Existence Today*, a book I dedicated to Adam, "In spite of what Aristotle rightly says about the unlikely possibility of true friendship between fathers and sons, Adam is my good friend. That is a gift I had no right to expect in this life but it is one for which I praise God daily." That was true. Adam is what made my life livable.

After the initial episode at Duke, life did become functional. Anne saw Dr. Loosen every other week. Adam was adapting to the new school and friends. I was going to school every day, teaching my classes and getting to know my colleagues. But life for us would never be normal. Indeed, it was not long before I experienced one of Anne's more frightening episodes.

Before leaving Notre Dame, I had accepted an invitation from the Sisters of the Holy Cross to give a lecture at a conference on medical ethics in South Bend. The sisters had an extensive hospital system. They wanted to explore the role ethics should play for that system. I had often tried to get Anne to accompany me on trips. She always refused, noting that she did not want to have to play at "being my wife." However, when I told her I had to fly back to South Bend, she said she would like to go with me. I thought maybe this was a positive development. In fact, however, Anne had entered another episode. I just could not see it. She had become quite good at disguising them. I agreed to have her come with me to South Bend. I had no idea that she had no intention of returning to North Carolina.

We flew to South Bend. As soon as we got to our room in the hotel, Anne told me that she was not going to go back. She had come to marry Jim. She was clearly in an episode. Not only had I missed it, but it turned out that she had left all her medications in Durham. She walked out to get a cab and find Jim. I called Dr. Uribe, the psychiatrist who had cared for her after Dr. Shriner's death, and explained the situation. I begged him to prescribe something I could get her to take to bring her down. He phoned in a prescription to a nearby pharmacy.

I ran to pick up the prescription. When I got back to the hotel, Anne had not returned. I had to give my lecture. I told the organizer of the event, whom I knew well, what was happening. Somehow I got through the lecture, then immediately went to search for Anne. It turned out that Jim was out of town. Thank God. Unable to find him, Anne had returned to the hotel. I begged her to take the medication I had gotten from Dr. Uribe. Depressed at missing Jim, she agreed. She took the pill and went to sleep. The next morning I managed to get her on the plane back to Durham. But her anger at me and her fixation on Jim would not go away.

I SOMETIMES WONDER IF I WAS ABLE TO PUT UP WITH ANNE BECAUSE OTHERwise I had such a good life. At Duke, I found that I had a wonderful new place to work. In particular, I had new colleagues from whom I could learn. I am a sponge. I soak up the water around me. It was clear that Duke was different from Notre Dame. I was in new water. There was much to absorb. That Fred Herzog was at Duke meant that I could not avoid liberation theology. I had read liberation theology at Notre Dame, but now I had a colleague who *was* a liberation theologian. John Westerhoff occupied the office next to mine. John taught Christian education and read everything. He was a wonderful discussion partner. It was soon clear that I had much to learn much from Rick Lischer. We really did not have anyone at Notre Dame who thought theologically about preaching the way Lischer did. I began to realize that when done well, homiletics was an interesting field.

Beginnings and an Ending

I was a bit surprised, however, to discover that Catholicism did not exist at Duke. To be sure, David Steinmetz, who quickly became a cherished colleague, made sure that students were well acquainted with the great Catholic tradition. And Roland Murphy was a Carmelite who taught Old Testament. But Roland, one of the loveliest people in the world, radiated Catholicism; he did not teach it. Despite David and Roland, Catholicism did not exist at Duke because no one thought it important to know Rahner, von Balthasar, or Catholic moral theologians such as Richard McCormack and Charles Curran. In time that would change with the appointment of Teresa Berger. But even then Catholicism did not exist at Duke, just as Protestantism had not existed at Notre Dame.

I was also surprised that few faculty read Wittgenstein and Mac-Intyre. Bill Poteat in the Department of Religion knew his Wittgenstein better than I did, but he was in the department, not the divinity school. I learned that this distinction mattered, and I began to see that Notre Dame had formed me to be a citizen of the university. I was now discovering that I worked in a seminary. I was confused. Seminaries rightly have specific responsibilities, but I saw no reason why those tasks should be intellectually limiting. Indeed, I thought the opposite to be the case. Given the demands before the church, I thought it all the more important for theology to avoid being identified as a discipline of a profession.

Despite the difficulties of making the transition from a Catholic university to a Protestant seminary, my classes were going well. I liked my students. I particularly liked a young divinity student whom Dennis had assigned to assist me. His name was Greg Jones. He was bright, personable, and he loved baseball. I had no idea he was the son of Jamison Jones, a former dean of the divinity school who had died after serving as dean for less than a year. All I knew about Greg is that I enjoyed discussing baseball and theology with him. And I thought he was well read for a divinity student.

In addition to being theologically astute and a baseball fan, Greg was also a worker. I do not know how he learned to work, but he knew how to work hard and well. With the help of Susan, his wife, who was also finishing her degree in the divinity school, Greg soon had my office organized in ways that allowed me to actually find stuff.

Greg still loves to tell the story of one of the first tasks I gave him. At a meeting at the Hastings Center, Alasdair had told me I would benefit from reading Hans-Georg Gadamer's *Truth and Method*. I sent Greg to the library to check out *Method and Truth*. Since I had given him the wrong title, he could not find the book. He did not think to check for similar titles because he assumed I knew what I was asking for. After all, I was Stanley Hauerwas. He had not yet learned that I cannot spell and that I have a penchant for getting word order wrong. Indeed, graduate students still debate whether or not I am dyslexic. I insisted that the library must have a book by Gadamer. Armed with the name of the author, he discovered my mistake and found the book.

At the time, neither of us could have anticipated that our lives would be intertwined for years to come, making it impossible for each of us to tell our own story without also telling the story of the other. Greg and I are different from one another. I am not as smart as he is, nor do I have any of his administrative gifts. Yet I believe God has found a way for our strengths and weaknesses to complement one another, making each of us more than we otherwise would be. I know for certain that Greg has made me a better theologian. I learned much from his dissertation and book, *Transformed Judgment: Toward a Trinitarian Account of the Moral Life*, although perhaps this is not as evident to others as it is to me.

Years after Dennis assigned Greg to assist me, after Dennis had served as dean for fifteen years and Greg had been appointed dean in his place, I took Greg's sons, Nathan and Ben, to a Bulls game. Nathan must have been about ten. He was trying to find out who I was. I explained that I had been one of his father's and mother's teachers and that I had directed his father's dissertation. Without missing a beat Nathan said, "I see, but now my dad is your boss." I told him he was certainly right about that, and that it was a good thing.

The events that led Greg to become my "boss" are both sad and important. Greg was a student in the divinity school when his father, only in his fifties, died. His death was unexpected and was a crushing blow for Greg and his family. It was also a major catastrophe for the divinity school, which had had only two deans from 1958 to 1981, when Jamison Jones was appointed after a frustrating national search.

It was in the wake of Jamison Jones's death that Dennis Campbell became dean. The story of how Dennis became dean starts with Tommy Langford, who became dean after Robert Cushman had been forced to resign. Tommy would become one of my best friends, though, again, many thought us an odd pair. Like Stuart, Tommy was a North Carolina native who had gone to Davidson, then the divinity school at Duke, where he completed his Ph.D. under Mr. Cushman. He was a philosophical theologian deeply influenced by Michael Polanyi, but his scholarly field concentrated on the theological developments in Methodism. I almost hesitate to indicate his knowledge of Methodist theology because it might suggest that he had a parochial mind. In fact, Tommy was expansive in both mind and spirit. He was also a gifted administrator.

I am sure Mr. Cushman never forgave Tommy for being his successor as dean. From all reports, Tommy negotiated that complex task as well as it could have been done. Tommy was a wonderful dean because he exercised excellent judgment about people without being judgmental. He could see clearly the foibles and weaknesses of others, but he refused to use their limits against them. Instead he sought to bring out the best in everyone for the good of the institution.

Tommy was dean for ten years. He loved teaching and wanted to return to the classroom. He finally got the administration at Duke to let him resign as dean. A nationwide search was undertaken to find a new dean. All reports of the search suggest that it was a difficult process, for no other reason than the discovery that the talent pool for the position was not deep. Finally Jamison Jones, then dean at Iliff School of Theology in Denver, was offered the job. When he died before having really had a chance to begin, the president and the provost were concerned, given the difficulty of the search that ended with his appointment, about launching a new search. The solution was to appoint an internal candidate.

Before Jamison Jones had arrived, Tommy had appointed Dennis Campbell as director of continuing education. This was not a faculty position. Dennis had his Ph.D. from Duke, but from the perspective of some faculty, Dennis's credentials did not warrant an appointment to the faculty. Before being appointed to the position at Duke, Dennis had taught at a women's college in South Carolina. He was so anxious to get back to Duke that the position in continuing education was attractive to him even without a faculty appointment.

Dennis had one great skill. He knew how to live among powerful and important people. Terry Sanford, who was then president of Duke and who had also served as both governor of North Carolina and a U.S. senator, was impressed by Dennis. And so following the untimely death of Jamison Jones, Dennis became dean. Of course, I had no knowledge of that history when I fielded the query from Dennis about joining the faculty and then agreed to come to Duke. All I knew was that he wanted me to come to Duke. That was enough to make me like him. I was ready to be liked by a dean. During my first two years at Duke, I found some of Dennis's judgments odd, given my assumption that he was committed to the reform of Methodism by returning the church to its Christological center. As it turned out, this assumption was simply a testimony to my ability to deny reality in the interest of a theological fantasy. Dennis and I were destined to conflict, but that was still in the future.

ENCOUNTERS WITH PEOPLE LIKE TOMMY AND GREG AND A WIDE VARIETY OF faculty began to have an impact on my formation as a theologian. I am not at all sure that the kind of work I have done in books such as *Cross-Shattered Christ* would have been possible if I had stayed at Notre Dame. It has been at Duke that I have discovered that I am first and foremost a theologian. This discovery, I think, has everything to do with taking on the responsibility of training people for the ministry. It also has everything to do with Paula, whose own commitment to the ministry has come to serve for me as a constant reminder of why training people for the ministry matters. Some people may find it odd for me to suggest that I became a different kind of theologian at Duke. After all, had it not been my task from the beginning to display how theological language was necessary to think about the moral life? Indeed, it had, but what I began to discover at Duke was a richer theological palette.

For example, after coming to Duke I paid increasing attention to the importance of Scripture. I had preached at Broadway, but now I was expected to preach in the divinity school's worship services. Preaching requires you to attend to the text. Coming to Duke forced me to read the Bible, which I had not read closely since teaching Bible courses at Augustana.

Beginnings and an Ending

Preaching was part of it, but students also made a difference. Mike Cartwright, who had been the catalyst that got me to Duke, entered the Ph.D. program at Duke. He and Greg had gone through the divinity school together. Mike served a church in Townsville, North Carolina, for a few years before coming to do his Ph.D. He was determined not to let me avoid the implications of my own arguments concerning the significance of Scripture. His dissertation and book, *Practices, Politics, and Performance toward a Communal Hermeneutic for Christian Ethics*, helped me see that I could not just talk in the abstract about Scripture. I had to perform it.

Will Willimon was another influence. He not only would become one of my closest friends but also would change my life. We had met originally through an exchange of letters. When I was at Notre Dame, I wrote someone named Will Willimon to commend him for his book *The Service of God*. At the time, he was serving a church in South Carolina, but he became minister to Duke University the same year I joined the faculty of the divinity school.

Will and his wife, Patsy, were a godsend for me. First and foremost, Will is just fun to be around. And I needed such people in my life. He is also smart, and as we got to know one another, we discovered that we shared much in common. For example, we had both gone to Yale and were influenced by Barth. However, there were also major differences, aside from his complete lack of interest in baseball. Will is far more Methodist than I am, which means that he would like for people to like him. He also has less philosophical ability than anyone I have ever met. I think that is one of the reasons he is such a good preacher — he never lets the truth get in the way of a good story.

Will once told me that he was going to make me famous. And I have no doubt that if I have become famous, it is his fault. We were sitting in my backyard when we came up with the idea for an article that would try to characterize what we took to be an alternative to the liberal/conservative divide in Protestant theology. George Lindbeck's *Nature of Doctrine* had just been published. In the light of this book, we saw an opportunity to describe an emerging theological development associated with people as diverse as Hans Frei, David Kelsey, Will Campbell, John Yoder, Walker Percy, and Flannery O'Connor. We wanted to argue for a theological transformation that would involve the recovery of the centrality of the church and the liturgy for Christian formation. As we talked about it in my backyard, we concluded that the problem with most pastors and theologians was that the way they went about their business did not require the existence of God. We did not think of this as a controversial judgment.

We wrote the article and published it in the *Christian Century*. We had no idea that our little article would ignite a firestorm. That so many people disliked the article gave us perverse pleasure. We got a sense that we might be on to something. The seeds for *Resident Aliens* had germinated. To be sure, those seeds had been planted from the time I first read Yoder, but thought takes time. Moreover, I had to rethink what I had learned from Yoder in light of the reality in which I now found myself, that is, establishment Protestantism. I was a full professor in Duke Divinity School. Will was the minister to both Duke University and the attendants of Duke Chapel. You cannot get more established and Protestant than that. Will and I were servants of that form of life that Yoder identified as neo-neo-Constantinianism; that is, we served a church that had lost its legal and social power but tried to stay established by identifying with what was assumed to be "progress."

Will and I thought that this project was no longer viable. We were, however, not trying to deny that we were mainstream Protestants. Rather, we were trying to understand how to go on after Christendom. Neither Yoder nor I had ever suggested that there might be a place to start over again. From the beginning, it was a question of how to go on from here, which is why I have always found the charge of "sectarianism" odd. Yoder and Willimon and I were not saying that those who forged the various forms of the church's accommodation to the world were bad or unfaithful people. No doubt there were bad and unfaithful people among them, but I suspect that most of the time they were doing the best they could. But that "best" simply no longer made sense.

One of the ways I began to explore how to go on was to suggest to Harmon Smith that we teach the core course in Christian ethics together. Harmon was my senior colleague in ethics. He was a Methodist from Mississippi. He had graduated from Millsaps College in Jackson and come to Duke for seminary and eventually his Ph.D. After he had joined the faculty, he had been hired by Mr. Cushman to be his assistant. Mr. Cushman often hired people, good people at that, without consulting the faculty. Ironically, Harmon played a crucial role in the later revolt that resulted in Mr. Cushman's resignation as dean. Along the way, Harmon left Methodism to become an Episcopalian priest.

Harmon could be an antagonistic son of a bitch. He did not suffer fools. He feared no one. He had been one of the courageous people who had been arrested at the sit-in in Chapel Hill. Moreover, he was a substantive theologian. He had done some important work in medical ethics. I knew Harmon before I came to Duke through interactions in meetings of the Society of Christian Ethics. He had even arranged for me to give a lecture at Duke some years before I joined the faculty. He was extraordinarily gracious about my coming to Duke. He could have vetoed my appointment, but he looked forward to having me as a colleague. Of course, I liked Harmon because he liked me and wanted me to come to Duke. But I also simply liked Harmon.

Harmon responded positively to my suggestion that we teach together. He was even more enthusiastic about the idea that we organize the course around the liturgy. As I began to understand that my task, even as a layman, was to train people for the ministry, the liturgy loomed large in how I thought about Christian ethics. The center of the ministry is word and sacrament. We were training people who would spend the rest of their lives presiding at the Eucharist. By organizing the ethics course liturgically, we hoped to defeat any temptation students might have to ignore the fact that what they would do at the altar is determinative for the witness the church must make in the world. The very fact that a people must be gathered to worship God not only is significant for how one thinks about "ethics" but also provides the appropriate context for considering what it means to be a human being. In this regard, Harmon's lecture on the significance of "greeting" was a classic.

Harmon's book *Where Two or Three Are Gathered: Liturgy and the Moral Life* was the fruit of that course. We taught the course together several times, but when our other colleague who taught ethics retired it was no longer possible to do so. At the time, there was a rule that students should be able to choose different instructors for their basic courses, so Harmon and I could no longer teach together. I continued to teach the course around the liturgy, which I think benefited not only me but many of the graduate students who assisted me in the course.

I think the most important training these students received happened not in the graduate seminars I taught, but through helping me in that course. Many of the essays in *The Blackwell Companion to Christian Ethics*, which I edited with Sam Wells, were written by people who had assisted in that ethics course.

I ASSUME IT IS OBVIOUS BY NOW THAT I CANNOT SEPARATE WHAT I THINK from who I know. People make all the difference. It seems to me that one of my gifts is my incessant drive to introduce to one another people who otherwise might not meet but who share much in common. Although I have made it a habit to connect people far and wide, many such introductions happen through my work with graduate students. My second year at Duke, I became director of graduate studies, a wonderful position from which to connect people to one another. Indeed, if I had any administrative strategy it was to help students find one another, because I assumed that graduate school was that strange place where professors get paid for students to educate one another.

It is interesting that my highest administrative role at both Notre Dame and Duke has been director of graduate studies. Perhaps this is an exemplification of the Peter Principle, that is, we each rise to the level at which we are incompetent. I think, however, that I was pretty good at it. And at Duke I had Gay Trotter, the longtime administrative assistant to the graduate program, to make sure I did what I was supposed to do. I served as director for six years.

The graduate program at Duke is a joint enterprise between the Department of Religion and the divinity school. When I came to Duke, I was told that there was a great deal of tension between the department and the school. Originally the Ph.D. had belonged to the divinity school, but Mr. Cushman had finally relented and let the department's faculty be included. Tommy Langford was chair of the department at the time. Tommy told me that he had to threaten to resign to get Mr. Cushman to broaden the graduate program.

As hard as I tried as director of the graduate program I was never able to overcome the history that seemed to put the divinity school and the department at odds. I once asked a member of the department if he would agree to appoint Maimonides, Avicenna, and Aquinas to the

Beginnings and an Ending

department, if by some odd twist in time such a thing were possible. He said he would not make these appointments because these figures were "confessional thinkers." It seems that the last refuge for modernist epistemological conceits is in departments of religious studies. I am happy to say, however, that when it came to the training of students, the tensions between the faculties of the department and the school did not come into play.

Not all departments of religious studies are quite as ideologically determined as the Duke department. In particular, I discovered that the department at the University of Virginia thought theology was not only a legitimate subject but also a necessary one. My third year at Duke, I was fortunate to have Jim Childress, who was then chair of the Department of Religious Studies at the University of Virginia, ask me to teach a graduate seminar for their students. I was more than happy to do it. In fact, I needed the money because I had not been at Duke long enough to get their tuition benefit. I had to pay for Adam's college. One day a week, I would drive up to Charlottesville, run a three-hour seminar, and then drive home. It made for a long day. I must have taught at Virginia in this way five or six times. Over time, we began to have yearly meetings at which the Virginia and Duke students would read and respond to one another's papers. We had done a similar thing at Notre Dame with the University of Chicago graduate students.

I liked getting to know the graduate students at Virginia. I served on a number of their dissertation committees. I have always thought that the strong theological presence in the Department of Religious Studies at Virginia was a manifestation of God's sense of humor. It is hard to imagine that Jefferson could have imagined people like Julian Hartt, Gene Rogers, Langdon Gilkey, and John Milbank teaching at Virginia. For that matter, I suspect he could not have imagined me teaching at Virginia. One of the most memorable of my Virginia seminars was what I called my "big book" course. We read Charles Taylor's *Sources of the Self*, Alasdair MacIntyre's *Whose Justice? Which Rationality?*, and John Mibank's *Theology and Social Theory*. I was fortunate to have a student in the class who knew more than I did. His name was David Hart.

LIFE IN THE WORLD WAS GOOD. LIFE AT HOME WAS TENSE. I NEVER KNEW what might set Anne off. She increasingly kept to herself. Her anger could be volcanic. At times it bordered on becoming violent. I knew she was sick. I knew chemistry and probably genetics had a role. But the language that increasingly seemed to describe her was "possession." She simply seemed possessed. How else could I account for a cruelty I did not think she was capable of?

I fear sounding overdramatic, but I began to worry that she might physically attack me. I went to bed often thinking that I might not wake up in the morning. My one comfort was that I did not think she was capable of hurting Adam. At least she was not capable of hurting Adam physically. But the older Adam got, the more difficulty she seemed to have in identifying with him.

It was Adam's senior year. Adam had been nominated for a national merit scholarship. He told me, and, of course, we celebrated the accomplishment. He told his mother. She responded, "You had better get it." When he made the next round, he told me that he was going to wait until his mother was in a good mood and, hopefully, could receive the news well. One night at supper things seemed congenial. Adam told his mother the news. She responded "Oh." That was it.

It is not easy to be a teenage boy in the best of circumstances, but Adam had the added burden of negotiating a difficult family. One night early in his senior year I heard him cry out. I rushed from my bedroom to find him in a grand mal seizure. He was as white as a sheet. I desperately tried to hold him on the bed, but he shook off, landing on the floor. I shouted for Anne to call the EMT for help. She did so, but before they arrived he went completely still. I thought he had died. I was beyond despair. But the emergency team arrived and assured me he was alive.

We took him to the emergency room. He was given a complete examination by a Dr. Massey, a wonderful Duke neurologist. After extensive tests, he was diagnosed as suffering from idiopathic epilepsy. I discovered that this diagnosis simply meant that Adam was prone to seizures, but no one knew why. A week later he seized again and was put on an anti-seizure medication. He never had another seizure, but that he had the seizures meant he could not drive. What a horrible fate for a senior in high school. Fortunately, his girlfriend lived close by.

We took a trip to look at colleges. Princeton and Haverford were high on the list. He also was considering Southwestern, because of John Score. We had a lovely visit at Haverford. Ron Thiemann, whom I knew well, had become the provost there. That at least suggested to me that Haverford might not disdain theology. Moreover, given its Quaker background, I thought Adam might find it a good place to think through what it means to be nonviolent. Adam decided to go to Haverford.

I shall never forget driving Adam to begin school at Haverford. We owned a 1984 Toyota station wagon. We had packed it to the gills. Adam was excited, and I was excited for him. He had been away before for a week at Governor's School, but this was different. We unpacked the stuff into his dorm room. There was then nothing for me to do but return to Durham. I cried most of the way. I had no idea what Adam's leaving would mean.

At the time, Anne was on Tegretol, an anti-seizure medication that seems to help keep people with bipolar disease level. I have nothing but admiration for the doctors who try to help people suffering from various forms of mental illness, but what a crap shoot. It seems you never quite know what may or may not work. For example, EST (electrical stimulation therapy) was not used widely during the years of Anne's illness, but it now seems to be one of the best therapies available for people with her peculiar set of problems.

The Tegretol combined with Lithium seemed to make Anne more stable. She even felt good enough to try to hold a job. She got a job working in a men's clothing store. She lasted only two days before being fired. From what she reported to me, I gather she thought she should run the store. I am sure that was not well received. That she felt increasingly in control, however, meant that her anger toward me became more intense. Her psychiatrist suggested that we should go to a marriage counselor to see if we could work out a better relationship. Anne resisted the suggestion, but I thought it a good idea. She finally agreed.

Adam had finished his first semester at Haverford. He had been with us at Christmas and then returned to school in January. We began to see the counselor after he left. For some reason, the presence of a third person seemed only to make matters worse. Anne dominated every session by pouring out scorn on me. The counselor, without trying to defend me, tried to help Anne see that this was getting us nowhere. Anne walked out midway in the third session, declaring that she was not coming back. In fact, she said she was going to leave me.

I was exhausted. Adam was gone. When Anne declared that she intended to leave me, she did not seem to be crazy. I finally told her to do what she had to do. She was determined to return to South Bend. We had two cars. She chose to take the Toyota sedan. I gave her most of the money we had. I arranged for the brother of one of my students who lived in Indiana to drive a panel truck with furniture and her clothes to South Bend. I had a meeting in New York City at the Center for Religion and Public Life. Adam came over from Philadelphia. He knew his mother was leaving. We went to the Museum of Modern Art to see a Paul Klee exhibit, had a meal together, and knew we had one another.

I returned home. The house was empty. I broke down in tears. After all those years, I mourned. I had no idea what the future held, but there would be no going back. The marriage was finally over. I was not sure what that meant, but I would do what I had always done. I would put one foot in front of the other and keep going. I got up the next morning and did what I always did. I went to work.

Returning to an empty house did feel odd. But in fact the house was not empty. I had the cats. I am an unapologetic cat lover. We had bought two Siamese kittens in Niles, Michigan, when we lived in South Bend. Adam named them Nip and Tuck. Nip was "not smart," but Tuck was both smart and had dignity. As odd as it may seem, knowing that they were in the house gave me a sense that I was not completely alone. But I was still lonely. Of course, I had been lonely for years. But this was different. I was not lonely because Anne was gone, exactly, but because for the first time in twenty-four years I was no longer married.

What that meant, I think, came home to me in a counseling session after Anne was gone. I continued to see the counselor Anne and I had been seeing for our marriage. Her name was Joann Turnbull. She was a wise lady. In our first session, she asked me what it was like to live with Anne on a daily basis. I told her how I would watch Anne's facial ticks because they sometimes indicated she was going into an episode. Joann responded, "You have certainly lost a job." She was right. I had lost a job. And even though it was a job I would rather not have had, I missed it. I continued to go to counseling with Joann because I knew the years with Anne had created some scars. I did not want those scars to determine my life.

I continued to function well in the everyday. I am not sure how the news got out that Anne had left, but I certainly let Dennis know. He was my dean, and I did not believe that such matters were "private." What was going on in my life could affect the school. I wanted to be as up front as I could be. I also told my friends and students. I remember, in particular, Greg and Susan having me over for a meal. When we prayed, I could not control my tears. Thank God I had friends who knew how to just be there.

IN A SESSION WITH JOANN, I TOLD HER HOW LONELY I FELT. SHE SUGGESTED that I should invite someone out. I was forty-six. I had not been on a date since college. But there was that mysterious person named Paula Gilbert. As far as I knew she had never been married. She seemed unattached. I had no idea how old she was, but it was clear that she was much younger than I. It turned out she was thirty-four. I could not help but be attracted to her, but I had no idea how even to begin to approach her.

We saw one another not only at school but at church. She was coming to the new church Adam and I had begun attending before he went to college. I suspect that, like us, she thought the church had a promising beginning. For example, we hoped that this might be a church that simply assumed celebrating Eucharist every Sunday was the rule. I had once preached in the divinity school chapel when Paula was the celebrant. She was extraordinary. When Paula celebrates you know that you are in the presence of a person who knows God is going to show up. I sensed that God was just "there" for Paula. That God was so present for her at once frightened and intrigued me. It still does.

It was the start of the baseball season. The Bulls were playing a Sunday afternoon game that was to start at two. The church was meeting in a daycare center. I think the service began at ten. There were not that many of us. I suddenly asked Paula if she would like to go to the game. She said she would. I told her I would pick her up at one thirty. I went home, not sure what I had done. The closer it got to one thirty, the less sure of myself I became. I called Greg to see if he could go with us. He could not. Paula and I were going on a date. It was April 12, 1987.

When I drove up in front of her house she was outside inspecting her plants. I may have already been in love with her without knowing it, but the moment I saw her carefully attending to what she had planted I fell completely in love. That I did so was, of course, irrational. But it was also right. Paula does have a love for the particular. She takes the time necessary to see each petunia for its particular beauty. She was going to slow me down.

Paula told me later that she was unsure if it was a date. All she remembers about my picking her up is that I made a disparaging remark about the brickwork on her house. Off we went to the ball game. All my friends at the ballpark immediately fell in love with Paula. One even retrieved a foul ball so that she could have a souvenir.

We stayed through the seventh inning. She had never seen the lemur colony. We went to see the lemurs. She loved the lemurs and wondered about the strange man she was with. She had not suspected I would love animals. I suggested we have supper. We went to my house and made a chef salad. I am not sure what we talked about other than our backgrounds. She had never been married. She had been through some significant relationships, but she was currently attached to no one.

We ate the salad. The evening was still young. I suggested that we go to a movie. We saw a Danish film in Chapel Hill. Then we ate some gelato, went back to my place, and held one another. I did not want to let her go, but this endless date, which may not have even been a date, needed to end sometime. I finally took her home, but not without first making plans to have supper together the next night. That was more than twenty years ago.

When we had supper the next night, I asked her to marry me. She thought I was crazy. She pointed out that I had no idea who she was. I responded that of course I did not know who she was. But I knew she was a Christian. I loved and lusted after her. The rest we could work out. Paula is wise. She understands the complexity of human relationships far better than I do. The great gift she gave me was not to run away from this extraordinarily needy guy. We began to see one another almost every day either for lunch or supper or both. God, how I loved to be with her.

Of course, I was still officially married. I realized that dating Paula might offend some people in the divinity school. Paula and I went to see Dennis to tell him we were dating. I told him I intended to marry Paula, if I could convince her to do so. I let him know that if he thought that was a problem, I would begin to look for another job. He assured us that as long as we conducted ourselves appropriately in the divinity school there was no problem with our dating. The problems would come later.

Anne had gone back to South Bend, still planning to marry Jim Burtchaell. She had set up an apartment and set about the task of convincing him that she was not going away. He made it clear to her that he was not going to marry her. I had put the house in Durham up for sale in order to split the equity with her. Anne wanted to be divorced as soon as possible. North Carolina is a no-fault state, but it takes a year from the last time the couple shared a roof.

I got a lawyer in Durham to prepare a separation agreement. Anne was ready to sign the agreement, but I did not want the divorce to be contested, and I wanted to make sure Anne would not be destitute. So I also hired a good lawyer in South Bend to act on her behalf. Even though my lawyer protested, the separation agreement obligated me to pay Anne monthly alimony. She signed the agreement.

I had been out of town lecturing. When I returned, Gay Trotter told me that Anne had called while I was gone and wanted me to call her back. I called. Her brother David answered the phone. David was a mental health counselor in Lansing, Michigan. I expressed surprise that he had answered. He said, "Oh! You don't know? Anne tried to kill herself. She stabbed herself in the chest. The knife blade broke off, so she didn't bleed to death. She became frightened and called 911. She is in the hospital, but she is going to be OK." I absorbed what he was saying in silence. It took me some time to respond. When I was able to speak, I said, "I am not coming."

It had taken years for me to be able to say that sentence.

CHAPTER 9

Paula

I do not remember how I got through the day after I learned of Anne's suicide attempt. I called Adam that evening so that he would know. I do not remember how I slept. I kept to my routine. I got up early the next day and went to work. As was often the case, John Westerhoff was already in his office. John and I were early risers and usually in our offices before anyone else even considered getting up, except maybe Stuart Henry. We often spent a few minutes at the start of the day catching up or discussing books we were reading.

John, who had his own demons to negotiate, had originally been a UCC minister but was then an Episcopalian priest. John was older than I and was a valued advisor and friend. We even edited a book together, *Schooling Christians*. It deserved more attention than it got. John would eventually retire and move to Atlanta, but that was still in the future. He was there for me that morning. John gave me many gifts but none more important than his response to the news that Anne had tried to kill herself.

I had often shared with John the life I lived with Anne. He knew she had left. I told him of her attempted suicide and my decision not to go to South Bend. This decision, if it even makes sense to call it that, reflected my sense that when Anne left there could be no returning. After years of responding to her illness, I could not let even her attempt to kill herself draw me back into that set of habits. The decision also marked my recognition that as long as Anne had me to blame she would not do what was necessary for her to live with her illness. But it was hard not to go. This was a human being with whom I had lived for twenty-four years. We had been young lovers. We had forged a life together. She had prepared many meals that we had shared. We had bought houses and furnished them. This was Adam's mother. She had, as best she could, cared for him and loved him. Even worse, as I explained to John, was my deep sadness that Anne was now absolutely alone.

John said, "No, she's not. God is with her." We then prayed for her. I believe that God was — and is — with Anne. That does not mean that her life got better. David took her to Lansing. I told him that he needed to be prepared for her to turn her anger on him. She would, I suggested, hate anyone who she thought had control over her life. I would get sporadic phone calls from her suggesting that this is exactly what happened.

Her father called a few years later asking if I was paying her alimony. I assured him that I was. It seems she had not paid her rent for some months. The owner of the apartment building in which she lived had called Mr. Harley to tell him he was going to have the sheriff evict her. He explained that he had to use the sheriff because both he and her neighbors were frightened of her. Mr. Harley told me that he was going to fly to Lansing to see if he could straighten it out.

I will not let myself even try to imagine how Anne lived after she left Durham. She called once to express an interest in knowing what had happened to Adam. I assured her that he was doing well in college. She asked for his phone number. Adam had told me that he did not want any contact with his mother, but I felt so sorry for her. I gave her his number. I phoned him to tell him to expect a call. He was quite angry with me. I said I would pay to have his phone number changed. Before that could happen, she phoned and left a message on his answering machine.

Adam called to tell me he was going to return her call. "I want to get it over with," he said. He wanted to make sure I was available because he would need to talk with me after he had talked to his mother. He recorded the phone call and played it for me: "Mom, this is Adam." "Adam who?" "This is Adam, your son. You called and I'm returning the call to see what you want." "Oh, I was just wondering how you're doing." By this time I can hear Adam breathing. He is hyperventilating. He said, "Mom, this is too hard. I am going to hang up." All she said was, "OK."

Paula

Poor Anne. "Adam who?" Poor Adam. Poor everyone connected with someone who is unable to tell her son she loves him. It was only with that phone call that I finally understood what living with Anne had meant for Adam. I would often counter his complaints by pointing out that many people have much more difficult challenges than living with a mentally ill mother. But as he later said to me, "You were in your thirties. I was seven." I suddenly realized that he did not have the defenses that were available to me. He was right to be angry. But Adam did not become an angry person. He is a wonderful human being.

Anne has been dead for almost ten years. Like her mother, she died in her late fifties of congestive heart failure. She had been living in a controlled living arrangement that allowed her some independence. I know this only because her brother David called to see if I could find her dental records. After she had died some days passed before her body was discovered. The coroner thought he needed her dental records to establish her identity. I tried to get them, but the dentist she had used in Durham had died. Without such records, the coroner finally declared that she was dead.

David explained that he had tried to stay in contact with her, but she often drove him away. I admired him and his family for trying to include her in their life. But the way she died served only to make me acutely aware of how lonely her life had been. That her loneliness was self-imposed does not make it any less sad. What possibly can be said about a life so lived?

I am a Christian theologian. People assume I am supposed to be able to answer that question. I have no idea how to answer that question. If anything, what I have learned over the years as a Christian theologian is that none of us should try to answer such questions. Our humanity demands that we ask them, but if we are wise we should then remain silent. I do think I was writing autobiographically when I wrote *Naming the Silences: God, Medicine, and the Problem of Suffering*. The argument of that book against theodicies was hard learned. When Christianity is assumed to be an "answer" that makes the world intelligible, it reflects an accommodated church committed to assuring Christians that the way things are is the way things have to be.

Such "answers" cannot help but turn Christianity into an explanation. For me, learning to be a Christian has meant learning to live without answers. Indeed, to learn to live in this way is what makes being a Christian so wonderful. Faith is but a name for learning how to go on without knowing the answers. That is to put the matter too simply, but at least such a claim might suggest why I find that being a Christian makes life so damned interesting.

DESPITE MY OWN SENSE OF THE KIND OF CHRISTIAN, AND THE KIND OF THEOlogian, I was becoming, others began to understand me differently — in particular, Jim Gustafson. Largely thanks to Jim, people were beginning to stereotype me as a theological and political reactionary. This was even before Will and I wrote *Resident Aliens*. Jim delivered his first broadside aimed at Lindbeck, Yoder, and me in 1985 at the Catholic Theological Society. According to Jim I was a "sectarian, fideistic, tribalist." Jim, who does not have a conservative bone in his body, had discovered a strategy not unlike those who use the charge of political correctness to put academic liberals on the defensive. The very denial of the charge only confirms the analysis.

I probably have let Jim's and other similar characterizations of my position set the agenda for much of what I have written. No matter how often you deny the choices created by dualistic presuppositions — for example, creation or redemption, sect or church — every denial seems to reproduce the problem. I still think my response to Jim in the introduction to *Christian Existence Today*, which came out in 1985, says what needs to be said, but I suspect that book remains one of my least read books. David Steinmetz and Ed Mahoney, a philosopher at Duke, had started Labyrinth Press. I wanted to be supportive, so I gave the book to them. I do not regret that I did so, but it was not the path to wide readership.

Even if the book had been read widely, I doubt that it would have made much difference. When you are trying to change the questions, you have to realize that many people are quite resistant to such a change. They like the answers they have. People who reacted so strongly against my work thought it unthinkable that I would criticize H. Richard Niebuhr's types in *Christ and Culture,* or that I would question Reinhold Niebuhr's theological legitimating of "democracy." Over time it was probably the case that many such critics had not even read

Paula

Richard or Reinhold, because their answers had become the air and water that sustained mainstream Protestantism in America. I wanted to change the questions because I thought these answers were suffocating the church.

Yet I was teaching in a seminary created by and dedicated to the continuation of mainstream Protestantism. I saw no reason to bite the hand that was feeding me, but neither did I want to lick it. I was not trying to tear down the liberal Protestant establishment, an unnecessary task in any case. It was doing such a good job self-destructing. Rather, I was trying to help Christians begin to develop the habits necessary to sustain the church when most people assumed that "being religious" was a good thing only if you did not take it too seriously. I was trying to suggest that Christianity is a good thing only if you do take it seriously, which means, at the least, that Christians should raise their children to understand that they are part of a people who have a problem with war.

My assumption was that wherever Christians exist they are constituted by words and actions that should — but may not — make their lives difficult. Given, among other things, that Jesus and Paul provide obvious biblical warrant for this assumption, I thought it quite odd that *Resident Aliens* was received as a radical book. All Will and I did was suggest that actions as basic as preaching had radical implications. It is not as if we thought we were reinventing Christianity. We assumed the exact opposite. God can use even a church as accommodated as liberal Protestantism. We were trying to remind Christians that, in the words of Peter Maurin, we were sitting on a keg of dynamite.

Of course, such a position can seem quite threatening to anyone committed to the status quo. I began to sense that Dennis Campbell was beginning to feel some ambivalence about my presence. I had initially been a feather in his cap. Along with a few other faculty he had recruited, I was a strong hire. Initially, it seems he wanted to bring the strongest minds in Methodism to the divinity school. He certainly deserves credit for having done so. But I am not sure he anticipated just how strong a position I represented.

I remained full of enthusiasm for the job I thought Dennis was doing. I suggested to Will that we dedicate *Resident Aliens* to Tommy Langford and Dennis. I noticed a slight hesitancy, but Will did not object. I thought it was important to thank the people who were doing the work to sustain the institutions that made me and my colleagues possible. After all, people like Tommy and Dennis often had to sacrifice their own intellectual passions and work for the good of the school. What I failed to realize was that Dennis had never had that kind of passion for the work of theology. What Dennis had a passion for was to be the dean. That is not a bad thing to want, as long as it is accompanied by the desire to do something as dean. It became increasingly clear to me, however, that as dean Dennis had nothing he wanted to do other than be the dean.

At first Dennis was thrilled that we dedicated the book to him. But later, perhaps after he had read at least parts of the book, he made clear to me that he disagreed with some of the things that Will and I had said. He did not tell me which parts of the book he thought ill considered, but I was not particularly troubled that he was troubled. I had a much greater challenge facing me. How could I get Paula Gilbert to marry me?

I WAS COMPLETELY AND TOTALLY IN LOVE. IT WAS WONDERFUL. I AM SURE I must have been disgusting, but I did not care. I think Paula was also quite happy to be loved. I certainly felt that she loved me. Of course, I was the guy who had argued that love was an insufficient basis for a couple to think that they should be married. I continued to think that I was right about that, but I was also sure that Paula and I should be married — if for no other reason than that it would make our friends happy.

In particular, it would make Stuart Henry happy. Paula was one of his favorite people in the world. He loved her, and he loved seeing us together. We would often share meals with Stuart, usually after we had picked him up at his apartment. Stuart lived in one of the ancient apartment buildings close to Duke. Every room was painted "Henry Gray." He loved monkeys and had a collection of monkey figurines that he had bought on travels he took every summer with his sister, Adelaide. Stuart's existence ensured that our love for one another had to include those who loved us.

Love, particularly in its early stages, is intoxicating and isolating. You are so absorbed in the sheer wonder of the one you love that it seems unnecessary for anyone else to exist. Paula and I were drunk on

Paula

one another, but somehow we avoided cutting ourselves off from other people. Particularly important during the early stages of our learning to love one another were Kelli Walker Jones and Logan Jones.

That Kelli and Logan had to put up with us was fitting, because Paula had originally engineered their relationship. As director of admissions, Paula knew everyone in the divinity school. Occasionally, she would suggest to one person that he or she might like to get to know another person. She thought Kelly, a Methodist, and Logan, a Moravian, would find much in common. She was right. They got married. Kelli later became Paula's assistant, while Logan completed his CPE training. We often went out with them, which was important, particularly for me. I was, after all, the "old guy," but Kelli and Logan treated me like I was part of the gang.

For some people, however, my and Paula's relationship did take some getting used to. For example, some of my graduate students were stunned when they discovered we were dating. I suspect they simply had never imagined that we might be attracted to one another. Greg Jones and Michael Cartwright had known Paula as director of admissions when they were students in the divinity school. So they had to come to see her in a new light. I am happy to say they responded to this "epistemological crisis" in a manner for which I will always be grateful.

David Jenkins, a student who had first come to Notre Dame to study with me but who was now at Duke, was also particularly important for our relationship. David had studied for the ministry at Yale. I first met David when I was teaching in London. At the time, he was serving as pastor in a United Methodist church in Oriental, North Carolina. He was in London leading a tour of Methodists who came to "follow in the steps of Wesley." We took a long walk — not, I am happy to say, in Wesley's footsteps — during which he told me that he was considering doing graduate work at Notre Dame. I liked him and encouraged him to apply. Some years later I asked David why he was so anxious to meet me before applying to the Ph.D. program at Notre Dame. He said he realized that graduate work was an apprenticeship, and he did not want to apprentice under a son of a bitch. Such a judgment I took to be an indication that David was a serious human being.

He did not stay long at Notre Dame. He left to explore what it might mean to become a monk at Taize. He wrote to me, observing that there was not sufficient laughter at Taize. Instead he went to London to work as an assistant at the Vine, a L'Arche community. I think it was David's involvement with L'Arche that first caused me to realize that this was a movement I needed to learn more about.

David did finally decide to return to Ph.D. studies, only this time at Duke, not Notre Dame. During the time he worked on his Ph.D. he also served as the director of the Wesley Foundation. Before David, the Wesley Foundation was more or less dead. He brought it back to life through Eucharistic celebration and mission trips to Central America. He recruited Paula to celebrate the Eucharist for the Wesley undergraduates. He knew us both well before we were dating, and therefore it was significant when he told Paula that he thought we would be good for one another.

Many people thought otherwise. People like David who knew us both knew just how different we were from one another. To say that Paula is an introvert and that I am an extrovert does not do justice to those descriptions. Paula is contemplative. I am not. In another life, in another time, Paula would have been an abbess. There is a quietness at her center that reaches out to God. I have no doubt that she is rightly a priest. I have no doubt that I am rightly not a priest. Few things are more important in my life than supporting her calling.

But her calling was part of the problem. She was sure she was called to the ministry. She was not sure she was called to be married. The very fact that she used the language of "calling" with regard to marriage indicated that she was different. I liked the difference, but I did not want that difference to mean that she might not end up marrying me.

For all our differences, Paula and I have similar backgrounds. We both come from conventional, good people who knew how to work. Her dad worked for the railroad. Her mother worked as a volunteer in organizations like the Girl Scouts. Paula grew up assuming that unions and Methodism were good ideas. Her middle-class roots probably place her a bit higher on the social hierarchy than my working-class roots place me, but we both assume that you have to work for a living.

Indeed, I think one of the things that attracted me to Paula was the dedication she brings to her work. Paula works. In particular, she does what needs to be done without assuming she will be rewarded for doing so. She never forgets, moreover, that the people for whom and with

Paula

whom she works are people. She has a "pastoral sense" that to care rightly for people requires that you tell them the truth.

That is the Paula I encountered at Duke. She was a "strong woman." She had somehow negotiated a largely male world without becoming angry or bitter. I have no idea how she did that. Nor do I have any idea what it meant for Paula to have been young. She told me that I would not have liked her when she was young. Perhaps she was right. But I knew I certainly liked her now that she was grown up. Of course, she was still young when we began dating, but in many ways she was wiser about the ways of the world than I was. That has not changed. I can be quite unrealistic. Every time I have trusted someone whom Paula does not, she has been right and I have been wrong. It is damned aggravating.

Paula is from Mobile, Alabama, which means she is as Southern as they come. She went to Huntingdon College in Montgomery. Huntingdon was originally a finishing school to make Southern ladies out of young girls. By the time Paula got to Huntingdon, it had become a school much like Southwestern, that is, vaguely Methodist with a liberal arts curriculum. She took full advantage of her education, majoring in English and religion.

Paula never had my doubts about being a Christian, nor did she grow up thinking she might go into the ministry. That happened because she went "north" to go to divinity school. She went to Duke Divinity School because one of her professors told her it might be a good idea. If you are in divinity school you have to do summer fieldwork. That is how Paula discovered she was called to the ministry. People told her she should seek ordination. She was ordained in the Alabama/West Florida Conference of the United Methodist Church.

Yet she was also encouraged by her teachers at Duke to do a Ph.D. W. D. Davies wanted her to specialize in New Testament, but she chose to work under Stuart in American church history. After she completed her exams, Tommy Langford, then dean of the divinity school, asked her to serve as director of admissions. She was writing on Georgia Harkness, but progress on her dissertation was slowed because of her work in admissions. She finished her dissertation just before we began dating.

That someone goes into the ministry does not ensure that she is a serious Christian. It quickly became apparent to me, however, that Paula was a serious Christian. We began dating just before Holy Week. I discovered that going through Holy Week with Paula means that you really go through Holy Week. The heart of her life is the worship of God. I do not know whence that came. I do know that this is simply who Paula is. For her the ministry is not the name of a "helping profession." You do not need to be ordained to help people. Rather, she clearly thinks that she was ordained to preside at the Eucharist.

This is the Paula I was trying to convince to marry me, in spite of my own judgments that in fact marriage might be a bad idea. Yoder had persuaded me that singleness was the first way of life for Christians. To be a Christian means you do not have to marry or have a child. The church is constituted by a people who grow through witness and conversion, not through biological ascription. A church in which the single rather than the married bear the burden of proof is one that inexorably legitimates violence in the name of protecting "our" children from those who think they need to kill to protect "their" children. The problem is not children, but the possessive pronouns. Even as I found myself trying to convince Paula to marry me, I thought that she was quite right to assume that she might be called to a life of singleness. I was caught.

Of course there were other issues. She was thirty-four. I was forty-six. Not long before we began to date she had bought a house in which she took great pride. She did not want to give it up. She had developed habits of living alone. She did not want to have to negotiate someone else on a daily basis. Would her cat be willing to live with my cats?

There was also the little problem that I was Stanley Hauerwas. Why would she want to have to deal with that? What, moreover, would it mean for her to become an adult parent to an adult child? Then there was the problem that, as she put it, "I'm just not sure this is going to work. You just have so many people in your life." That was true.

During the time that Paula and I were dating the Society of Christian Ethics met in Durham. I am not an academic that enjoys going to academic meetings. I have, however, been a loyal member of the Society of Christian Ethics and have seldom missed a meeting since graduating from Yale. I have so many friends who have worked hard to make that society a place of genuine conversation. In spite of the differences in our training, people in the society usually share enough in common to have a good argument. I think the "ethics" espoused by members of the society is often too thin theologically. Nonetheless, I find the annual meeting congenial. I believe I have the distinction of being the only person not elected to be president — twice.

For the meeting in Durham, I was responsible for all the arrangements. Greg and Susan Jones did all the real work to make it happen. In conjunction with the meeting, we planned a banquet for Paul Ramsey. When Paul and I were working on *Speak Up for Just War and Pacifism*, I discovered that he had no place to donate his papers. One thing led to another, and Paul agreed to give them to Duke. The banquet was to be the formal occasion at which Paul was to bestow this gift to the university. The occasion carried added weight because soon after Paul and I had finished *Speak Up for Just War and Pacifism* he learned that he was dying. We decided to have the banquet just before the start of the society's meeting so that the many people in the society who were Paul's friends could attend. Paul was sick, but he came and gave a rousing speech.

At the time, Yoder was president of the society. It is expected that the president will give an address to the whole society. John gave as his presidential address an extraordinarily eloquent speech entitled "To Serve Our God and to Rule the World." Paula and I sat with Paul Ramsey, listening to John Howard Yoder. John told us that to learn to see the world doxologically, to rule the world in fellowship with the living Lamb, sometimes will mean humbly building a grassroots culture. Other times it will mean helping a pagan king solve one problem at a time. Still other times it will mean disobeying the king's imperative of idolatry. Paul Ramsey had ears better than most to hear what Yoder was saying. He was generous in his praise of John's speech. He would live only a short time past this momentous occasion.

Paula was rightly concerned that I had too many people in my life. But as she began to meet them, she discovered that she liked them, and that they liked her. That Paula and I were able to witness the regard these two giants had for one another remains one of the singular most important moments of our lives. I have strong doubts whether the very idea of "ethics" is a good idea, but I will continue to go to meetings of the Society of Christian Ethics because Paul Ramsey and John Howard

Yoder went to these meetings. Moreover, part of what it means for me to love Paula is to remember her sitting without fear next to my dying friend.

When you are in love, and I was deeply in love, it is difficult to see clearly the one you love. We are opaque mysteries to ourselves and one another. I do not know if I saw clearly who Paula was. But I knew she was good for me. And I hoped I was good for her. A single life can fold in on itself. I had no doubt that I was complicating Paula's life. I had no doubt that I continue to complicate her life. My life is noisy. Her life is quiet. My gift to her is a life filled with people. Her gift to me is stillness.

We were inseparable. I loved courtship. Most days we had supper together. What a joy it was to ask, "How was your day?" Love is constituted by the small things shared. Of course, baseball is not a small thing. When we began to date, Paula liked baseball. She did not, however, follow the Braves. I did. Paula quickly became a fan. In particular, she was enamored with Tommy Glavin. She admired how he never gave in. One night at supper she looked at me with loving eyes and said, "We're only three out." I thought this just might work.

We needed to meet one another's families. Laura, Paula's sister, came to visit us in Durham. My folks came and fell in love with Paula. At least my father fell in love with Paula. I am not sure what Mother thought, other than that she was glad to see me happy. We went to Mobile. I am sure Mr. and Mrs. Gilbert must have thought me quite strange, but they seemed to like me. I told Mr. Gilbert that I intended to marry Paula, with his permission, of course. I am at least that much of a Southerner.

Adam was a junior in college. He had known Paula because we went to the same church. I am sure he found it odd for his father to be in love. He and Paula seemed to like one another, but that I loved Paula, as well as wanted to marry her, could not help but change Adam's and my relationship. I think Adam sensed more than I did what such a change might mean to our relationship. He liked being with us, he enjoyed seeing me in love and happy, but he was not sure where that left him. Thus his observation at the time of our marriage that "this was the real divorce."

But I still had to convince Paula to marry me. Paula remained reticent. As a Southerner, she thought "maybe" was a definitive position.

Paula

I had sold the house. Paula had hunted for a new house with me. We found one we both liked. I bought it with her name joining mine on the deed. We had been dating for over a year. I had continued to be counseled by Joann. I once complained that I just wished Paula would make up her mind. Joann pointed out that I had either forgotten or never learned that relationships require constant work. My life with Anne had been difficult, but it had not really been a "relationship." Anne's illness perhaps had prevented me from learning that the work of love is never over.

I finally told Paula that I loved her but was unsure how much longer I could live with the "maybe." I was beginning to think it just might not work out. I did not want to think that, but by then I knew Paula well enough to know that her life could be lived without me. Then a miracle happened on October 27, 1988. We were sharing a plate of bad nachos in The Country Kitchen, a restaurant in the Indianapolis airport. She told me she would marry me. I had to ask her to say it again. She did.

I have no idea why Paula agreed to marry me over bad nachos in the Indianapolis airport. We were on our way back from DePauw University. By chance we had ended up there. Paula, as director of admissions, often went to represent Duke at colleges that sponsored "seminary days." She was scheduled to go to DePauw University in Greencastle, Indiana, for their event. I had been asked to deliver the Mendenhall Lecture and to receive an honorary degree at DePauw at the same time. Millard Fuller, the founder of Habitat for Humanity, was the other honoree.

The lectures were held in the Mendenhall Chapel, a Methodist church, which Jamison Jones had once served. I delivered two lectures that were early versions of material that made its way into *Resident Aliens*. As I delivered the lectures, I noticed that Paula was really listening. I had a sense that she was saying to herself, "This strange man really believes what he is saying." It was a lovely occasion, made all the more special for me because I was able to share it with Paula. I have no idea what, if anything, "happened" at DePauw that caused Paula finally to agree to marry me. But I returned to Durham a happy man.

We told our friends we were engaged. We bought her ring. Our lives were in Durham and Duke. It made sense that we should be married in Duke Chapel. It is not easy to be married in Duke Chapel. Too many people want to be married in Duke Chapel. But Paula found a date, May 18, 1989. Our friends and family were alerted. We asked Will Willimon and Nancy Ferree-Clark, one of Paula's close friends and associate minister of the chapel, to officiate.

With the wedding date set and wedding plans in motion, we were suddenly confronted by the possibility that Paula might not have a future in the divinity school. She had told Dennis Campbell previously that as much as she loved her work she would like to gain wider administrative experience in the divinity school. At the time, she served not only as director of admissions but also as dean of student life and minister to York Chapel. Moreover, she directed summer Course of Study for United Methodist local pastors, and taught the basic course in American church history. God knows how she did it.

Dennis offered her the opportunity to assume a new position that would have responsibility for planning and new programs. It was not clear exactly what Dennis wanted Paula to accomplish in this position. Nonetheless, we decided that it offered her an opportunity to become more familiar with what is involved in running a divinity school. Paula does what is asked of her, but she is not without ambition. She entertained the idea that one day she might like to be the associate dean of the divinity school. Moreover, even with the new position, she would continue to have many of her prior responsibilities, but she would no longer be director of admissions.

Dennis had expressed to me on several occasions that he was concerned about what he characterized as the "feminization of the ministry." The loss of status and prestige once associated with the ministry meant that men no longer found the ministry attractive. Women, however, who had been long excluded, were increasingly discovering the ministry. Seemingly working from these assumptions, Dennis hired a young man to serve as the new director of admissions.

In her new position, Paula found it frustrating that her work was largely undefined, but she stood ready to do what Dennis asked. Dennis had a different plan. As the second semester began, Dennis told her the position would not be renewed. She would have to find another job. Moreover, there would be no job for her in the divinity school. She was stunned. Neither of us had imagined that our marriage might involve a change in her status in the divinity school. But as Dennis put it to her: "Your husband has tenure. You do not. He stays. You do not."

Paula loved the divinity school. Her presence was particularly important for women going into the ministry. It was hard to imagine her doing anything else. She told Dennis she was completely unprepared for his unexpected decision. She was not even sure under the circumstances what it meant for our upcoming marriage. Dennis relented, assuring her of employment for the coming year. At the time, we did not suspect that Dennis did not think husbands and wives should be employed in the same unit of the university. Later he would tell me what a bad idea he thought it was for the English Department to have hired both Stanley Fish and Jane Tompkins. "What," he said, "do you do if they get divorced?" I could not understand the problem.

We knew we faced an uncertain future, but we hoped something could be worked out. We directed our attention to our upcoming wedding. All kinds of arrangements had to be made. I tried to be as much help as I could, but I am sure I was not much help. Still, I thoroughly enjoyed the planning and even more the wedding itself. We had fun at the rehearsal and the rehearsal dinner. Paula and I share a deep love of hot Mexican food. Indeed, Paula can eat me under the table when it comes to hot. David Jenkins had told us of a restaurant in Chapel Hill called the Flying Burrito. It was owned and run by Phil Campbell. Paula and I soon began eating at the Burrito at least twice a week. The Raging Bull, a jalapeño-stuffed burrito, was our favorite meal. We were the first to eat the even hotter Ultimate Raging Bull, a burrito Phil made with habaneros. Phil cooked our rehearsal dinner.

We wanted our marriage to be part of the liturgy. There was a full procession with a crucifer. Adam carried high the Scripture. Students from the divinity school had volunteered to be a choir. Will preached, making reference to the lion and lamb lying together, which elicited an unexpected uproar of laughter from those gathered to witness our marriage. We exchanged vows. Nancy Ferree-Clark celebrated the Eucharist.

Many of our friends were there. Greg, who now taught at Loyola College in Maryland, came with Susan and our mutual friend Jim Buckley. David Burrell and Jim Burtchaell came. What a gift their presence was. They had become quite fond of Paula. I had left Notre Dame, but they came to Duke to witness this special event in our lives. Robert and Carol Wilken came from Charlottesville, where Robert was now on the faculty at the University of Virginia. The whole Duke community turned out. More people came than we expected. We came close to running out of food at the reception.

We were married. I was married. I could not have been happier. We went to Ireland, Scotland, and England for our honeymoon. We must have still been young to have the energy for such a trip. In Ireland, we went to Glendalough, Cashel, the ring of Kerry, the cliffs of Moher, the Burren, and Galway, before ending up in Dublin. Enda told us one of his friends wanted to host a celebration of our marriage. So we found ourselves at a wonderful dinner hosted by Garret Fitzgerald, who had recently been Taoiseach, the Irish equivalent of prime minister. Only the Irish could have such a person as their leader. During the alcohol-fueled festivities, he leaned over to ask, "What do you make of MacIntyre's work?"

Enda had another engagement and was not able to be at Fitzgerald's feast, but the next day he entertained us at St. Patrick's, Maynooth. It was Sunday, so we went first to Mass, then to Maynooth. Enda often entertained his friends at Maynooth. Indeed he entertained so many one year that he used up his entire salary. We had a wonderful time. Sean and Gail Freyne were at Fitzgerald's and at Maynooth. I had met Sean when he came to teach at Notre Dame in the summers. Everyone loved Paula. I loved Paula being loved by friends that Notre Dame had made possible.

We took the train from Scotland to London but stopped in Durham. I had delivered the Pastoral Lectures at the University of Durham the March prior to our marriage. Learning of our honeymoon plans, Dan and Perrin Hardy, who would be gone during the time we expected to be in Durham, invited us to stay in their rooms in the cathedral close. We loved hearing Evensong sung in the cathedral. We then made our way to London, where we joined up with Stuart Henry and his sister Adelaide. They had just returned from Italy, as one stage of their annual vacation. On our way to enjoy a meal together Stuart saved Paula, who had looked the wrong way, from being run over by a bus.

Paula

OUR LIFE TOGETHER HAD BEGUN. IF OUR HONEYMOON WAS ANY INDICATION, it was going to be a life constituted by church, friendships, and travel. In Durham our church was Aldersgate United Methodist Church in Chapel Hill. Unfortunately, the church we had attended when we first began to date became tempted to use church growth strategies. We left quietly. Paula suggested that we go to Aldersgate, where the pastor was Susan Allred. Susan was a "late vocation." She and Paula had been friends in seminary. Paula rightly held Susan in high regard. Susan was not an intellectual, but everything she did would have been unintelligible if the God we worship as Christians does not exist.

I loved Susan. I loved the people who attended Aldersgate. We usually had sixty to eighty people in attendance. There was absolutely nothing obviously impressive about Aldersgate. I think that is one of the reasons I liked it so much. This small church took responsibility for cooking the Sunday evening meal at the homeless shelter. This small church had three people called to the ministry. This small church studied and discussed for a year whether we should become a "reconciling congregation," that is, a church that welcomed gay people. This small church had a softball team on which our best player was a woman and on which I played. This small church observed the liturgical year and celebrated the Eucharist most Sundays. This small church had moved to a full Holy Week set of services.

For many years, Paula and I gave all we had to Aldersgate. Paula often celebrated and preached. I sometimes preached. I particularly liked to preach when Paula celebrated. I even taught sixth-graders for a short period. The period was short because apparently I had no special gifts for teaching sixth-graders. We were humbled by the quiet and good lives of those who worshiped at Aldersgate. Wanda, for example, was a code breaker for the Navy during World War II. She told us on lay Sunday how in the process of teaching young Japanese women how to quilt she had discovered how horrible the bombing of Japan had been. She joined a protest movement of quilters against war. They encircle the Pentagon with peace quilts.

People often ask, "Where is the church you allege is so central for the world? Where is the church that is the necessary condition for rightly knowing the way things are? Where is the church that is the end of war?" I believe with all my heart that this church is present in congregations like Aldersgate. Aldersgate is not an exception. Such congregations exist everywhere, but we have to be able to recognize them for what they are. Susan would often begin her sermons by observing that she could not "think the church up." She could not imagine an Aldersgate, but God can and does. What a wonderful way to put it. Gathered together in churches like Aldersgate, we are God's imagination for the world. What a gift that Paula and I were welcomed by such a people. What a gift that they rejoiced in our marriage.

Susan's husband, Herb, was a wonderful man who for many years was a junior-high principal in Chapel Hill. Herb loved Susan, his students, and Carolina pottery. Forced to retire by a new school superintendent, Herb gave the church his gift of arranging flowers. He died of a stroke. He was so beloved in Chapel Hill that we knew our tiny church would not be able to accommodate the many people who would come to his funeral. Next door to Aldersgate was Saint Thomas More Catholic Church. They graciously loaned us their building, even though they knew a woman, Paula, would conduct the service and celebrate the Eucharist.

My life with Paula is constituted by the church. I have no idea how our marriage would work otherwise. We are different people. A friend once observed that we go to church a lot. That is true. We do go to church "a lot." We do so because we can think of nothing we would rather do than to go to church. There are many other things we love to do together, but finally what it means for us to be together involves our going to church "a lot."

Our marriage is also constituted by friends. Friendship can threaten as well as enrich a marriage. Friends change you. In doing so, they can change what it means to be married. We often think of marriage as quintessential friendship. But in fact marriage depends not upon friendship but upon an unconditional promise two people make to one another and to God that they will remain together to the end. Such a promise does not depend upon friendship. Rather, it enables the risks that make friendship possible. Of course, in good marriages two people do become friends with one another, but such marriages also thrive on the changes in the relationship that other friends can bring. I thank God that Paula and I are friends, and that our marriage and friendship are enriched through friendship with others.

Paula

Paula often has to help me "get" what a friend is trying to tell me. David Jenkins tried to tell me he was gay. He told me he had been invited to live with a young man who often came to church with him. I told him I thought that would be a good idea, because I worried that he might be lonely. He told me he was going to march in a parade supporting the mayor of Durham, who had signed a law against sexual discrimination in city hiring practices. Since I thought that such a law would be just, I commended his involvement. Paula finally had to tell me David was gay.

I remain unsure if we can call the relationship between gay people "marriage," but I know that David's friendship enriches Paula's and my marriage. I hope and pray for the day when Christians can be so confident in their understanding of marriage that we can welcome gay relationships for their promise of building up the body of Christ. That I have such a hope and that I pray such a prayer have everything to do with my and Paula's friendship with David. I think, moreover, that this is the way it should work.

We became particularly close to Tommy and Ann Marie Langford. When I first told Tommy that I was dating Paula and hoped to marry her, he said, "That might work." Tommy had become a close confidant the year before Anne left. After one particularly intense verbal assault that Anne had leveled at me, he even tried to help me imagine moving out. Ann Marie and Tommy were close friends with Stuart Henry, which meant we often shared meals together. Tommy was a wise man who would play a crucial role in enabling Paula and me to stay at Duke.

Grady and Rowena Hardin were also our close friends. Grady had retired from Perkins School of Theology, where for many years he had taught preaching. Grady and Rowena were originally from North Carolina. I suggested to Dennis Campbell that Grady's retirement gave us an opportunity to bring him back to Duke to teach preaching. He did come back, and Rowena worked in the bookstore, having run a Cokesbury store previously at Perkins.

I knew Grady and Rowena in Texas because Louise, their older daughter, was a student for a short time at Southwestern. I gave her rides from Georgetown to Dallas. Grady and Rowena had known my mother and father through church circles. And Daddy and I had laid the brick for an addition they put on their house in Highland Park.

Grady had also come to Southwestern to give a speech during a symposium we were having on race. I gave a speech at the event castigating segregationists. Grady told me later that I was so self-righteous that he had been tempted to become a segregationist. He was a wonderful man with amazing rhetorical gifts. Paula and I loved to hear him preach.

We loved the Hardins and their daughters. Their younger daughter, Nancy, lived in Durham. For a time, we were close to her and her partner. Grady was killed by a fast-acting cancer. Paula conducted the funeral, a sign of how deeply our lives were tied together. Rowena later suffered a stroke that made speech difficult. But for some years she played an important role in our lives.

Not all of our growing friendships were connected to the university. The undergraduates put on a spring festival for artists. Paula and I were nearing our first anniversary. We thought we might buy something we both liked. A young man came to the event to display his marble sculptures. You cannot sell marble sculptures to undergraduates. But Paula and I fell in love with him and his work. The next day he brought more pieces to our house. Thus began our long relationship with Bill Moore.

I have no idea how many pieces of Bill's work we have bought over the years, but our house and yard are full of his sculptures. Paula and I make a lot of money. At least, it seems like a lot of money given where we came from. What better way to get rid of our money than to help local artists. We buy a lot of art. We are fortunate to live in an area where so many good artists work. We also like to buy art when we travel. We like to bring home art that will remind us of where we have been. One of our favorite pieces is of Mary and the baby Jesus, by the Irish sculptor Imogene Stuart. Enda introduced us to Imogene and her work.

I am not sure we anticipated when we married how important beauty would be for us. We have remarkably similar tastes. We love abstract art. We love bold colors and graceful curves. Light, bright light, floods our home. Every week we go to the farmers' market to buy flowers that Paula arranges and stations throughout our home. We are fortunate people.

Friendship is often a matter of place. For several years we lived next door to Stanley Fish and Jane Tompkins. We liked them both. Stanley is one of the most competitive and kind people I know. I loved to run with Stanley. Once, as we ran the neighborhood, I told him I knew his secret. In spite of his criticism of liberals, he cannot help but be one. He stopped, looked at me, and said, "Don't you tell anyone."

Paula and I love to work in the yard. We are always planting something the deer end up eating. We can hardly blame the deer. We are living in their woods. Stanley found it completely mysterious that we were always doing something in the yard and that I did my own mowing. Jane, on the other hand, thought yard work was a way to work for peace. She was so upset by the start of the first war against Iraq that she bought a flowering tree to plant in their backyard. I dug the hole for it. Though Stanley and Jane have long since moved, we continue to enjoy Jane's peace tree.

We had not expected to be in Australia on the first anniversary of our marriage. Paula and I had often discussed places we might like to go. We both thought that someday we would like to go to Australia and New Zealand. So when I received a letter from Bruce Kaye, the master of New College of the University of New South Wales, inviting me to give the New College Lectures, we accepted. We had no idea how important going to Australia would be. Bruce and Louise Kaye would become our closest and dearest friends.

I THOUGHT THE INVITATION TO GIVE THE NEW COLLEGE LECTURES WAS A good opportunity for me to develop more fully the philosophical and theological background Will and I had assumed in *Resident Aliens*. The lectures thus became something of a sequel when they were published as *After Christendom?* It did not occur to me that some people would find this book more controversial than *Resident Aliens*. I thought my use of Rowan Williams's account of Augustine might indicate that the question mark in the title was not accidental.

In *After Christendom?* I was not trying to write a more scholarly book than *Resident Aliens*. Rather, I was trying to write a book to counter some of the easy dismissals of *Resident Aliens*. I ended up only making matters worse. But I am not sure it was entirely my fault. It also had something to do with what I think is a false distinction between popular and scholarly work. Not all Christians need to read the work of theologians, but some Christians outside the academy do need to be able to do so. And I write for those Christians as much as I do for other academics.

I find it frustrating that the arguments I develop in books like *After Christendom?* are often ignored by my scholarly critics. People who focus on my "exaggerations" too often fail to see how they function to invite thought. For example, critics who focused on the claim in the subtitle of *After Christendom?* that justice is a "bad idea" often failed to attend to the detailed arguments I developed in the text. The subtitle itself — *How the Church Is to Behave If Freedom, Justice, and a Christian Nation Are Bad Ideas* — was created by the publisher to give symmetry to the chapter titles. No doubt it is a provocative title. But it is frustrating that some people dismissed the book because of such provocation. Damn it, I did my homework. Some critics were upset by my title, but they did not go on to suggest that I got Richard Rorty or John Rawls wrong. Or that I misunderstood MacIntyre on craft and was thus mistaken about an alternative epistemology. Or that the relationship I posit between the sexual revolution and the growth of power of the nation-state was misplaced.

When I gave the lectures that became *After Christendom?* in Australia, they were well received. I have always found my work better received in England and places like Australia than in the United States. I am not sure why. I suspect that it may be due to the absence of a civil religion in a context like Australia. If Locke is the public philosopher of America, Bentham plays that role in Australia. The difference is stark because no one assumes that Australian society depends on some generalized religiosity. Accordingly, Christians in Australia are not burdened with the notion that the future of Australia depends on them.

Of course, I may also be better received in Australia because Australians bear an uncanny resemblance to Texans. Their history ensures that, like Texans, they do not have anything to live up to. It has become fashionable in Australia to show that your family can be traced to a convict. It is thus hard to be an Australian and live with pretensions. As a result, Australians are a lot like Texans — what you see is what you get.

Paula is a great reader. Much of the time we share is spent reading. We both love murder mysteries. Before we visit a country, we try to read some of their murder mysteries. In preparation for going to Australia, we discovered Arthur Upfield. Upfield was English but spent

Paula

most of his life in Australia. He wrote detective fiction, creating a won-derful investigator who was half aboriginal and half white. He solved mysteries by combining modern detective procedures and the arts of the aboriginals. We learned much about Australia from Upfield.

Bruce picked us up at the airport. We had flown through New Zealand because we planned a vacation there after I had lectured in Australia. That meant the trip had lasted thirty-six hours, but during the layover in Auckland we had been able to shower and rest a bit. We thought we felt good. We were glad to have supper with Bruce and Louise. I went to sleep in my plate.

Friendship between couples is a complex business. There is a lot going on, but we had suddenly found in Bruce and Louise friends. That we were Christians made all the difference. We also shared an analo-gous history. Bruce had become a Christian and a priest in the Anglican Church even though his family was not Christian. Quite disaffected with Sydney Anglicanism, he left Australia to do his Ph.D. in New Testament in Basel. He then taught at St. John's College in Durham, England. Tragically, his wife died, leaving him with two small children to care for. Offered the job of Master of New College, he returned to Australia.

Louise was an Australian trained to practice medicine in England. A dedicated Christian, she had been on the board of New College and was therefore acquainted with Bruce. Like Paula, she had never been married. Bruce soon set out to put an end to that. I do not know if Lou-ise made Bruce wait in the way Paula made me wait. By the time we met them, their son was already in university and their daughter was soon to enter.

On our first anniversary, Bruce and Louise took us to the Blue Mountains. On the way, Paula got to pet a koala, a wombat, and no telling how many wallabies. The day was magical. The brightly colored birds on the mountain captivated us. We loved being with Bruce and Louise. Returning, we stopped to have tea at an old hotel, during which we witnessed a beautiful sunset. We were entranced.

We were with Bruce and Louise for over a week. We had assumed that we would never return to Australia, but by the time we left them, we knew we would be back. We were friends. Our friendship meant that distance somehow had to be overcome. Bruce became general secretary to the Church of Australia. That meant he sometimes had to travel to England and America. He was once "stuck" with us for over a week because he could not get to the meeting he had come to attend. The meeting began on September 11, 2001.

We have been back to Australia twice, and we will return again. We have been with Bruce and Louise in England, seen the American West with them, shared a wonderful vacation in Ireland, toured Tasmania, and shown them parts of the American South. Whatever it means to be a Christian, it at least involves the discovery of friends you did not know you had. Bruce and Louise have been for us that grace.

The lecture circuit Bruce had planned for me took us across Australia. We went to Canberra, Melbourne, and Perth. From Perth, we flew back to New Zealand, rented a car, and set out to see that extraordinary land. Paula and I never plan a trip. We just go, quite happy to be surprised by what we find. No matter where you are in New Zealand you will be happy with what you find.

THE TRIP TO AUSTRALIA AND NEW ZEALAND GAVE US THE TIME AND SPACE we needed to adjust to the new reality we faced in Durham. When we returned, Paula would no longer work in the divinity school, although she would direct summer Course of Study one last time. Course of Study is the program offered during the summer for people serving Methodist churches who cannot go to seminary. Students in Course of Study include, for example, former truck drivers who have not gone to college but for whom Jesus has made all the difference. Course of Study students loved Paula, and she loved them. It was fitting that her last task in the divinity school would be to direct Course of Study.

Before going to Australia, I had been contacted by Southern Methodist University to see if I was interested in one of their newly established chairs in ethics. My friend Bill May had already assumed one of the chairs. I explained to Bill that not only was I crosswise with my dean, but Paula needed a job. It turned out that the provost at SMU needed an associate provost, and she thought Paula might well be a candidate for the position. We were interviewed in Dallas and offered the positions. The chair came with an annual salary of more than $100,000 and a course load of only two courses a year.

Paula

I informed Dennis Campbell and Tommy Langford, who was serving as provost. Dennis called me to his office. He was holding the offer letter from SMU with obvious disdain. He told me that the divinity school had no equivalent chair. He said he could not counter the offer from SMU. I would need to decide to stay at Duke or go to SMU. He had clearly decided that I was going to take the position at SMU. Had the decision been mine, he probably would have been right. But he had never really understood Paula.

I had been at Duke six years. I liked the university and the divinity school. I particularly liked my graduate students. The one thing I did not want to lose was my work with these wonderful people. The position at SMU had a huge research budget, which I was assured I could use to come back to Duke to work with the graduate students who had come to study with me. However, Dennis told me that he would not allow me to do that. I do not know if he could have stopped me, but the very suggestion made me mad as hell.

Even worse, he suggested that I was trying to force him to give Paula a job because she was now my wife. Nothing could have been further from the truth. I thought she should have a job in the divinity school because of how valuable her work was for the school. I explained that Paula thought her work in the divinity school was one of the ways her ordination found expression. Dennis told me that Paula had no ministerial calling. If she did, he said, she would go out and get a church. I said, "Dennis, this is the last serious conversation you and I will ever have." Then I left the room.

Tommy did not want us to leave. He was the provost but could not override a decision of one of his deans. He could, however, find Paula a job. There was an opening in the continuing education office, which was headed by a wonderful woman named Judith Ruderman. Paula interviewed with Judith and was offered the job. I still thought we would go to SMU. I did not give a damn about the money or the chair. I just did not like the way Paula was being treated.

We had several conversations with Tommy. I well understood that SMU and Duke were not in the same league, but I had never been impressed by pretension. Tommy was serving as provost because Phillip Griffiths, a distinguished mathematician under whose leadership as provost Duke had made such strides, was on sabbatical. I had come to admire Phillip by serving on several university committees he chaired. He asked to see us. He could do little, other than assure us that deans come and go. But he made it clear that he did not want us to leave.

We left his spare office in the physics building. We had to come to a decision. Paula loved Duke. Even more, she loved the church. She thought the work I was doing with the graduate students was important for the church. She did not want that lost. She decided we would stay. I was happy to do so, but I knew that I would now have to find a new way to negotiate the divinity school. I had assumed when I was hired that as a member of the faculty I would work with the dean to help determine the future of the school. I was now unsure what role I might play.

I deeply regret that I have had to tell the story about why we almost left Duke. I have never regretted that Paula decided we would stay. I regret that the grace of Paula has not had the presence I think it should have had for those studying for the ministry. On the other hand, her talents as an administrator were soon recognized. When Judith became vice provost, Paula became dean of summer session, director of continuing studies, and associate dean in Trinity College at Duke. The divinity school's loss was the university's gain.

The main reason I regret telling the story is that I think such conflicts diminish everyone involved. It is often remarked that academic battles are so nasty because so little is at stake. Such a comment is dead wrong. Often much is at stake. Battles in the university today will have effects on wider society in the next generation. Indeed, one of my main worries about current universities is that we are not having the conflicts we need to have for the good of future generations.

Of course, the conflict we were having with Dennis did not seem to involve anything so important. Most people internal and external to the university, and I suspect most of my colleagues at the time, would have regarded what was happening as no more than a personal issue. It certainly was that, but personal matters are intellectual issues. That is particularly true in matters Christian. That we were locked in such an intractable situation indicates that we could not discover the truthful speech demanded of us as Christians.

I also fear that telling the story as I have may suggest that Dennis was the "heavy." I have no doubt that he was doing what he thought he needed to do to be responsible to the office he held. I have a high regard for those who become chairs, deans, provosts, and other administrators in the university. I do not like the assumption that those who take on the responsibilities of those positions have given up on intellectual work. I think such positions demand the most serious intellectual work in the university. Moreover, there are peculiar moral demands on those who hold these positions. For example, people who occupy such offices cannot let their likes and dislikes of this or that person shape the decisions they must make for the good of the whole. The ascetic character of the rightful exercise of power is seldom appreciated.

I suspect that Dennis regretted losing my friendship and support. Given our deep differences, this was probably inevitable, but it did not have to occur in quite so dramatic a fashion. In the months and years that followed, I found myself trying to have sympathy for Dennis. This was not a matter of charity on my part. I simply did not want him to play an important role in my life. To stay angry at him made him more than he was. I had to find a way to go on.

I began to think that my future in the divinity school depended on me being what I said I was, that is, nonviolent. I am not by nature nonviolent. It is not a natural stance. But one slow step at a time I tried to learn not to live a life determined by what I was against. Peace is a deeper reality than violence. That is an ontological claim with profound moral implications. But it takes some getting used to.

I wanted to play a constructive role in the divinity school, but it was now clear to me that the future Dennis imagined for the school was quite different from what I thought we should be about. That Dennis had "fired" Paula was but a complication in our deeper disagreements. Dennis's "vision" for the school, as far as I could tell, assumed that the church's primary role, a role enshrined in the Methodism of the 1950s, was to support those who think they run the world. In contrast, I wanted a church capable of reminding those who think they rule the world that they are in the grip of a deep delusion.

But I did not want to become "the opposition." I cared deeply about the work of the divinity school. I wanted to be constructive. I discovered that this meant, in the language of nonviolent protest movements, that I would sometimes simply have to "go limp." I would not directly oppose Dennis, but neither would I support policies or appointments that I thought only perpetuated the mistakes of the past. I was not part of the dean's inner circle, nor did I desire to be. I made the arguments I could in faculty meetings and in conversations with friends and colleagues.

I confess that I sometimes found it hard for that to be "enough." I cannot resist wanting to make a difference in the institutions in which I find myself. I cannot resist wanting to run the world, even though I am obviously no good at it. People like Dick McBrien and Dennis Campbell always seem to know how to outmaneuver people like me. What I had to learn was patience. Change, if it is significant, takes time. At least change takes time if you remember that finally any change that is accomplished nonviolently comes about through honest persuasion.

Teaching is just another name for one form of persuasion. We had stayed at Duke so I could be a teacher. I had wonderful students. Of course, I was a teacher before we had made the decision to stay at Duke. But now there were no distractions. My primary task was to teach, not only the students in my classes and graduate seminars but anyone ready to listen to what I had to say or read what I had written. I had good work to do. I had little about which to complain.

I was married to Paula. For years I think I feared happiness. But now I was happily married, and being so made me happy. No longer would my life need to be lived as if it hung from a thread. Whatever it might mean for me to live a normal life, that was the life I now had before me. Thank God.

Paula

CHAPTER 10

Good Company

One might think that the decision to stay at Duke would have given me the time to take stock of my life. I was forty-eight, in good health, happily married. Adam was happy and would also soon be married. I had a good job. I was a "success." Surely it was a time for me to try to look inward, or at least to ask what I wanted out of life now that everything seemed "settled." But I am not an introspective person. I do not agonize about my life. No doubt, one of the reasons I do not worry about myself is that I am my mother's child — interestingly enough, an introspective remark. I assume my task is to make others happy, which means I am happy making others happy. Moreover, I have discovered over the years that my attempt to make others happy is somehow related to my academic drive.

The summer I came to Duke I ran one of the summer seminars for college teachers funded by the National Endowment for the Humanities. The seminar was entitled "Happiness, the Life of Virtue, and Friendship." We read *Adam Bede* along the way. At the end of the seminar, the participants gave me a gift of a framed quote from *Adam Bede*. The words they chose to frame are ones they knew I loved. They are uttered by the indomitable Mrs. Poyser. The seminar participants quite rightly thought that Mrs. Poyser expressed my basic attitude about life: "There's no pleasure i' living, if you're corked up for iver, and only dribble your mind out by the sly, like a leaky barrel."

I am not a "leaky barrel." I am more like a fire hose. In 1989, I was honored to be named the Distinguished Alumnus of Southwestern University. The commendation suggested that I could best be described as a paradox: "Friends have called you energetic and kind, controversial and thoughtful, abrasive and generous, shocking and sensitive, boisterous and tender, loud but loving. They've said you're like a man who's been kept in a cage for twenty years, and now it's your first day out. You surprise people." John Score, when asked about his influence on me, replied, "How could you be the mentor of a volcano?"

I may surprise people, but I also surprise myself. I am simply drawn into life. Moreover, the life into which I am drawn is a life without safeguards. I do not know how to hedge my bets. In the parlance of poker, I am "all in." I do not regard this habit as a virtue because it is not something I try to do. Indeed, there are times when I wish I lived a more controlled life, but I quite simply do not know how to do that. I may fear being out of control, but it turns out that the way I think and live makes my life uncontrollable.

Having married Paula, I told myself that I could slow down. I would not work so hard. I continued to write more than anyone would want to read. I continued to give lectures all over the world. I think one of the reasons I continued to work hard is actually quite mundane. Hard work had become a habit.

I have sometimes worried that I do not stop because I am afraid of what I might discover about myself if I were to do so. So far I have been able to overcome these worries and avoid introspection by convincing myself that my work is much more interesting than my life. That said, I have to admit that writing this memoir has caused me to take some steps toward introspection. One of these steps has been recognizing that I am, indeed, Hannah's child. I had not thought of my life in terms of Samuel's until I began this memoir. Having made the connection, it is quite fascinating to realize that, like Samuel, my life has been shaped by a time of transition. Samuel was caught between the judges and kingship. I am caught between a church that once assumed a kingly role and a church that now awaits an uncertain future. Of course, given my passions, an uncertain future was a wonderful invitation to try to make a difference. I wanted to make a difference. I am, after all, my mother's child. I wanted to make a difference for the church — by undertaking the hard work of writing theology. I wanted to make a difference in the university — by doing what I was asked to do. I wanted to make a difference in the divinity school — by teaching as well as I could and being a constructive colleague. I wanted to make a difference as a friend — by being faithful. For me, these ambitions added up to one thing: my life.

WRITING IS HARD AND DIFFICULT WORK BECAUSE TO WRITE IS TO THINK. I DO not have an idea and then find a way to express it. The expression is the idea. So I write because writing is the only way I know how to think. I write, moreover, because I have something to say. That I have something to say is not a personal achievement. I have something to say because I am a Christian. I also have readers who are obligated to care about what I write. They are called Christians. What an extraordinary gift. Audience makes all the difference. I am an academic, but I do not have to write only for other academics. I write for a people who, no matter how ambiguous the identification "Christian" may be, think that what theologians say should matter. I believe that God has given me something to say. I have been given the work of trying to imagine what it means to be Christian in a world that Christians do not control.

This imaginative task has everything to do with words. In this time of transition, Christians must regain confidence in the words that should determine our speech. Although I would like to think that I learned from Barth to avoid the apologetic mode, I nonetheless hope that when readers read what I have written they find it hard to resist thinking, "This is true."

Recognition of truthful speech begins when readers identify the words they encounter as an honest expression of life's complexities. The theological trick is to show that speaking honestly of the complexities of life requires words that speak of God. Theologians betray their calling when they fear using such words and begin to think that they are not necessary. Often the result is desperate shouting. Barth's theology is anything but desperate. It is the joyful celebration of the words we have been given to speak of God. As such, Barth stands as one of the great exemplars of theological speech.

Barth understood that the work of the theologian is word work, or, as John Howard Yoder would have it, that the task of theology is "working with words in the light of faith." The difficulty of the task is manifest by the misleading grammar of Yoder's observation, that is, one can draw from his description the conclusion that words do not constitute "the light of faith." In fact, faith is nothing more than the words we use to speak of God. And yet the God to whom and about whom we speak defies the words we use. Such defiance seems odd, because the God about whom we speak is, we believe, found decisively in Jesus of Nazareth, the very Word of God. Still, it seems that the nearer God draws to us, the more we discover that we know not what we say when we say "God." I suspect that this is why one of the most difficult challenges of prayer is learning how to address God.

For Christians, learning to address God is complicated because we do not begin by addressing "God" but rather "Father," "Son," and "Holy Spirit." "God" is the name we use to indicate the love that constitutes the relation of Jesus and his Father through the work of the Holy Spirit. Thus we know what it means to say "God" only because Jesus taught us to pray to the Father. Disputes between those who believe in God and those who do not often turn on the assumption by both parties that they know what they mean when they say "God." This seems unlikely, since Christians believe that we learn to use the word "God" only through worship and prayer to the One we address as Father, Son, and Spirit. Such a God is identified by a story that takes time, often a lifetime, to learn.

Theology is the ongoing and never ending attempt to learn this story and to locate the contexts that make speech about God work. How theology can at once be about God and about the complexities of human life is never easily rendered. Some theologians in modernity have tried to split the difference between speech about God and the complexities of human life, with the result that their theology is more about "us" than about God. When that happens, it is not at all clear that you need the word "God" at all. If my work has seemed to be "in your face," I think it has been so because I have tried to show that "God" is a necessary word.

Learning how to say "God" is hard but good work. It is good work because the training necessary to say "God" forces us to be honest with ourselves about the way things are. Our lives are but a flicker. We are creatures destined to die. We fear ourselves and one another, sensing that we are more than willing to sacrifice the lives of others to sustain the fantasy that we will not have to die.

The widespread confidence that medicine will someday "cure"

death is a fantasy. The attempt to develop and maintain a medicine so aimed, moreover, depends on the creation of wealth as an end in itself. A social order bent on producing wealth as an end in itself cannot avoid the creation of a people whose souls are superficial and whose daily life is captured by sentimentalities. They will ask questions like, "Why does a good God let bad things happen to good people?" Such people cannot imagine that a people once existed who produced and sang the Psalms. If we are to learn to say "God," we will do so with the prayer, "My God, my God, why have you forsaken me?" This is word work.

I do this work as an "ethicist." Some people assume that ethics is a subject more appropriate in the university than theology. For me, however, ethics is but a name for exposing the practical character of theological speech. My critiques of liberalism, my attempt to challenge the widespread confidence that someday medicine will get us out of life alive, and my calling into question the moral rationale for war are subsidiary themes meant to illumine what we do when we say "God." The challenge I have mounted against the accommodation of the church to the ethos of modernity is my attempt to help us recover our ability to pray to God, and to imagine what it might mean to be Christian in a world we do not control.

I HAVE TRIED TO PRACTICE THEOLOGY AS WORD WORK. I HAVE ALSO COME TO understand the work of the university in this way. Universities are built on words. I am an academic and a theologian. I hope I will be able to recognize any temptation that I might have to trim my sails as a theologian in the interest of appearing academically respectable, but I see no reason why the practice of theology so understood should be excluded from the university.

Universities are wonderful places to work. Duke in particular is a wonderful place to work. I joke that Duke has no idea what it wants to be other than excellent. Excellence turns out to mean that we can buy higher-priced intellectuals than others can buy. Duke does in fact attract extraordinary talent. You cannot avoid being pulled into a world of smart and interesting people.

One of the ways I got drawn into this world was by serving on the provost's advisory committee for appointments, promotion, and tenure. All internal promotions that grant tenure and all appointments of new tenured faculty must pass through the APT committee. As a member of the committee you are expected to read not only the peer evaluations of the people under review but also at least some of their work. APT is the one place where the university is a "university," that is, where academics in quite diverse fields must share judgments.

The work of the APT committee was onerous, but I liked it so much that I served on the committee for eight years under four different provosts. It was as if I had returned to college. For example, I had the opportunity to revisit controversies in modern historiography and to discover fascinating research agendas in other fields. I had no idea, for instance, that mathematicians study "random walks." Because the committee is made up of faculty from diverse disciplines, we had lively debates from which I never ceased to learn. I shall never forget the time one of the members of the committee from the science faculty, in an effort to gain some clarity about a file from the humanities, asked, "What is modernity?"

The significance of that question was brought home to me by a dispute occasioned at Duke by the hiring of Skip Gates. Stanley Fish had engineered Skip's appointment in the English Department. It was a wonderful hire for Duke. But some of the faculty, particularly from the sciences and social sciences, were quite upset. They started a chapter of the National Association of Scholars in order to oppose what they perceived to be a threat to the university from the postmodernists. I was asked to join the NAS but wrote the charter members to decline the "honor." I noted that the modernist epistemological presumptions that shaped their understanding of "objectivity" were the grounds that were often used to exclude theology from university curriculums.

The antagonism between the factions in the faculty was intense. Tommy Langford, who was serving as provost, thought it might be a good idea to get some of us together for a day to discuss our differences. There were probably fifteen of us. We introduced ourselves to one another by describing what we studied. The biologist talked of his fascination with butterfly wings. Barbara Herrnstein Smith made clear why relativism is true. A biochemist described the research he hoped would have therapeutic outcomes. I was one of the last to speak. I began by confessing that some of them might not regard me as a proper academic because I was not a free mind. Rather, I served a church that told me what I should think about. I offered the example of the Trinity, noting that, as far as it is possible to do so, I am supposed to think about that. I then observed that it is clear to me who I serve, or at least who I am supposed to serve. I concluded by asking my colleagues who they thought they served.

We had a good discussion, but they did not address my question. The next day, however, I ran into Frank Lentricchia from the literature program. In fact, we met in front of Duke Chapel. Frank and I had come to Duke at the same time, but I did not know him well. I was drawn, however, to his naturally abrasive character. Frank said, "I've been thinking about your question. I know who I serve. I serve myself." I responded, "God, Frank, I hope that doesn't mean you have to do what you want to do." Frank recognized a sermon when he heard one. Drawing on my experience at Notre Dame, I told Frank that with a name like Lentricchia he had to be a lapsed Catholic. I suggested that he needed a priest and that I knew just the one — Mike Baxter, one of my graduate students.

The three of us had dinner. Frank, in his inimical way, asked Baxter, "What have you been up to?" Mike said he had just gotten back from a retreat with the Benedictines at Mepkin Abbey. "Really," Frank asked, "what was it like?" Mike said simply, "They were happy." Frank replied, "I have to go there." He did. The rest is history, as Frank himself later recorded it in an article in *Harper's*. In ways that are not entirely different from me, Frank will probably always be an uneasy Christian, but hopefully God takes pleasure in our unease.

I was also drawn into the university by serving on the board of Duke University Press. The board approves every book published by the press. One of their acquisition editors, Rachel Toor, had acquired Jeff Powell's dissertation, *The Moral Tradition of American Constitutionalism*. I had directed the dissertation, and for some reason Rachel thought I should also write a book for Duke Press. I explained to her that I really did not write books. Instead, I put essays together to make them look like books. Rachel, however, was forceful and persistent. Eventually she talked me into rewriting some of my essays to make it look like I had actually written a book. The result was *Dispatches from the Front*.

Sitting on the board was my first introduction to the review process associated with university presses. I had published a number of books with Notre Dame. But Jim Langford, the editor of University of Notre Dame Press, ran the press well by trusting in his own judgment. Over the years that I published with Notre Dame, Jim and I became good friends. After all, he is a Cubs fan and author of *The Cub Fan's Guide to Life,* one of the more important unacknowledged texts in ethics. I am in his debt for all he did to help get my work out. But Jim had not prepared me to understand how university presses now perform the role of gatekeepers.

I was already a member of the board when Stanley Fish became the executive director. He asked me to serve as chair, which I was glad to do. I enjoyed learning how presses and acquisition editors quite literally work to produce knowledge. There is a selflessness about the work of editors that I deeply admire. They are seldom credited for the imaginative work they do in order to force authors to see what they should write and how to write more clearly.

My experience on the APT committee and on the board of Duke Press revealed to me that the review process has had the effect of making recent scholarship, particularly in the humanities, far too conformist and conventional. It is not simply that the process encourages young academics to know more and more about less and less, but also that the "less" about which they know is overdetermined by their dissertation director. What dissertation directors know, moreover, is overdetermined by the scholarly guild to which they belong. I worry about this process, knowing that Wittgenstein would have never received tenure at Duke, nor would the *Tractatus* have been published by Duke Press.

Of course, these are the kinds of worries that you would expect from someone who is hopelessly in love with the university. In *The State of the University* I develop an account of why I think the university as we know it is in trouble. But the reasons for this trouble do not justify abandonment. I learned from Tommy Langford that patience is required if we are to discover alternatives that we otherwise overlook under the threat of necessity. I cannot even imagine what my life might be if it were divorced from the university, and for that I am profoundly grateful.

Paula decided we would stay at Duke, even though her own future was at the time unclear, because she thought the work I was doing with graduate students and seminarians was important for the church. I hope she was right. I certainly think that the work I do with graduate students is the most important work I do, but it is time consuming.

The students who come to study with me are often brighter than I am. Moreover, they usually understand me better than I understand myself. They are thereby able to write more interesting books than I am able to write. I am not being humble but simply reporting what I have learned from directing over fifty dissertations. I have no idea how many preliminary exam committees or dissertation committees I have served on. What I do know is that much of my life has been consumed by my work with graduate students.

When John Milbank left the University of Virginia, Gene Rogers called to see if I might be interested in taking his place. Gene, whom I love dearly, was simply testing an imaginative possibility. I told him I was perfectly happy at Duke and that, in any case, I could not replace John because I am not intellectually in that league. Gene acknowledged that this was true — God, how I love an honest man — but said that, nonetheless, the most interesting dissertations in theology were being written by my students. I have never received a higher compliment.

I try to let students write dissertations shaped by their deepest passions. That means that my students are allowed to take risks in a manner that is unusual, given the power of disciplinary expectations that usually determine the way things are to be done. Trust is the heart of the matter. Students have to learn to trust me, and I have to learn to trust them. Trust is forged through work we do in common. Such work often happens in graduate seminars, as well as in courses the graduate students help me teach for those preparing for the ministry.

Prospective students often come to explore what it might mean to do a Ph.D. at Duke. They usually arrive after having visited other institutions. I often ask them what they hear about me during these visits. They report that I am considered a good mentor, but also that I have a reputation for making students think like me. I assume this means that students who go to Harvard, Yale, or Chicago are not expected to think like the faculty at Harvard, Yale, or Chicago. Apparently they learn instead not to think like Hauerwas. That they do so is appropriate. All good graduate programs in theology should be about the intellectual formation of students. It does not get more serious than training other human beings to do work that will, or at least should, determine the rest of their lives.

The truth of the matter is that I try not to dominate the life or thought of those who study with me. I let students determine the kind of relationship they would like to have with me, and every student is different. I find that I cannot help but become friends with most of my students, but I do not want to make that a condition for their study with me. The professor-student relationship centers on power. Friendship can be a form of manipulation. But what I want is for students to care about what I care about. I want them to discover the joy of the work of theology. That does not mean I want them to replicate my thought. I have no desire for my students to write dissertations confirming what I already think. Life is too short for that.

I have discovered that there is nothing quite like training graduate students, particularly in theology, to make you take your life seriously. They rightly expect that there should be some relationship between how and what you think and how you live. Of course, I have made a career of trying to think through the complexities and ambiguities of the relation between thought and behavior. And I can say with complete confidence that we are subtle creatures capable of infinite modes of self-deception. It may be that this memoir is just an attempt at self-justification and that it will fall short of the kinds of expectations graduate students have of their teachers. In any case, that is a judgment for others to make.

If I learned anything from John Howard Yoder, it is not to trust yourself to know yourself. You learn who you are only by making yourself accountable to the judgment of others. Ironically, I learned this not only from John's thought but from his life. John always struck me as living what he preached. He lived modestly and in his own way was generous toward all whom he met. So I was a bit taken aback when I learned that John had been involved in a pattern of behavior with women that was, to say the least, problematic.

Before I left Notre Dame, John and I had begun to plan a book on marriage. John wanted to write a book at the popular level in which we would explore various "laws" that exemplify "Hauerwas's law," that is, "You always marry the wrong person." John thought we should write under a nom de plume, making it possible to quote third-person authorities, such as Yoder and Hauerwas.

In order to get us thinking about the book, John wrote a wonderful long memo. He observed that Hauerwas's law is actually good news. It suggests that it is perfectly normal for partners in a marriage to discover, in time, that each person has some trait about which the other had not bargained. John went on to outline how our culture trains us to assume that for a marriage to succeed we need to be "right" for one another. Hauerwas's law frees us from that demanding requirement.

In contrast, Yoder argued that, until recently, Christians have not assumed that the things we undertake as humans are best considered in terms of what makes them go right. Rather, Christians are people who know what to do when something goes wrong. Accordingly, Christians should understand marriage as an institution for resolving conflict, and marriage should be structured toward that end. In the memo, Yoder observed that "the commitment to hanging together, i.e., lifelong fidelity, is a prerequisite for taking conflict resolution seriously: otherwise every conflict becomes an occasion for fantasies of escape."

We never wrote the book. I do not remember any decision we made not to write it. I think I assumed that because we were no longer in daily contact it just proved too hard to continue with our plans. Perhaps I also thought that my divorce and remarriage made such a project ill advised. I brought John to Duke to lecture, but I do not remember if we even talked about the book. It never occurred to me that there were developments in John's life that made it impossible for him to be involved in such an enterprise.

I found out what was going on only because I began to receive invitations to give lectures that John had been scheduled to give. I had no idea why John was being disinvited, for example, from giving a lecture at Bethel College in North Newton, Kansas. But I was asked to come in his stead. There I learned from those close to John that he was under a ban initiated by Prairie Street Mennonite Church because of inappropriate relationships with some Mennonite women.

Only someone as heady as John could have gotten himself into such a mess. I had long had in my possession unpublished papers of John's in which he argued that the mainstream church was wrong to assume that the only alternatives available for men and women in the church are celibacy or marriage. John, who thought that, first and foremost, Christians are called to be single, argued that for brothers and sisters in the faith there should be other ways of relating bodily with one another. In short, he thought there might be "nonsexual" ways that Christians could touch one another short of intercourse. It seems he set out to test his theory. Of course, such testing could not be done in public. Of all people, John should have recognized the problematic nature of such an "experiment."

John began "experimenting" sometime in the Sixties. It is important to note the timing, because Mennonites were not immune from the cultural forces that caused many people of the time to think that new possibilities in human relationships might be possible. John began his seductions of "weighty" Mennonite women — women of intellectual and spiritual stature in the community — by asking them to help him with his work. He would then suggest that they touch him, and that he touch them, without engaging in sexual intercourse. John was intellectually overwhelming. He may have convinced some women that what they were doing was not sexual, but they later came to recognize that John was clearly misusing them. They somehow made contact with one another, compared notes, and John was in a heap of trouble.

God knows what John thought he was doing. I have often observed that no one taught us more about community than John, but the power of his intellect as well his shyness and personal awkwardness meant that he often seemed "alone." I hope I learned to invade John's loneliness, but there is no question that you had to work at it. Annie, John's wife, is a wonderful person and their children are equally impressive, but John seemed to need something else that I suspect neither he nor those who loved him quite knew how to describe. Annie supported John throughout the process set in motion by the church.

John was supposed to submit to a discipline laid out by a discernment committee of the church. They were enacting Matthew 18:15-20. It was not clear if John would submit. He did not think the process was following the rule that he should be allowed to confront his accusers. I am not sure what would have happened if it had not been for the intervention of Jim McClendon and Glen Stassen. Glen and Jim were colleagues at Fuller Theological Seminary. Glen, the son of Harold Stassen, had been deeply influenced by Yoder and was a good friend. Jim was a Baptist from Louisiana who had done most of his work at Southwestern Seminary in Fort Worth. He was especially crucial to the effort to convince John to submit to the church's discipline.

Jim was essentially self-educated, which meant that he exhibited an independence that Baptists are alleged to value. He had taught at Golden Gate Seminary, but it turned out he was too "liberal" for that institution. He also lost his job at the University of San Francisco, because he used university stationery when he wrote a letter protesting the Vietnam War. Before going to Fuller, he taught for many years at the Episcopal Seminary in Berkeley. He heard J. L. Austin lecture at Berkeley, which led him to go to England to study with Austin.

Jim drew on Austin's understanding of the self-involving character of language to coauthor an extremely important book in philosophical theology called *Convictions*. This book led him to write *Biography as Theology*, which I read while at Notre Dame. I realized that this was someone with whom I shared fundamental philosophical and theological judgments. We became good friends, leading Jim to spend a sabbatical at Notre Dame. That is how Jim came to know John and to become one of his best friends. I think it is fair to say that Jim and John understood one another better than I understood either of them. They were not only close in age but committed Baptists.

That they shared a commitment to being Baptist was extremely important for the role Jim played to help John decide to submit to the disciplinary process. Glen arranged for the three of us to have a conference call with John just prior to the time he had to make a decision about submitting to the discernment committee. Jim led the way. Jim pointed out to John that no matter how bad the process might be, he had to submit. He had to submit because too much was at stake for John to insist on ill-defined procedures. Jim pointed out that John had convinced us to be advocates of Christian nonviolence. We now expected him to live out what he had taught us. John agreed to submit.

In 1992, I was asked to give the commencement address at Goshen College. I was not necessarily thinking of John's situation, but I entitled my speech "Why Truthfulness Requires Forgiveness: A Commencement Address for Graduates of a College of the Church of the Second Chance." The Church of the Second Chance is a church portrayed in Anne Tyler's novel *Saint Maybe*. The relationship between memory, forgiveness, and truth is a theme that runs through my work, in particular in *Dispatches from the Front*. I think what is most destructive for living truthful and good lives is not what we do, but the justifications we give for what we do to hide from ourselves what we have done. Too often the result is a life lived in which we cannot acknowledge or recognize who we are.

During my stay in Goshen I met with the committee charged with the responsibility to restore John to the community through appropriate discipline. Confronted by John's intellectual power, they knew they were at a disadvantage. But they loved John. They loved what he meant for their community. They were determined to reclaim him. Four years later, in 1996, the process had done its work and John was reconciled. On the last Sunday in December 1997, John and Annie were warmly reunited in worship at Prairie Street Mennonite Church. John died on December 30, 1997. He was seventy years old. I have no doubt that he would have responded unemotionally to the suggestion that he had died early by saying, "It was biblical — three score and ten."

There is now a minor publishing industry trying to show the ways I may be different from John, or even the ways I have misinterpreted his work. I will leave that project to others. What I know is that John taught me a way to think that I could have learned from few others. For that I cannot help but be grateful. How John's community responded to his inappropriate relations with women, for all the ambiguities and confusions associated with that response, is also a lesson in its own right. It is a testimony to a community that has learned over time that the work of peace is slow, painful, and hard.

One of the things I learned from John is that the apocalyptic character of our faith in Christ requires that we learn how to recognize how extraordinary the ordinary is. To be baptized into Christ is to be made a citizen of a new age in this age. To so live sometimes tempts Christians to try to force God's kingdom into existence through violence. But that is to betray the time we have been given. The great paradox is that the apocalyptic character of our faith not only makes the everyday possible but also enables us to see how extraordinary it is. It is extraordinary, for instance, that we can take the time to welcome children into this world and to enjoy the time called friendship.

I hope that the extraordinary character of friendship, which we often see only in its ordinary guise, helps account for lives like John's and mine. If his life and mine make anything clear, it is that to be a Christian is not something you do alone. Our lives are possible only because of what others make of them. As theologians, we must say more than we can be in the hope that others will make us more than we are. What is crucial is that we not write to justify the limits of our lives.

In 1995 I published a book entitled *In Good Company: The Church as Polis. In Good Company* gave expression to how my life has been enriched by people who claim me as a friend because of something I have written. Paula was right. I do have a lot of people in my life. Countless people write me to say that what I have written is of help to them as they try to be church. They often ask questions. I try to respond as helpfully as I can. As a result, I have a lot of people in my life.

I sometimes worry that my hunger for friendship may be pathological. During the years with Anne, I could not have survived without friends. Moreover, I depend on friends to help me think and write. So I seem to live assuming that my capacity for friendship is without limit. I probably should be more protective of my time. But I seem to lack any capacity to know what the limits might be. Most of my friends try to respect the time I need with other friends, as I try to respect the other friendships that they have. I have no reason to deny it is a tricky business to have so many friends, but it is a business that I believe lies at the heart of what it means to be Christian.

Writing and lecturing are for me the discovery of community. I have learned that life is not a zero-sum game. Through friends I discover other friends. In the process, they discover one another, making us all more than we would otherwise be. Many of my friendships begin with a letter. If you care enough to write, I will write you back. It often takes me at least an hour a day to answer the letters I receive. I am extremely fortunate because I can dictate a response that is then typed by a secretary. Of course, as many of the people whom I have corresponded with know, it does not do justice to the reality that is Sarah Freedman to call her a secretary. Sarah, who assisted me for a decade, is a force of nature. She is always ready to tell me, the people she came to know through my correspondence, and whoever happens to be president of the United States how to conduct their lives. Sarah, now retired, often became friends with my friends through the correspondence she made possible.

I once received a letter from a strange group of folk who identified themselves as members of the Church of the Servant King. They had read *Resident Aliens* and posed questions about what such a community might actually look like. After an exchange of letters, they asked me to come to one of their retreats in California to discuss matters further. I do not believe in California, but these were people who had formed a church that had the makings of something interesting, so I agreed.

It seems they had been living quite normal lives. They were Christians denominationally associated with the Disciples of Christ. Then they decided they were too normal, so a number of them entered into a covenant to found an intentional community. They took jobs that would allow them more time to be church, and they read voraciously. They were gathered into three different communities scattered from Southern California to Oregon. Many of the members had a history that was anything but respectable, but as a result they had no time for bullshit, nor were they in awe of me. I came to their retreat. They beat the hell out of me intellectually for two days. I liked them a lot.

That is how I met Jon Stock. Jon is an unlikely friend. He lives in Eugene, Oregon, where people who say they are anarchist may actually be anarchist. He is from Oregon logging culture, has been through hell and back, and is a Yankees fan. The latter is unforgivable. Moreover, I do not trust intentional communities or people associated with them. They have to spend too much time reinventing the wheel. But Jon makes the Church of the Servant King in Eugene work. The church works because Jon does not have a pious bone in his body, so he and the church know they are no "ideal." The community stays healthy because with Jon at their center they have an appropriate sense of humor.

Another unlikely friend whom I encountered initially through a letter is Rodney Clapp. He wrote me to investigate doing a Ph.D. He was from Oklahoma, had gone to Wheaton, and worked for *Christianity Today*. Not exactly someone with a background you might associate with me. But he wrote an article on me in *Christianity Today* that seemed to make a few evangelicals think I might have something to say. As it turned out, Rodney never came to Duke to do his Ph.D. Instead, he has started his own press, which has linked us together in ways that probably exceed anything that might have happened had he come to Duke.

After looking at one of the early catalogues of books to be published by Brazos Press, David Burrell remarked to me, "How clever, Stanley, now you even have your own press." I hesitate to report David's remark because some people might be tempted to think it an accurate characterization of what Rodney is trying to do with the press, which is not simply to publish books by me and my friends. However, I cannot deny that many of the books Rodney has published are by my students or friends. I am not going to apologize for that anymore than I am going to apologize for our friendship.

I sometimes meet people not because of a letter but because they attend a lecture I have been invited to give. That is how I met Kyle Childress, no more likely a friend than either Jon or Rodney. Kyle is a short, round man who serves as the pastor of Austin Heights Baptist Church in Nacogdoches, Texas. Kyle was a student at Southwestern Seminary in Fort Worth, Texas. He took me to the airport after I lectured at Southwestern. Kyle is a Southern Baptist. I do not like Southern Baptists, which is only fair because most Southern Baptists do not like me. But Kyle has some things going for him. For one thing, he is from West Texas. For another thing, he drove a pickup truck. He had to drive like a bat out of hell so that I would not miss my plane back to South Bend. I liked Kyle. It was clear that he would never have the smoothness to make it big in Southern Baptist life. He not only was from West Texas and drove a pickup, but also, like me, had been influenced by Will Campbell.

Few people might suspect that Austin Heights is an outpost of radical Christianity, but appearances are deceiving. I was honored to be asked to preach at the service celebrating Kyle's tenth anniversary at Austin Heights. Preaching at Austin Heights or participating in a retreat with the Church of the Servant King is for me every bit as important as giving a lecture at Yale or Cambridge. I may well spend more time working on a sermon for Austin Heights than I do writing a lecture for Yale. In fact, I often learn what I need to say at Yale or Cambridge because I have visited the Church of the Servant King or preached in Nacogdoches.

Not all my friendships start because people write or ask me to speak, nor do they all start smoothly. My friendship with Peter Ochs, for example, started in disagreement at a conference on narrative at the University of Dayton. Peter and I had a terrific argument about prayer in the public schools. Peter became one of my closest friends, and he has never let me forget that God has joined us, Jew and Christian, in an ongoing dispute that we dare not repress in the name of being nice. One result of our friendship has been the book series Radical Traditions, which we started to enable younger Jewish, Christian, and Muslim scholars to publish work that challenges the reigning academic paradigms of theology. A book series is hardly a revolution, but you have to start somewhere.

Another place to start was the Ekklesia Project. Mike Budde, a political scientist at DePaul University, had read a number of my students' books. Mike, a Roman Catholic, sensed that there was a birth of a fresh way to think about the church. He got a number of us together, and, in 2000, the Ekklesia Project was born. We meet annually, publish a scholarly series, sustain a project in congregational formation, and have a pamphlet series. As a result, we each discover that we are not as crazy or alone as we might feel. Though often unclear about what we think such an organization ought to be about, we find through the discovery of one another that any church capable of challenging the powers depends on sustaining friendships.

In Good Company begins with an epigraph from C. L. R. James: "The aesthetics of cricket demand first that you master the game, and preferably, have played it, if not well, at least in good company. And that is not the easy acquisition outsiders think it to be." I do not pretend I have learned to play the game of Christianity well, but I have certainly played it in good company.

IN GOOD COMPANY WAS THE FIRST BOOK I DEDICATED TO PAULA — WHO CERtainly is my "good company." Marriages are forged from the everyday. We are given time through our promises to have our lives joined in a common history that does not require the loss of our differences. Given the differences between me and Paula, there is little chance of that happening in our marriage. Yet our marriage "works."

Good Company

Paula and I live wonderful, privileged lives. This can be a problem. You have too much time to get on one another's nerves. Small matters can assume more importance than they should. Paula and I can get on one another's nerves, but how wonderful it is to be able to tell one another that we do so. Paula also has given me the gift of knowing that I do not have to try to please her. Sometimes when she is out of sorts, she makes clear that it has nothing to do with me, so I should just leave her be. It turns out that the world does not depend on me. What a relief!

Our marriage works because we love one another, of course, but also because we love others whose lives become constitutive of our marriage. Stuart Henry was such a person from the beginning of our relationship. We had not been married long before it was obvious that Stuart was failing. Stuart had always lived an independent and dignified life, but it became increasingly apparent that his ability to live on his own was coming to an end. He could no longer be sure that some of the basic functions of his body could be trusted to work. He had to recognize that he should no longer drive, which was difficult for him to do. He had to give up his beloved Buick. One of Stuart's great gifts to me was to let me be present as he negotiated the narrowing of life that aging brings.

Paula and I tried to be present to Stuart as he made his way toward death. He had moved to a retirement community. Of course, he had his apartment painted "Henry gray." For a time, he was able to live independently, but it was not long before he had to move to assisted living. Stuart hated the idea that his living had to be assisted. I tried to visit him two or three times a week on my way home at the end of the day. Stuart loved to know what was happening at the university, with Paula and Adam, and how the two of us could solve the world's problems. With some sadness, he once told me that, after all his years in the divinity school, I was his most constant friend. The university can be a lonely place.

Stuart became increasingly confused. His family was extremely supportive. Paula and I tried to be present, but being present was painful. How Stuart's body fought death. He needed to die, but he had loved life so much that his body was captured by the habits of living. His dying took time, and when it came we could only be thankful. Paula and I mourned, but we thanked God that Stuart's life was part of ours.

We also had another death to negotiate. Tuck had taken one look at Paula and fallen even more desperately in love with her than I had. They shared a special bond I tried to respect. As cats go, Siamese live long. Tuck was twenty-one. But like Stuart, Tuck began to fail. In particular, his kidneys began to fail. Still, he remained the dignified cat that he had always been. He had just slowed down. We kept him alive for a year by daily infusion of water. We never thought it a burden. He was such a wonderful friend. He lived to be twenty-two. Then, as he suffered from seizures, we finally asked a compassionate vet to help us help Tuck die.

I cried as I dug his grave. Paula and I buried him in the front yard. Bill Moore carved a marble slab with his name embossed under a cross. We placed it over his grave. I wrote this prayer:

Passionate Lord, by becoming one of us, you revealed your unrelenting desire to have us love you. As we were created for such love, you have made us to love your creation and through such love, such desire, learn to love you. We believe that every love we have you have given us. Tuck's love of us, and our love of him, is a beacon, a participation, in your love of all your creation. We thank you, we sing your praise, for the wonderful life of this cat. His calm, his dignity, his courage, his humor, his needs, his patience, his always "being there," made us better, made our love of one another better, made us better love you. We will miss him. Help us not fear remembering him, confident that the sadness such memory brings is bounded by the joy that Tuck existed and, with us, is part of your glorious creation, a harbinger of your peaceable kingdom. Amen.

For all my talk of friendship, I seldom speak or write of love. But as this prayer suggests, I believe that we were created to love God and one another. I seldom focus on love because, given the character of contemporary Christianity, the word is subject to sentimental distortion. But that I could write this prayer suggests that I was beginning to love God, though I may not have recognized it at the time. I do not know how our marriage may have unleashed that love, but I began to sense that the love that moves the sun and the stars was sustaining my life.

What a pleasure it is to create a space to live with one another. We have a beautiful home. We have been fortunate to be able to surround ourselves with beauty — and cats. We waited after Tuck died. He was such a special cat that we feared bringing another animal into our lives. We knew that we would inevitably compare a new cat to Tuck. But then we noticed an advertisement in the paper for Siamese kittens. They were seventy-five dollars each. They were clearly not "with papers," so they were perfect for us. That is how Eden and Enda came into our lives.

Paula and I were married, but it takes time to be a family. That Paula was there when I learned of my father's death meant that sadness could be shared. That we could rejoice at Adam's graduation from Haverford in 1992 meant that happiness could be shared. That Adam asked Paula to celebrate at his wedding in December 1993, a year after the death of my father, meant that we were learning to be a family.

Paula never tried to be Adam's mother. It is not clear that he ever wanted her to be that. But she has been for him a parent who does not forget that he is an adult child. As a result, she was much more help than I was when Adam got married. I had always recommended that Adam marry a rich Catholic. Instead he fell in love with Laura Boynton. Laura is a Bryn Mawr graduate and a member of the United Church of Christ who grew up in Dover, Massachusetts. She has many gifts, but in particular she brought to her marriage with Adam a wonderful family: her parents, Bob and Sandy, and two brothers, Jamie and John. The Boynton family knows how to be a family in ways that Paula and I had never experienced. Adam needed more family than the two of us. I thank God for the Boyntons.

Laura did a Ph.D. at Northwestern in a research and clinical program in psychology designed to diagnose and offer the appropriate intervention for children with disabilities. Toward the end of her doctoral work, she became pregnant and Joel was born. We went to visit. Adam picked us up at the airport. As we made our way to Evanston, I asked him how it felt to be a father. Without hesitation he said, "I always felt something was missing in my life, and this is it." Adam was not afraid to be a father. What a gift. On September 20, 1998, Paula baptized Joel at Aldersgate. Adam and Laura are wonderful parents, not only of Joel but also of Kendall, who was born two years later.

Laura now has tenure at Providence College. Adam, who had done his M.A. in computer science during their time in Chicago, works in information services for the college. So our family remains intertwined in the work of the university. I love my son. I love his family. To love Adam and his family means that I am happy Adam has more than "me." I have no idea what our grandsons will ever make of their grandparents, but I hope they will think, "Granddad and GG sure went to church a lot."

We forgot we go to church a lot when we bought a mountain house in the Blue Ridge Mountains. Because we work hard, we thought it might be a good idea to buy a place where we could get away from our everyday routines. We found a lovely place on Groundhog Mountain three hours from Durham. It had a spectacular view over the Carolina Piedmont. The one problem was that we had forgotten we go to church. We cannot leave town on the weekend because we go to church. We soon discovered that we did not use the lovely place we owned more than twice a year. It took us forever to sell it.

WE NOT ONLY GO TO CHURCH, BUT I TRY TO BE A CHURCH THEOLOGIAN. I AM not interested in what I believe. I am not even sure what I believe. I am much more interested in what the church believes. I have discovered that this claim invites the skeptical response, "Which church?" I can reply only by saying, "The church that has made my life possible." The name of that church is Pleasant Mound Methodist, Hamden Plains Methodist, the Lutheran church at Augustana, Sacred Heart, Broadway Christian Parish, Aldersgate United Methodist, and the Church of the Holy Family.

I am well aware that many people will find such a response inadequate, but it is the only response I can give. One of the inadequacies of this response is the way in which it underscores the fact that I have no ecclesial home. I have "belonged" to all the congregations named above, but that they represent such diversity (Catholic, Methodist, Lutheran, Episcopalian) accents my homelessness. I have described myself as a high-church Mennonite — a description that is meant to be funny. But it also points to the fact that, although I have belonged to many congregations, I have never had a home in a particular ecclesial tradition. God knows why God has made some of us ecclesiastically homeless, but I hope and pray that our being so may be in service to Christian unity.

In Good Company was an attempt to express the ways in which my work has developed in response to people who have claimed me as a friend, people like Jon, and Kyle, and Peter. But it was also an attempt to make some sense of my ecclesial homelessness. Clearly one of the reasons I have so many people in my life is that I do not have an ecclesial home. Instead I have friends in diverse ecclesial homes. That is one of the ways I live out being homeless, but I also resist homelessness by trying to be at home in a particular congregation. In this sense at least, my home is in the church, although that is a claim Paula can make and live much more truthfully than I can. She is ordained. Even though she is dean of summer session and director of continuing studies at Duke, she never forgets that she is ordained. I, however, am an academic. You would think that teaching in a divinity school would be sufficient to remind me that I serve the church, but I do forget. Sometimes Paula reminds me what I am supposed to be about. For example, she asked me if I prayed before class. I confessed that I did not. She said, "You should." That was a major challenge. Prayer has never come easy.

At Hauerwas family gatherings, it was assumed that my father would be the designated "pray-er." As a young boy, I was quite impressed that my father was so designated. He prayed simple but eloquent prayers. My problem began, however, when I discovered that the family thought that the gift of prayer was genetic. I simply am not a natural "pray-er." But I thought I ought to do what Paula told me to do. At least, I ought to do what she told me to do when I taught the basic course in Christian ethics, because I could assume that the students in the course were people preparing for the ministry.

I do not trust prayer to spontaneity. Most "spontaneous prayers" turn out, upon analysis, to be anything but spontaneous. Too often they conform to formulaic patterns that include ugly phrases such as, "Lord, we just ask you . . ." Such phrases are gestures of false humility, suggesting that God should give us what we want because what we want is not all that much. I pray that God will save us from that "just."

So I began to take time before my lectures to write a prayer. Writing the prayer often took more time than writing the lecture. I discovered in the process that I pray the way I talk — plainly and straightforwardly.

When I write prayers, which may be as close as I get to prayer itself, my fundamental rule is never to think that my job is to protect either God or us from the truth. For example, I wrote the following prayer during the celebration of the five hundredth anniversary of Columbus's "discovery" of America:

> Dear God, our lives are made possible by the murders of the past — civilization is built on slaughters. Acknowledging our debt to killers frightens and depresses us. We fear judging, so we say, "That's in the past." We fear to judge because in judging we are judged. Help us, however, to learn to say "no," to say, "Sinners though we are, that was and is wrong." May we do so with love. Amen.

Students began asking me for copies of my prayers. It was as if the prayers were more important to them than the lectures. I was not sure what to make of that. Some students even asked me to collect my prayers in a single volume to see if I could get them published. So I did. At the time, Rodney Clapp was an editor for InterVarsity Press. I sent the manuscript to Rodney, and *Prayers Plainly Spoken* was the result. I am an academic, but I pray before class and have been published by InterVarsity Press. That is a lot to overcome if you want academic respectability.

I do, of course, want academic respectability. I must want academic respectability, because I have it. I am a chaired professor at a major research university. I can tell myself that I am simply using the university to serve the church, but such a justification is surely an invitation to enjoy the delights of self-deception. I can play the perpetual outsider — a working-class kid and a Christian — but like it or not, I am an insider. I am no longer the working-class kid from Texas who almost got lost in New Jersey on the way to Yale.

Paula and I continued to go to church at Aldersgate. Under Susan's leadership we had the Eucharist at least twice a month. We had a full Holy Week climaxing in the Vigil. This was no small accomplishment for a small church. One Easter, Susan called to ask Paula to celebrate and me to preach. Because of Herb's illness, she needed help.

Jane Tompkins was looking for a place to go to church. She came to Aldersgate. I do not think Jane was particularly impressed by my sermon, but she could not get over seeing Paula celebrate. "Magic" was the way she described it.

Later, we began to notice that when Susan preached she would sometimes lose her train of thought. There would be long, pregnant pauses. The death of Herb had been wrenching. She began to think she needed to retire. None of us wanted to see her retire before she needed to do so, but that was not easily discerned. She went on leave. Paula and a retired minister kept the church going. I was chairing the pastoral-staff committee. We met often to help Susan discern what she needed to do. She decided to retire. It was not long after her decision to retire that it became apparent she had Alzheimer's.

Alzheimer's is a cruel disease. We live by memory. The central act of the church is an act of memory. That act makes possible our being memory for those who can no longer remember. Susan, whose last years were spent in a Methodist nursing home, was ministered to by those her ministry had made possible. Paula and I often joined others in sharing the Eucharist with Susan.

Susan died shortly after I had completed a draft of this memoir. Paula and I were fortunate to have time with her hours before she died. Susan often said what an honor it was to be allowed to hold the hand of the dying. I was honored to hold her hand as Paula read psalms and prayed. I was asked to speak at her funeral. This is part of what I said:

> Susan often began a sermon with the observation, "I could not have thought the church up. I could not have imagined 'church.' " That we existed, that Aldersgate United Methodist Church existed, that this modest collection of people existed, Susan thought to be a miracle. So she would tell us that she was honored that we desired to have her lead us in the worship of God. She was honored because she thought that God had "thought us up." She thought we were God's imagination for the world. . . .
>
> I could not have thought Susan Allred up. I could not have imagined that such a person could exist. But she undeniably existed. That she did so is a miracle. It is an honor to have been in her presence. She was and is, and she continues to be, God's imagination for the world.

It would not have been easy for anyone to follow Susan. But we had no idea that the district superintendent thought that Susan had not sufficiently tried to increase the size of Aldersgate. Methodism was losing members. A general strategy of church growth became the order of the day. It was assumed that Aldersgate had potential for growth. Accordingly, we were sent a young person to be our pastor who was as ambitious as she was misdirected. In college she had majored in drama. She applied her theatrical skills in her sermons, which only made them harder to bear. Having more experience in Methodism than I do, Paula has lower expectations. But she was even more upset than I was. It was that bad. At the time, Paula was head of the worship committee. The pastor told her that we were too small a church for full services during Holy Week. She said that instead of Maundy Thursday, Good Friday, and the Vigil, we would perform a play on Wednesday. Paula told her that she simply could not be part of such a farce.

The outreach and pastor-staff committees were called together to hear her plan for the future. She had been to a church-growth seminar. She told us she knew how to make the church grow. First, we needed two services. We would have a contemporary service at nine and a more traditional service at eleven. Second, we would have a phone-a-thon, during which we would call 20,000 people at random. That would ensure that the church would attract two hundred new members. Sociologists had confirmed such a result. Finally, we would need to learn that we had been far too close-knit as a church. New people who came to the church might feel strange. Accordingly, we needed to get used to being a congregation in which people did not know one another well. Most new people would be attracted to the church because of the activities and pastoral services the church could provide, not because of a sense of belonging to a community.

I was stunned by her plan for the church. I said little at the meeting, other than blurting out "over my dead body" when she said that she was going to lead a delegation of our members to Willow Creek Church in Chicago to see how a church that had utilized these methods works. The pastor at Willow Creek is said to have once declared that there is no cross in the church because "it gets in the way of the gospel." I could not believe this was happening. It seemed like a joke. Everything I detested about mainline Protestantism in both its liberal and conservative modes had come to roost in the church I loved.

I waited a few days and made an appointment with the pastor. I told her that what she was proposing was against everything I was about. She accused me of being against evangelization. Surely I wanted to bring people to Jesus. I hate that kind of pious language. But I told her the problem was not that she wanted to bring people to Jesus, but that she wanted to do so with means shaped by economic modes of life incompatible with the gospel. She asked me how I could be so critical of what she was trying to do. She had, after all, graduated from Duke Divinity School. I told her that I found it profoundly embarrassing that she was a graduate of Duke Divinity School. What in the world were we doing to produce people who did not seem to have a theological clue about what they were ordained to do?

Our conversation went nowhere. Her sail was set. Moreover, the good people of Aldersgate were Methodists. They assumed they should do what their pastor wanted. If Paula and I had stayed, we would have split the church. That was the last thing we wanted to do. I told her that we would not be back. Ironically, the difference between Dennis Campbell's and my understanding of what we should be about in the divinity school had just played itself out at Aldersgate.

DENNIS HAD BEEN APPOINTED TO A THIRD TERM AS DEAN. THAT WAS NOW coming to an end. For a time, he had desperately wanted to be considered for the presidency of Duke. That was not about to happen, but it meant his energies were directed elsewhere. Slowly but surely my perspective was beginning to have some traction for the future of the school.

Three terms as dean were enough. We needed a new dean. The provost and president appointed a search committee. Much to my surprise, I was on it. The pool of talent for such a position was not deep. It soon became apparent that there were only two viable candidates. One of them was Greg Jones. Greg had not only published his dissertation but had written two books, *Reading in Communion* and *Embodying Forgiveness*. They are both good books, but the latter is rightly considered to be a major contribution to the field of theological ethics. The recent discussion about the centrality of reconciliation for the work of peace owes much to Greg's work, even if not everyone in the discussion knows it. He was also one of the editors of *Modern Theology* and chair of the Department of Theology at Loyola College in Maryland.

Greg had three problems — he was young, he was Jamison Jones's son, and he was my student. Somehow he overcame all those disadvantages. Tommy told me later that he was asked when he appeared before the APT committee in support of Greg's tenure file if Greg was one of my clones. Tommy replied, "You cannot clone Stanley." I hope that is true, but I certainly know that Greg is no clone. For one thing, Greg will never share my enthusiasm for Yoder. For another, he will be able to tell you why. I was going to have a dean with whom I could work. I would have a dean who thought the divinity school could make a difference for the church. This was going to take some getting used to.

CHAPTER 11

Patience and Prayer

I turned sixty on July 24, 2000. Many people say they notice their fiftieth birthday, but I was too busy to notice I had turned fifty. I was no less busy at sixty, but for some reason at sixty I realized I was growing old. I was not sure what it meant for me to grow old. I did not feel old, but then I had no idea what it might mean to feel old. I had aches and pains that I had not had when I was younger. I had worn out my knees, making it impossible for me to continue to run, but that just meant I spent more time on the elliptical machines. Yet at sixty I began to realize that death was not just a theoretical possibility — even for me.

Given my addiction to work, I was not planning to coast for five years and then retire at sixty-five. I have been going to "the job" since I was seven or eight. I have no idea what it might mean for me not to show up for work at six every morning. But even if I had been planning retirement, it would not have worked. Our lives are constituted by contingencies. All life is timing. And timing determined that as 2000 turned into 2001 and I entered my sixties, I would forget that I was growing old. Three events occurred in 2001 that ensured that this was so. In February and March I gave the Gifford Lectures at the University of St. Andrews in Scotland. In the September 10, 2001, issue of *Time* magazine I was named the "best theologian in America." Then September 11, 2001, ensured that few would notice that I had been so named.

I HAD NEVER EXPECTED THAT I WOULD BE ASKED TO GIVE THE GIFFORD LECtures. The lectures, which had been endowed by Lord Gifford in the

1880s and were to be given in the great Scottish universities, had become over the ensuing century the most prestigious lectures philosophers and theologians can give. I am from Pleasant Grove, Texas. I had assumed that I was not in the intellectual league of most of the scholars who have given the lectures. The names of William James, John Dewey, Reinhold Niebuhr, Karl Barth, and Paul Tillich are sufficient reminders that the Gifford Lectures are different.

I was stunned, therefore, when I opened a letter inviting me to give the 2000-2001 Gifford Lectures at the University of St. Andrews. I remember thinking, "This must be a mistake." After I got over my initial shock, I called Paula and read her the letter. Paula, quite rightly, is seldom impressed by such things. In this case, however, she responded, "This is big."

It was big, and "big" can be a burden. It is one thing to be asked to give the lectures but quite another to have to write and deliver them. The fact that the invitation came four years before I was to give the lectures was itself intimidating. I began to prepare by systematically reading through what past Gifford lecturers had said. This proved to be a fruitful exercise to free the imagination. By reading what had been done by others, I realized that the Gifford Lectures had been as diverse as they had been interesting.

However, I did have one big problem. Lord Gifford had wanted the lectures to "promote and diffuse Natural Theology," but I have little sympathy with natural theology. At least I have little sympathy with natural theology understood as Lord Gifford understood it, that is, as the attempt to prove the existence of God by unencumbered reason. Thankfully, however, Lord Gifford was extraordinarily generous in declaring that Gifford lecturers should be "under no restraint whatever in their treatment of their theme." I took advantage of Lord Gifford's generosity to argue that Karl Barth is the great natural theologian of modernity. I could not have made a more counterintuitive argument. No one engaged in more unrelenting attacks on natural theology than Barth. Yet I was determined to show that Barth's theology was implicated in robust metaphysical claims that make necessary an alternative reading of that time we call history. I tried to show how Barth's strong claims about the ways things are might be construed as a "natural theology."

Patience and Prayer

Admittedly, to do this I had to work against the grain of modern theology's great temptation to make what we believe as Christians intelligible on terms set by the world. On these terms, any claims Christians make about God or the world must be accessible to anyone. In this way theology is "natural." For Barth, the task is not to make the gospel explicable in terms set by the world, but rather to show that the world can be rightly known only if Jesus has been raised from the dead. In other words, to privilege Jesus' cross and resurrection is to make a claim about reality that invites and requires Christians to see the world differently than others. And, as Yoder suggests, this difference concerns time.

For the world, time is simply a causal sequence that makes what appears to have happened seem a matter of necessity. "Things just turned out that way." For Christians, however, time is apocalyptic, that is, it concerns the otherness and priority of God's cosmic and historical act through Jesus' singular life. In an essay called "Armaments and Eschatology," Yoder observed that the point apocalyptic makes is not only that those who wear crowns and claim to foster justice by the sword are not as strong as they think, but "that people who bear crosses are working with the grain of the universe." When it came time to title my Gifford Lectures, I chose *With the Grain of the Universe* because it summarized so well the cosmic character of the historical claim that Jesus' death and resurrection determine everything, even our understanding of time and of the retrospective narration of events that we call "history."

When MacIntyre gave the Gifford Lectures in 1987, he used the opportunity to tell the philosophical story that had shaped much of the work done in the Gifford Lectures since the first lecture in 1888. Following Alasdair's lead, I decided I would try to tell the theological story of this century-long period by focusing attention on three decisive figures: William James, Karl Barth, and Reinhold Niebuhr. Although I was principally interested in Barth and the resources he provides us for doing theology in an apocalyptic mode, James and Niebuhr were equally important. James, whom I came to admire deeply, provided the most humane account possible of how we could live in the face of a purposeless existence. Niebuhr's theology is then the best we can do once James's world is assumed. In contrast, Barth exemplified a way of doing theology in which theological speech makes possible a world and a time that grant none of the assumptions of James and Niebuhr.

In *With the Grain of the Universe,* I was able to articulate the way in which Barth's recovery of the apocalyptic character of Christian convictions was a rational acknowledgment that we cannot divorce our descriptions of the way the world is from how we are to live and what we must be if we are to describe the world rightly. Barth, through his own theological speech, provided us with the ongoing training to help us recover the basic grammar that should constitute our lives as Christians, a grammar rooted in the cross and resurrection of Jesus.

The argument I developed in the Gifford Lectures shaped my response to September 11, 2001. I knew we were in deep theological trouble as soon as politicians and commentators made the claim that September 11 had forever changed the world. Most Americans, Christian and non-Christian, quickly concluded that September 11 was a decisive event. That was exactly the problem. For Christians, the decisive change in the world, the apocalyptic event that transformed how all other events are to be understood, occurred in A.D. 33. Having spent decades reading Yoder and four years writing the Gifford Lectures, it was clear to me that September 11 had to be considered in the light of the crucifixion and resurrection of Jesus.

In some ways, I felt as if my whole life had been preparation for September 11, 2001. Of course, like everyone else I was not prepared for the sheer horror and terror of that day. But because I had learned to think theologically and apocalyptically about time I was prepared to resist the apocalyptic descriptions of September 11. It had taken sixty years of training to give me something to say, or at least pray, in response to September 11.

It was clear to me what needed to be done, but I did not feel adequate to the task. I kept thinking that McClendon and Yoder had died just when we so desperately needed them. It felt like they had left me holding the bag. I knew I had to say something. But I also knew I had to say it carefully. The wound of September 11 was real and could not be denied. Any hint of self-righteousness or self-importance would betray what I had to say as a Christian. At the same time, there was the challenge that to read September 11, 2001, in the light of A.D. 33 entailed a quite demanding alternative politics. Such a politics had become almost impossible for Christians in America to imagine. The seductions of worldly power had sapped the habits necessary to imagine what it would mean to provide a theologically disciplined response to the "attack on America."

The morning of the attacks, I was scheduled to give the regular lecture in the basic course in Christian ethics. Sarah Musser, one of the graduate students assisting me in the course, came to tell me a plane had crashed into the World Trade Center. I then got a call from Paula. She told me about the second plane. Like most Americans, I found a television and saw tapes of the second plane crashing into the building. It became clear that this was no accident but a carefully planned attack.

Sarah asked if we should have class. I decided we should, if for no other reason than to pray. So I went back to my office and wrote the following prayer:

Vulnerable — we feel vulnerable, God, and we are not used to feeling vulnerable. We are Americans.

Nor are we used to anyone hating us this much. Such terrible acts. Killing civilians. We are dumbfounded. Lost.

We are good people. We are a nation of peace. We do not seek war. We do not seek violence.

Try to help us remember that how we feel may be how the people of Iraq felt when we bombed them. It is hard for us to acknowledge that "we" in "we bombed them."

What are we to do? We not only feel vulnerable but helpless. We are not sure what to feel except shock, which will quickly turn to anger and even more suddenly to vengeance.

We are Christians. What are we to do as Christians? We know that anger will come to us. It does no good to tell ourselves not to be angry. To try not to be angry just makes us more furious.

You, however, have given us something to do. We can pray, but we wonder for what we can pray. To pray for peace, to pray for the end of hate, to pray for the end of war seems platitudinous at such a time.

Yet when we pray you make us your prayer for the world. So, Lord of peace, make us what you will. This may be one of the first times we have prayed a prayer for peace with an inkling of how frightening it would be for you to grant our prayer. Help us.

I think this prayer was at least on the way to being honest. I dismissed the class after a brief discussion. A few days later I would pray before the class:

September 11, 2001, we are told, forever changed our lives. What are we, the people of your cross, to make of such a claim? We are alleged to believe that Jesus' death on the cross forever changed all that exists, including us. In truth September 11, 2001, seems more real than the hard wood of your Son's cross. That cross, your Son's cross, seems "back then," lost in the mists of history. The horror of September 11, 2001, dwarfs Christ's crucifixion. Yet, surely, if we are able to acknowledge such evil and still know how to go on, we will do so only by clinging to the cross of Christ. So, we pray that you will teach us to pray as a cruciform people capable of resisting the attraction and beauty of evil that September 11, 2001, names.

As the rhetoric of "the war against terror" increased, the perspective embodied in this prayer would force me to "go public." I do not like the idea of "public intellectuals." I certainly have never desired to be one, even though I suppose I have played this role within the church, insofar as the church is a "public." But September 11, 2001, meant that I was now going to be called upon to represent the public character of the church in the wider public. This was not an entirely new role but seemed to have a different significance. Like it or not, I had been named the best theologian in America by *Time,* and my commitment to Christian nonviolence meant that I was supposed to have something to say. It seemed my time had come.

One of the first public occasions at which I was asked to speak took place at the University of Virginia. John Milbank, Ken Surin, and I spoke. In different ways, we were each quite critical of the American response. I argued that the Christian understanding of the cross required the church to be a counter-community capable of challenging the presumption that "we are at war." The "we" in "we are at war" could not be the Christian "we."

Patience and Prayer

I ended my talk by reading a prayer I had written for a devotion to begin a general meeting of the Divinity School a few weeks following September 11, 2001. I was able to write the prayer because of an article in the *Houston Catholic Worker* by Jean Vanier, the founder of L'Arche, about what it means to learn to live with those the world calls "retarded." This is the prayer:

> Great God of surprise, our lives continue to be haunted by the specter of September 11, 2001. Life must go on and we go on keeping on — even meeting again as the Divinity School Council. Is this what Barth meant in 1933 when he said we must go on "as though nothing has happened"? To go on as though nothing has happened can sound like a counsel of despair, of helplessness, of hopelessness. We want to act, to do something to reclaim the way things were, which, I guess, is but a reminder that one of the reasons we are so shocked, so violated, by September 11, 2001, is the challenge presented to our prideful presumption that we are going to get out of life alive. To go on "as though nothing has happened" surely requires us to acknowledge that you are God and we are not. It is hard to remember that Jesus did not come to make us safe, but rather he came to make us disciples, citizens of your new age, a kingdom of surprise. That we live in the end times is surely the basis for our conviction that you have given us all the time we need to respond to September 11 with "small acts of beauty and tenderness," which Jean Vanier tells us, if done with humility and confidence, "will bring unity to the world and break the chain of violence." So we pray, give us humility that we may remember that the work we do today, the work we do every day, is false and pretentious if it fails to serve those who day in and day out are your small gestures of beauty and tenderness.

I was not prepared for the reaction to the panel. I knew, of course, that what we had to say was "against the grain." But I had not thought that what we said would invite such a strong reaction from friends. In particular, I was taken aback by Robert Wilken's response. Robert and I were old friends, having gone through the wars at Notre Dame together. After suggesting that we were nothing short of traitors to the very country that made our lives possible, he stormed out of the room.

Robert's reaction made it clear to me that this was going to be "different." These were going to be days of tension. I did not want to lose Robert as a friend, but our differences were deep. Robert wrote soon after the event, asking me if I disdained all "natural loyalties." He argued that our lives are interwoven with the lives of others whom we rightly use force to protect. We are a better people, he said, because of the sacrifices made in World War II. He was angry that I failed to acknowledge the ways in which our relationships with others bind us to protect them. He was angry that I seemed to be forsaking all forms of patriotism. That Robert wrote to challenge me I regard as a profound act of friendship.

I responded by acknowledging that I do disdain all natural loyalties. Moreover, I refuse to accept the presumption that patriotism is a "natural loyalty." I also suggested that he, too, must recognize some limit to "natural loyalty," else why would he and Carol have had their children baptized. I assume that the light of baptism reconfigures the "natural love" between parents and children. After all, we and our children are baptized into the death and resurrection of Jesus. At the very least, this means that we might have to watch our children suffer for our convictions.

Robert and I had not only shared the joys and struggles at Notre Dame but also were often together at board meetings for the magazine *First Things*, edited by our common friend Richard Neuhaus. Other friends, not the least being Paula, have long given me grief for being associated with the neo-conservatives. I have always responded that as long as the neo-conservatives are willing to put up with someone as radical as I understand myself to be, then it is incumbent upon me to put up with them. Moreover, I regarded Richard as a friend. I found his "Americanism" a bit hard to take, but then I have always thought that if Richard ever had to choose between America and Jesus, he would go with Jesus. I simply wanted him to make that decision earlier than he thought was necessary.

It was not long before an editorial appeared in *First Things* in response to September 11, 2001. The editorial suggested that "those who in principle oppose the use of military force have no legitimate part in the discussion about how military force should be used." Clearly the authors did not take me and what I had learned from Yoder seriously.

Instead, they reproduced Niebuhr's understanding of liberal pacifism, such that nonviolence is divorced from its Christological and ecclesial home. I thought I had no choice but to resign from the board of *First Things*.

Robert and I remain friends. We are united by our commitment to Christ and his church. We may even have deeper agreements in judgments about our current political situation than we each suspect. I think Robert senses that the very economic policies favored by the neo-conservatives make the practices they most abhor, like abortion, morally intelligible. I do not think Richard, whose friendship I continue to value, carries this sensibility. Ironically, I think the magisterial office that Robert and Richard, as Catholics, now acknowledge understands more profoundly than many conservatives that to conserve economic liberalism is antithetical to the formation of communities capable of caring for one another in the name of the common good.

As the "war on terror" unfolded and turned into a war against Iraq, I continued to receive invitations to respond. One of these invitations came from the editors of *Time*. Perhaps because they had not forgotten that they had named me "the best theologian in America" on September 10, 2001, they asked me to write a piece about why I thought a war against Iraq would be immoral. Apparently they were not persuaded by the editorial in *First Things* that suggested a pacifist had no legitimate place in the discussion.

My article appeared in the February 23, 2003, issue of *Time*. I began the short piece trying to defuse the language of "evil." I pointed out that such language is incompatible with any presumption of a limited, and thereby just, war. I noted that I saw no reason that, as a representative of Christian nonviolence, I could not remind just-war advocates of the implications their position entails. I concluded the essay with these words:

G. K. Chesterton once observed that America is a nation with the soul of a church. Bush's use of religious rhetoric seems to confirm this view. None of this is good news for Christians, however, because it tempts us to confuse Christianity with America. As a result, Christians fail to be what God has called us to be: agents of truthful speech in a world of mendacity. The identification of cross and flag after September 11 needs to be called what it is: idolatry. We are often told that America is a great country and that Americans are a good people. I am willing to believe that Americans want to be good, but goodness requires that we refuse to lie to ourselves and our neighbors about the assumed righteousness of our cause. That the world is dangerous should not be surprising news to Christians who are told at the beginning of Lent that we are dust. If Christians could remember that we have not been created to live forever, we might be able to help ourselves and our non-Christian brothers and sisters to speak more modestly and, thus, more truthfully and save ourselves from the alleged necessity of a war against "evil."

Indeed, death, in particular the fear of death, is at the heart of the American inability to sustain a less murderous presence in the world.

About the same time I was writing for *Time*, Frank Lentricchia and I edited *Dissent from the Homeland: Essays after September 11*. Many of the essays in that book challenged the death-denying policies that were shaping the American response to September 11. I remain quite proud of the book. It was one of the few books published after September 11 that began to provide a critical perspective on the general presumption that a war against terror makes sense. We had asked people as diverse as Fred Jameson, Rowan Williams, Dan Berrigan, Wendell Berry, Catherine Lutz, Slavoj Žižek, Jean Baudrillard, Peter Ochs, and Susan Willis to write essays. But the book also made it clear that theologians, in particular, had something of significance to say about September 11, 2001. That was due in large measure to the extraordinary work of John Milbank, who I am honored to describe as a friend. The book included the unforgettable photographs of the World Trade Center by James Nachtwey. I had met Jim because *Time* had sent him to photograph me for the September 10, 2001, issue. Jim describes his work, so powerfully collected in his *Inferno*, as "after war" journalism. He helps us see what war is.

THE POSITION I WAS TAKING ON THE WAR WAS NOT WITHOUT COST. FRIENDships make my life possible. Jean Bethke Elshtain and I were longtime friends. Because of arguments we had in the wake of September 11, 2001, this friendship has ended.

Patience and Prayer

I do not remember how our friendship began, but I do remember a memorable conference on the ethics of nuclear war at which we both spoke at the University of Montana in 1986. The conference was memorable in part because of an excursion we made to a nearby Indian reservation. On the trip back to Missoula, the transmission of the car we were in ceased to function. Reverse was the only gear that would work, so we ended up backing up in the snow for miles. We finally reached a roadside cafe, where our host called for help. To be with Jean in such circumstances was a delight, because her whole life has been an energetic overcoming of the odds.

I have always admired Jean's energy, her intellectual vitality, and her courage. It is not easy being a feminist against abortion, but Jean is a person of strong conviction who is not about to compromise in the interest of gaining the approval of those who style themselves as morally enlightened. That she and Christopher Lasch, who was also at the conference in Montana, were such close friends was not accidental, given their deep moral commitments.

As fate would have it, *Time* called upon Jean to write the article on me in the September 10, 2001, issue of the magazine. She emphasized my "contrarian" character and my insistence that Christians be what they say they are. She observed that "before communitarianism became a buzzword, Hauerwas addressed community. Before the Americans with Disabilities Act, he wrote perhaps his most engaging work on persons with disabilities and how, as a community, we react to their presence. Before talk of 'the virtues' became widespread, Hauerwas wrote about the need for an account of our habits as members of community." That she highlighted those aspects of my work was not accidental, because they were also characteristics of her work in political theory. Indeed, in some ways they were the heart of her argument that radical feminism was in some tension with aspects of liberal political theory.

Despite all of our intellectual affinities, Jean did not share my commitment to Christian nonviolence. Nonetheless, I admired her book *Women and War*, which helped us see how women can be no less seduced by war than men. Given her critical perspectives on war, I assumed that she would be less than enthusiastic about the American response to September 11. I was wrong. In fact, she was deeply impressed by President Bush's concern for the safety of the American people, and she was one of the "religious leaders" invited to the White House after September 11. In 2003 she published *Just War against Terror: The Burden of American Power in a Violent World,* which drew on the just-war tradition to underwrite the notion of preventive war and to legitimate the coming war in Iraq. I read the book with dismay.

Paul Griffiths and I discovered that we shared similar negative judgments about the book. I am a pacifist, and Paul stands in the just-war tradition. Together we wrote a sharply worded negative review in *First Things.* We sent the review to *First Things* because we knew they would let Jean respond in the same issue. She was extremely upset, not only by our criticisms but by the tone of the review. In retrospect, I regret the tone, which was far too personal, but I do not regret the criticisms that Paul and I leveled against the book.

I need all the friends I can get. I did not want to lose Jean as a friend. But we are both people who believe that what we think matters. And we both care deeply about such matters as war and peace. I fear, therefore, that we will never be able to recover the friendship we once had. I suspect that we are each quite sad about that. But that we were once good friends now makes it impossible for us to pretend to be friends. That does not mean, however, that we are enemies. Rather, it means that as people of strong convictions we cannot pretend that the differences between us do not matter.

Not long after September 11, 2001, Paula and I were in Ireland visiting Enda. Enda had retired but was as lively as ever. He said he thought he had three to five years of active life left — an estimate that fortunately has been proven to be incorrect. He was not complaining about growing old but simply providing a realistic report about his life. He observed that he wanted to devote the time he had left to an effort to eliminate war. He explained that even though he had always seemed to support a just-war position he was really much closer to pacifism. Accordingly, he asked me to join him in an effort to "abolish war."

I responded that I was more than happy to join him, even though a call to abolish war could be construed as a strategy inconsistent with the kind of nonviolence I had learned from Yoder. Yoder desired a world free of war. But he also saw quite clearly that Christians are committed to nonviolence not because nonviolence is a strategy to free the world of war. Rather, in a world of war, faithful followers of Christ cannot be anything other than nonviolent. An appeal to abolish war might suggest that nonviolence can be translated into public policy based on grounds that do not require the cross and resurrection of Jesus.

Still, I thought Enda's project well worth the risk of such a misunderstanding. Yoder had spent his whole life trying to show that the boundary between church and world is permeable. I saw no reason, therefore, why I should not join Enda in an attempt to draft an appeal to abolish war. We addressed the appeal to Christian leaders and theologians and began with this paragraph:

> As Christians called out to serve the church in differing Christian traditions, we appeal to our Christian sisters and brothers to join in a campaign to abolish war as a legitimate means of resolving political conflict between states. Though our Appeal is addressed to the Christian community, we fervently believe that if our witness is true, many not part of that community may want to join our appeal to abolish war. God has after all created us to desire the Kingdom of Peace.

We then called attention to John Paul II's appeal in *Centesimus Annus* for "War Never Again." We also pointed toward those in the Christian tradition who have assumed that when Christ disarmed Peter he disarmed all soldiers for all time. And we appealed to advocates of just war to help us find alternatives to war. We concluded our appeal by acknowledging that our call for the abolition of war will take time, but this is not an argument against taking first steps. As long as it is assumed that war is always an available option, we will not be forced to imagine any alternative to war.

I am aware that joining Enda's effort to abolish war may seem foolish. But his proposal was especially appealing to me in the wake of September 11, 2001, because my life and thought had become dominated by war. To let your enemy, even the enemy called "war," determine your life is a mistake. I am a pacifist. But pacifism is just one piece of a complex web of interconnected philosophical and theological convictions that makes no sense if nonviolence is isolated from what it means to worship Jesus. Enda's effort to abolish war served for me as a reminder that my work is not about war but about Jesus.

The worship of Jesus is the central act that makes Christians Christian. It is that center that connects everything together. My work is about such connections. I have tried to show that how we live together in marriage, how and why we have children, how we learn to be friends, and how we care for the mentally disabled are the ways a people must live if we are to be an alternative to war. To find alternatives to war will take time. The effort to abolish war presumes that we have all the time we need to persuade others that war can be abolished. War is impatience. Christians believe that through cross and resurrection we have been given the time to be patient in a world of impatience.

Of course, I am the personification of impatience. I am sure that many people have the impression that I am always in a hurry, or at least always busy. I am often in a hurry and busy, but this is not the same thing as impatience. Patience does not mean "doing nothing." Rather, patience is "sticking to" what you are doing because you believe that it is worthy and worthwhile. It took some doing, but I have come to learn that my own practice of patience plays out within the two institutions that have defined my life: the church and the university.

It is all too easy to think of these institutions as empty containers within which we then carry on with our business, whatever that might be. In fact, however, I have learned that my daily practices and encounters within the church and the university are themselves integral to the life of these institutions. I have learned, in other words, that the patience and time it takes to build and sustain institutions like the church and the university are themselves an alternative to war. This is a lesson I learned from Tommy Langford.

The year I received the invitation to give the Gifford Lectures is the same year that Greg Jones became dean of the divinity school and that Tommy Langford retired. Although the events of my own life seemed to have prepared me for the increasingly public role I was called upon to play in the aftermath of September 11, 2001, I was not prepared to play this role without Tommy's counsel. But Tommy had died on February 13, 2000. I could not help but feel that Tommy died, like John Yoder and Jim McClendon, just when I most needed him.

I loved to discuss philosophy and theology with Tommy. Even more, though, I depended on Tommy to teach me how to be an institutional being. Tommy joined the faculty at Duke in 1956. By the time he retired in 1997, he had served the divinity school and the university as department chair, dean, and provost. He was an institutional creature, and I never ceased to learn from him. He was invaluable to me during the years when Dennis Campbell was dean, and the lessons did not end when Greg Jones, my own young student, replaced Dennis. Tommy understood how to live in, and love, institutions, which turns out to mean learning how to be a human being amidst other human beings.

I was with Tommy the day before he died. I asked him if he was frightened to die. He said, "No, that would be a philosophical mistake. I do think, however, that I will miss my friends." I loved Tommy deeply, though we were different people. He left instructions that I was to speak at his memorial service. This is what I said:

I have to tell people that I am committed to Christian nonviolence. I have to tell people that I am so committed because my life belies that conviction. You do not have to be around me long to know that I am not exactly a peaceable guy. As far as I know, Tommy never said he was a pacifist. He did not have to say that he was formed by the habits of Christian nonviolence, because he was so obviously a person of peace. He was so, I believe, because he was, as we Methodists put it, sanctified, which is but a reminder that sanctification names the rest — the habits shaped by the conviction that God has redeemed the world through the cross and resurrection of Jesus Christ.

Tommy did not have to change the world. He knew that the world had been changed, so that in a world as dark as war and as petty as the envy between academics, he could take the time to listen — to receive. Tommy could listen. He could hear what the other person was saying, not what he might want them to say. He could listen even to me. I would rage into his office, an office that I now happily inhabit in the hope that his memory will inhabit me, and he would absorb my rage. He never told me to calm down. Rather, I calmed down because he listened.

Yet there was nothing sentimental about Tommy. In fact, there was a hardness at the center of his soul. Because he knew that his life from minute to minute was sheer gift, he also knew that neither he nor those he loved could afford to live lies. So he sought to be truthful, knowing that truth but names the arduous discipline that we must undergo if our speech, and the life our speech makes possible, is to be a truthful witness to the God who is the beginning and end of our existence. After all, what good would a peace be that was not truthful?

Joy, the exhilaration that is ours in response to God's grace, was the hallmark of Tommy's life and theology. He loved theology, he loved the church and the university that made his work as a theologian not only possible but necessary, because he knew that the God he worshiped as a Christian delights in truth. That is why, I think, he never feared asking himself or us questions to which neither he nor we knew the answer. He was quite capable of making himself and his friends uncomfortable by truthful questioning. He was so because he knew that whatever answers we might have in life must reflect our willingness to befriend and be befriended by the mystery that the other exists not to please us, but to please God. How else can we explain Tommy's extraordinary ability to be a friend with people as peculiar as you and me without ever wanting us, in the interest of getting along, to be anything other than who we are?

Tommy's life was, in truth, a witness to the God whom he knew could be trusted to be the truth. I know no more fitting way to remember Tommy than to ask you to join me in a prayer of thanksgiving for his life:

> Lord of life and Lord of death, we give thanks for the life of Tommy Langford. Tommy was wise, but he was so because you taught him early how to wait, to be patient. He lived knowing each day could be his last, so why not use that day to plant a daffodil, talk to a friend, read a book, or pray — all of which for Tommy may have been the same thing. Of course, he did much good work. He ran the divinity school and even the university, whatever it may mean to run those things. More importantly, you somehow gave him the gift not only to put up with fools,

but to love them into being at least less foolish. God, we will miss him. He was one of those who make the world better because he was just there. He could just be "there" because he never doubted that whatever he was, he was nothing without you. So, help us who are left behind. May we learn to be there for one another. One last thing — when his eyes are closed, he often really is listening hard to what you have to say. He listened to us, thereby, making it possible for us to shout, to celebrate, this life with a grateful amen.

AFTER I TURNED SIXTY, I NOTICED THAT I WAS GROWING OLD, BUT I DEALT with that the way I have dealt with most of my life — I worked all the harder. And the combination of the Gifford Lectures and September 11, 2001, gave me good reason to do so. Still, I did begin to notice a difference. I do not know if the difference was different enough to say that I was "changing," but I noticed I was able to write and speak with less hesitancy about God. I noticed it first when I wrote sermons on the seven last words of Christ for the Good Friday service at Saint Thomas Church Fifth Avenue in New York in 2003. I found that to be an exacting assignment. It was as serious as it gets.

The subsequent book was entitled *Cross-Shattered Christ*. I dedicated the book to Peter Ochs. I was worried that I might put Peter, as a Jew, in difficulty by dedicating a book to him on the seven last words of Christ. So I sent him the manuscript, trusting him to tell me if he did not want me to dedicate the book to him. Peter wrote in response: "These seven words *(dibberot)* show how much you have been brought up not only to the Son's service, but also to Israel's — to his flesh in both senses. May His resurrection shine in you as much as the unrelenting facticity of his death, which, I see, drives you past the human self-centeredness that envelops all of us in modernity, much of the Church and the Synagogue too. But of course we see the Light in you too, the laughing joy that is as much fully God fully human as the other, is it not?"

Peter is a religious person. Could he really see the Light in me? Such a thought at once encouraged and frightened me. At best, I have never imagined myself to be more than a "broken light." But it may be the case that if you hang around people like Peter Ochs, David Burrell, and Paula Gilbert, something finally happens.

Another indication that perhaps something was "happening" to me came in the form of a dissertation on my work by a priest in the Church of England. The priest was Sam Wells, and the dissertation was later published as the book *Transforming Fate into Destiny*. I found the book illuminating because Sam was able to plot how my work had forced me to finally write about God. I found this to be a stunning insight, because it exposed the fact that I have not always written about God, even though I have imagined myself to be a theologian. Even more, however, Sam's account of my work struck me with the same force as Peter's declaration that he sees the Light in me. Could it be that after all these years of writing and teaching about theology and the church, I have come to believe in God with sufficient intensity that others can now see in me a faith I did not even know I had?

I do not want to overplay any "signs" of change or a "difference" that became apparent as I entered my sixties because I worry that such accounts might be deceptive. Nonetheless, in addition to noticing less hesitancy in speaking about God, I found that I increasingly enjoyed preaching. In particular, I like wrestling with the texts. For some reason, when I preach I feel free and joyful. I am free because it is not up to me to make it up from whole cloth. I am under the authority of the Word.

I also think the difference I started to notice had everything to do with where Paula and I had been going to church. Paula and I left Aldersgate the Sunday before Palm Sunday. We needed a place to go for Holy Week. Before Aldersgate had begun Holy Week services, we had sometimes attended services during Holy Week at a nearby Episcopal church that bore the name the Church of the Holy Family. As we left Aldersgate, Paula declared that she was not going to go to a church that did not have the Eucharist every week. We went to Holy Family for Holy Week. We have never left.

I had given talks at Holy Family before Paula and I became members of the church. I had told them that I wondered about the church because Holy Family is usually the name of a Catholic church. But as soon as they called the basement in which I was to speak the "undercroft," I knew they were Episcopalians. After all, Episcopalians are people who refuse to let any pretension go unused. God's little joke on me is that now I am an Episcopalian or, more accurately, a communicant at the Church of the Holy Family.

Paula and I like to think that we are simply bringing Methodism home. Methodism was a reform movement in the Church of England that by accident became a church in America. Methodists attending an Episcopal church, therefore, are not an anomaly. Moreover, our rector, Timothy Kimbrough, comes from deep Methodism. His father, S. T. Kimbrough, is a Methodist minister, an extraordinary musician, and a Charles Wesley scholar. In Timothy, we have the best of all possible worlds — an evangelical Anglo-Catholic.

Even more, Timothy is a priest who is clearly in love with God. Paula was director of admissions in the divinity school when Timothy, having graduated from Duke, came through the school. He is an extraordinarily talented jazz musician. By his own account, he aimlessly came to divinity school because he had nothing better to do. He was assigned to St. Philip's Episcopal Church in downtown Durham, a church with a ministry to the poor. There he discovered the essential connection between that ministry and the Eucharist. That connection has formed his life and ministry.

The principle that "like knows like" is exemplified by Timothy's recognition of Paula as a priest. He invited her to consider being appointed to Holy Family as an assisting pastor. She was so appointed, with the approval of both the bishop of her United Methodist conference and the local Episcopal ordinary. She is a vital part of the liturgical life of Holy Family and responds to the needs of the congregation.

That she is an ecumenical appointment is not without pain. She cannot celebrate at the altar at Holy Family, except at times clearly designated as ecumenical. She continues to celebrate every Thursday for the Wesley Fellowship, but not being able to celebrate at Holy Family for a people she loves is not easy. Paula carries the pain of our disunity as Christians in her body. She does so with a dignity and grace that often moves me, particularly during the liturgy, unexpectedly to tears.

My tears are unexpected even though I often cry in church. I usually cry at baptisms at Holy Family. We immerse adults and infants in a cross-shaped baptistery. I am not sure why I cry at such times. You would think I would be used to it by now. I have spent my whole life in church. Thank God, however, that I have never gotten used to being a Christian. I think that is why I cry. I simply cannot get over what a surprising and wonderful life God has given me.

CHAPTER 12

Last Things

I am a Christian because at some point early in her own life my mother heard the story of Hannah and Samuel. Of course, the story I have told about my life should make it clear that nothing has been quite this simple. Yet when all is said and done, it remains true that I am a Christian because of that story.

I am quite certain that my mother knew little about the details surrounding Hannah's prayer. I doubt she knew what it meant for Hannah to promise that the child would be a Nazirite, or the details surrounding Samuel's service in the house of Eli. But she knew enough of the story to pray Hannah's prayer. My life has been determined by people who know how to pray.

I have spent a lifetime learning how to pray. Yet I did not become a theologian to learn how to pray. I became a theologian because I found the work of theology so compelling. Along the way, I discovered that the work of theology is the work of prayer. That Paula told me I should pray before class may have been the most important instruction I have been given in my work as a theologian. I confess, however, that prayer still never comes easy for me. But I hold no conviction more determinatively than the belief that prayer names how God becomes present to us and how we can participate in that presence by praying for others.

Although it is true that I got through the years with Anne in part because of my boundless energy and stubbornness, I would not have survived if I had not had friends praying for me. I "knew" God was with me because I knew I had friends all over the world praying for us. Prayer did not mean that I thought everything would work out for the best. Prayer meant that God was with us. Prayer meant that Anne did not die alone. Prayer means that none of us will die alone.

In 1 Samuel 25 we are told, "Now Samuel died; and all Israel assembled and mourned for him. They buried him at his home in Ramah. Then David got up and went down to the wilderness of Paran." An anticlimactic ending for a life caught in the transition from judges to kings — amidst Israel's desperate attempt to secure its existence. Samuel did the work he had been called to do, and then he died. That is the way it is supposed to work.

I have not written this memoir in preparation for my death. I am not finished. I have work to do. Still, I know that in the not-too-distant future someone will write, "Now Stanley died." I think often about dying. I had imagined that I would be quite frightened as I aged and the reality of death became just that — a reality. But I have been surprised to discover that to the degree I have contemplated my death, I have not been frightened.

In front of my desk I have a poem by the Irish poet Monk Gibbon. I read it every day. Imogene Stuart, the sculptor and friend of Enda's whom we met in Ireland, sent me a lovely drawing on which she had beautifully inscribed the poem. She did so in response to a discussion of death we shared with Enda. Gibbon's poem is entitled "The Last Thing" and reads:

> Who'd be afraid of death.
> I think only fools
> are. For it is not
> as though this thing
> were given to one man only, but all
> receive it. The journey that my
> friend makes, I can
> make also. If I know
> nothing else. I know
> this, I go where he is.
> O Fools, shrinking from this little door,
> Through which so many kind and lovely souls have passed
> Before you,
> Will you hang back?

Last Things

Harder in your case than another?
Not so.
And too much silence?
Has there not been enough stir here?
Go bravely, for where so much greatness and gentleness have been
Already, You should be glad to follow.

I do not speculate about what life with God after death might be.
I am quite content to leave that up to God. Nor do I intend to plan my
funeral. Not only does that seem rather silly, but I trust those who love
me to do what the church has taught us to do at such times — gather
and pray. I hope, moreover, that a people will assemble who will not
only mourn but also celebrate that God gave me such a wonderful life.
I know the church has already prepared a prayer for such occasions. In
the Book of Common Prayer there is a prayer included in The Common
of Saints entitled "Of a Theologian and Teacher":

> Almighty God, you gave your servant Stanley special gifts of grace to
> understand and teach the truth as it is in Jesus Christ: Grant that by
> this teaching we may know you, the One true God, and Jesus Christ
> whom you have sent; who lives and reigns with you and the Holy
> Spirit, one God, for ever and ever. Amen.

It may seem presumptuous of me to identify myself with this
prayer. But then, the point of the prayer is that of gratitude for the good
work God has given. It is not about me. It is about Jesus Christ. Moreover, I believe that such prayers reflect the church's wisdom. As a theologian, I cannot read that prayer without being reminded that the work
I have been given is pure gift. That it is so means that I must take all
the more care to live up to the vocation of teaching "the truth as it is in
Jesus Christ."

I hope the story I have told of being Hannah's child makes no sense
if the one true God is not fully present in Jesus Christ. I have come a
long way from Pleasant Grove. Admittedly, there are times I would like
to lose "Stanley Hauerwas." I sometimes feel trapped by that identity.
The trick, I believe, is to be who I am without being held captive by being so identified. There is a kind of forgetfulness at the heart of what it

means to be a Christian. I do not pretend to have mastered the ability to live with such forgetfulness, but at times I have intimations that I am so enthralled by what I have been given that I almost forget who I am. Another name for such forgetfulness is humility. Humility is a virtue that rides on the back of a life made possible by having been given good work to do.

As I shared this manuscript with friends along the way, someone asked me what I had learned in the process of writing *Hannah's Child*. I am tempted to say that I have learned how fortunate I am to have had such good friends, but that would be stating the obvious. I might also reply that I now realize how lucky I have been, but that would be killing time in the hope of discovering something to say. There are other possibilities. But in fact what I have learned is quite simple — I am a Christian. How interesting.

Epilogue

I never imagined I would write anything like *Hannah's Child*. Friends, however, particularly younger friends, began to ask me to give an account of my life. I resisted that request for some time, but then the thing got into my imagination and it seemed like something I had to do. I am a bit taken aback by the fact that I did it, but now that it is done I cannot imagine not having written this book. *Hannah's Child,* a title I found along the way, I hope exemplifies the title Sam Wells gave the book he wrote on my work, *Transforming Fate into Destiny.*

I know that once I began to write *Hannah's Child,* it became something like an obsession. In his lovely book *Waiting for Snow in Havana: Confessions of a Cuban Boy,* Carlos Eire reports that once he began writing his book he could not stop working until he finished. I cannot pretend to have Eire's literary gift, but I found I also could not stop writing this book. I could not stop because every day was a day of discovery. The word that comes closest to describing the nature of what I discovered is "gratitude."

That does not mean, however, that I know what I have done. I do not know if it is a memoir, but then it is not at all clear to me what that genre names. I know it is not an autobiography. I tried to avoid "then I did that . . . and after that I wrote this." Such accounts may be useful, and even interesting, but I had little interest in producing that kind of history.

I would like to think that this book might fall into the category of "testimony," but I am not confident that what I have done deserves that description. When I was a child, I often heard testimonies in church.

They usually came during services on Sunday night. A member of the congregation would suddenly "feel moved" to declare to those assembled what God had done in her life. Such heartfelt testimonies made by unsophisticated people in straightforward language impressed me then and impress me now. I trusted their testimonies.

I am a theologian. I have been trained too well to be able to trust claims that I might make about what God may or may not have done to make my life possible. I believe, however, that God has made my life possible. Yet how do you write a testimony, a witness, to testify to God's presence in your life that does not make more of you than your life has been? How do you testify to God in a manner that does not tempt you to say more about God than you know? These were the conundrums I faced.

That I was able to write this book at all is a testimony to friends. I quite literally could not have survived without friends. *Hannah's Child* can be read as one long acknowledgment, even if I was not able to name all the friends who have made my life possible, which is my only regret. Friendship is a central theme in my "work." More importantly, friendship is a reality in my life. I was tempted, therefore, to use as a subtitle for the book "A Testimony to Friends." But God matters for the friends who have made my life possible, which made it impossible for me to avoid gesturing toward God in the subtitle. By calling *Hannah's Child* a "theologian's memoir," I hoped to indicate that my tale has something to say about the God who has made my life and work possible.

That said, there are certain friends who had a direct impact on the writing of *Hannah's Child,* and I would be remiss not to name them here. Alonzo McDonald seems an unlikely benefactor. He is a former marine, served as President Carter's chief of staff, and is a capitalist. But he is also a Christian who thinks it important to have theology done without apology in the contemporary university. Al made it possible for me to have the time to write by giving me support from his Agape Foundation. I am grateful for that support, but I am equally gratified to have gotten to know the character who is Alonzo McDonald. Al takes an interest in those he aids. That could be a problem, but Al is too interesting to be a problem. He cares about what I care about.

It was Al's idea to convene a group of my friends before I began my sabbatical so that they could tell me what to do with my time. On

November 12, 2007, such a meeting took place. Those present were David Aers, Rom Coles, Paula Gilbert, Eric Gregory, Kelly Johnson, Greg Jones, Timothy Kimbrough, Travis Kroeker, Therese Lysaught, Al McDonald, Jerry McKenny, Jenifer McDonald Peters, Peter Ochs, Sam Wells, and Jim Wetzel. Sheryl Overmyer organized the meeting and made extensive notes.

Greg Jones chaired the daylong meeting. I shall never forget the substantive suggestions made in the first hours of the gathering. Greg began the meeting by asking each person to introduce himself or herself and then make a suggestion about what I should do. Each of the people named above did that. I listened and learned a great deal. *Hannah's Child* grew from the seeds planted in that meeting. I do not think any of those present suggested that I should write what I have written, but I do not think it unfair to blame them collectively for what I have done.

I began to write without quite knowing what I was doing. So I asked Greg Jones and Sam Wells to read the chapters as I completed drafts. Their reactions and criticisms were invaluable. Carole Baker, who has to read and make available everything I write, was essential for my ability to go on. When Carole told me, "This is really good," I thought I might be doing something worthwhile.

While I was on sabbatical, I was often asked what I was writing. I was a bit sheepish at first to acknowledge that I was working on a memoir. But the more I wrote, the easier it became to say what I was doing. By the time I was finished with a draft, many of my friends asked to read what I had done. I decided that the thing was public property, so whoever wanted to read it could. Only Carole knows how many people read drafts of the manuscript, but I have a lot of friends. I am grateful not only for their interest but also for their advice about how to make the book better.

There are two people in particular whom I need to single out for making the book better. Lauren Winner is a wonderful writer, which means that she is also a great reader. She made extremely important suggestions about the manuscript. But David Toole deserves the lion's share of credit for making me rewrite what I had already rewritten in the hope that I would write better. David was the editor for *With the Grain of the Universe*. He now has many other responsibilities, but because he is such a good editor and knows me so well I asked him to edit *Hannah's Child*. He graciously agreed, and the book, particularly the last chapters, owes much to his skill.

I tried to tell the story in as straightforward a manner as I could. I relied on my memory, and memory is a tricky business. We often remember what we hope we did rather than what we did in fact do. We forget and then remember incorrectly what happened when. I do not think I willfully distorted anything on which I reported, but I may have made mistakes. If I have, however, the mistakes may be true.

I also tried to be honest about myself, my friends, those who are not my friends, and what "happened." It is not easy to see ourselves truthfully and without illusion. The difference between a loving but honest description and cruelty is often not easily determined. Son of my father, I have no capacity for cruelty, though at times I may be stupid. I hope the descriptions of my life and those who have made my life possible are determined by love, but I will have to trust the reader to tell me where I have been stupid.

Toward the end of his life, Henri de Lubac described his work this way: "Almost everything I have written sprang from unforeseeable circumstances, scattered, without technical preparation. In vain would one look for a true, personal philosophical or theological synthesis in the ensemble of such diverse publications, whether to criticize or approve it. And yet, in this many-colored fabric, occasioned by the condition of the most various lectures, commissions, situations and calls, I nevertheless believe I can find some traces, a pattern that constitutes its unity." As a theologian, I am not in de Lubac's league, but I could not wish for a better description of how I regard my life and work. *Hannah's Child* is my attempt to find in my life "a pattern that constitutes its unity."

I asked Paula and Adam to read *Hannah's Child*. In quite different ways *Hannah's Child* is not an easy book for either of them to read. Harder for Adam than for Paula. However, I gave each of them veto rights over the book. They did not exercise these rights. For obvious reasons, the book is dedicated to them.

Epilogue